In the Running

In the Running
The New Woman Candidate

By

Ruth B. Mandel

New Haven and New York

TICKNOR & FIELDS

1981

Library of Congress Cataloging in Publication Data
Mandel, Ruth B
In the running.
Includes bibliographical references and index.
1. Women in politics—United States.
2. Women—United States. 3. Feminism—United States.
4. Electioneering—United States. I. Title.
HQ1391.U5M36   305.4'2   80-24190
ISBN 0-89919-027-8

Printed in the United States of America
Designed by Ann Gold

00   10   9   8   7   6   5   4   3   2   1

For Ida and Betsey

Contents

Acknowledgments

This book is indebted to collective support to a greater extent than is usual in such matters. It has been written and published because numerous people who care about the issue of women's political leadership devoted time and thought to the materials I have presented in these pages.

During the period from 1975, when the original project to study women's campaigns began (see Preface), until the manuscript's completion about five years later, a core group of people has been critical to the book. Foremost in importance are the journalists who observed and described the campaigns of selected women running for office in 1976. Without their contributions, there would be no book. Each journalist met demands for time and effort above and beyond anyone's initial expectations of what would be required. Their work is described in the Preface, and they are named in a separate section. What must be added here is an acknowledgment of the commitment and professional integrity they brought to their work, the extent of their willingness to cooperate in a challenging and demanding group enterprise, and the patience they have exhibited through the years it has taken to complete this book.

Three other people whose importance to the book is incalculable are Betsey Wright of Washington, D.C., Avery Russell of the Carnegie Corporation of New York, and Pat Irving, a free-lance editor currently living in Georgia.

Throughout the years the book has been in the making, Betsey Wright has been a professional partner—specifically, in her role as co-director with me for the project to study women's campaigns in 1976; more generally, as former Executive Director of the National Women's Education Fund and as one of the most knowledgeable persons in the country about women in politics. Her insights and expertise have been profoundly important to the book's development. Above and beyond her direct involvement in the project, Betsey Wright is the person from whom I learned much of what I had to know to consider writing this book. Her knowledge of politics and talents as a political activist, her profound yet realistic feminist idealism, and her unwavering support have been invaluable during the years we have known each other as close professional associates and personal friends.

Avery Russell is one among a small number of women occupying influential positions in national foundations who is deeply committed to the advancement of women's opportunities and status in society. She has provided professional guidance, material resources, and moral support from the time the idea for this book was conceived until the manuscript's completion. She has been the ideal patron—willing to take risks, consistently encouraging, never oppressively demanding, always ready and able to help.

Avery Russell understands me and the process of shaping a book well enough to have said, after she read the first draft, "I know the perfect person to work with you to get this manuscript ready for publication." Pat Irving was that person. She brought to the task not only her considerable skill and experience as an editor, but the infinite good humor and patience it took to grapple with the mass of verbiage she confronted when we began working together. During our collaboration—cutting, pasting, shaping, and honing drafts—I had the pleasure and benefit of her tutelage and friendship. From Pat Irving I have gained new admiration for the talented people who can discover order in disarray, build sequence, discard the inessential—and, most of all, who respect language so much that they themselves use it with the precision and affection its power deserves. Pat Irving's contribution to *In the Running* has enhanced it immeasurably and has been constrained only by my own limitations as an author.

A number of other people have been enormously helpful. Susan Carroll, Assistant Professor of Political Science at George Washington University, remained a very generous colleague and encouraging friend throughout the time I worked on this book. In addition to sharing the results of her research about women as political candidates, she was always ready to rearrange her own busy schedule to talk with me and even to compile special data for answering my inquiries. Her belief in the importance of the subject we were both studying and her careful, intelligent reading of the manuscript pointed up important issues which needed attention and contributed significantly to improving the final draft.

The book also profited from the insights and useful suggestions offered by Nevada State Senator Jean Ford, who brought to her reading of the manuscript years of experience on the campaign trail and in elective office. Jo Freeman not only contributed directly to the book as one of the journalists who worked on the original study of women's campaigns in 1976, she also read an earlier draft and challenged me to confront a number of troublesome problems. While I have not solved them all, the final product has benefited from Jo Freeman's usual perspicacity. Alan Rosenthal, Executive Director of the Eagleton Institute of Politics, Rosalie Whelan, Executive Director of the National Women's Education Fund, and Nancy Seifer all offered helpful suggestions at various stages of the manuscript's evolution. Alan Rosenthal, himself managing to complete two books during the time I labored on this one, expressed steady confidence in this project and stood ready to throw out a lifeline when I called for help. I did, many times.

Staff members and associates of the Center for the American Woman and Politics and the National Women's Education Fund provided all manner of direct assistance when the need arose to check data, organize reference materials, make phone calls, or accompany me on interviews. Chief among them at the Center is Kathy Stanwick, who has been a constant source of unqualified support and has willingly taken on many extra tasks at the office to free me for writing. Ruth Ann Burns and Lora Fong have also taken on extra burdens and adjusted their schedules to favor my needs, always graciously. Cynthia Ulman, formerly of the National Women's Education Fund, provided valuable research assistance on many occasions. Her work was always reliable and accomplished cheerfully. Beverly Braun, Barbara Bleichner, and Katherine Kleeman also contributed to the process of gathering and verifying information about the candidates described in the book. It has been a pleasure to work with them all, particularly because each one respects and cares deeply about the subject we are tackling together.

Nancy Hamilton joined the Center's staff just when I needed someone to convert messy draft pages into clean typed copy. She similarly transformed successive drafts for three years—always quickly, accurately, and working with high standards for professional self-respect. Without her steady assistance, my job would have been infinitely more burdensome. I am also grateful to Martha Casisa for bringing her typing skills and cheerful encouragement to the task of making clean copy at one point during the process.

At one stage or another, other persons have made important contributions to *In the Running.* Eli Evans, former program officer at the Carnegie Corporation of New York and currently president of the Revson Foundation, encouraged Betsey Wright and me to design the study of women running for office in 1976. His conviction that the story of women's changing political roles (and especially their experiences in campaign politics) must be told remains a source of inspiration. Pat Berens, literary agent for the book, and Fred Whitmer, my attorney, used their impressive professional skills and lent their patient support to moving the book forward at critical moments. So did Dana Adkins, my editor at Ticknor and Fields. Her interest in this book and the obvious satisfaction she derives from her own work with authors and manuscripts made the publication process a pleasure in itself.

During the many months of writing, I have been less available as a mother and friend than I would like to be, and I have been blessed with a daughter and friends who gave much more than they received. "Some day I might be interested in reading that book," said my daughter, Maud Mandel, in a day when her tastes ran more to Enid Blyton's fiction. I hope so. In the meantime I look forward to weekends away from the typewriter and to resuming our Sundays at the ice-skating rink. Two special friends must be singled out. Barrett John Mandel for always helping me to recognize that a moment's despair or a day's paralysis is nothing more or less than one chooses to make it. And Ida Schmertz, whom for many years it has been my rare good fortune to count as a warm, loyal friend and wise colleague. In every conversation, I learn something from her. At every difficult moment, she is there to offer encouragement or consolation. Her reading of an early draft of these chapters and her generosity in serving as a sounding board and advisor throughout the writing process have been immensely important to me and the book.

Finally, *In the Running* is about the experiences of real women who are named in its pages. Not only did they permit my colleagues and me to observe and interview them, they were always eager to help us, willing to make themselves available at our request, and convinced of the general importance of the subject we were attempting to illuminate. Without their cooperation, we could not have proceeded. But beyond cooperation, their support and enthusiasm made our work a pleasure. For that we are doubly grateful.

Preface

For almost a decade I have been privileged to work professionally in an area where individual aspirations and broad social change are intersecting dynamically. As Director of the Center for the American Woman and Politics,* I have observed and studied women's political experiences at a turning point in women's history, one which promises to change the dramatis personae of public life in the United States.

Meeting and working with hundreds of women who are entering the political arena has been an enormously enlightening and stimulating educational experience. It is an experience which I value highly enough to wish to share with women and men interested in public affairs and the democratic electoral process, and particularly with women who may not realize how their own latent political aspirations or individual campaign histories are mirrored in the experiences of others across the country.

This book was also written for young and old alike whose textbook and mass-media acquaintance with elective politics has left them feeling removed, unconcerned, powerless, and often hostile regarding that part of our social contract which manifests itself seasonally in candidates, campaigns, and votes. The political process affects everyone's life no matter how little responsibility individuals take for it. What we miss in remaining

---

*The Center for the American Woman and Politics is a research, education, information, and public service center which was established in 1971 as a unit of the Eagleton Institute of Politics at Rutgers—The State University of New Jersey. The Center's programs are aimed at developing a body of useful knowledge about women's participation in public life and at assisting efforts to increase women's numbers and effectiveness in politics and government.

aloof is not only the real opportunity to influence the course of events, but also the opportunity to participate in a highly spirited, dramatically exciting, and genuinely satisfying communal activity. Watching and listening to political women waging campaigns for all levels of public leadership has taught me that we lose much more than we gain by keeping our distance from the rough-and-tumble of politics.

While this book deals exclusively with women running for elective office, its analyses and implications should be relevant to men and women in other public roles and professional situations where they encounter the restraints imposed by stereotypes, the problems of discrimination and minority status, the conflicts and challenges of belonging to a vanguard.

In the Running draws heavily on firsthand accounts of experiences women have had while competing for various elective offices across the country. It also incorporates findings from research conducted between 1972 and 1979 by the Center for the American Woman and Politics and a number of independent researchers, and it utilizes information gathered by the National Women's Education Fund, an organization established in Washington, D.C., in 1973 to develop programs for increasing the numbers and influence of women in politics.

The specific project from which this book grew began in 1975 when the Carnegie Corporation of New York awarded a grant to the National Women's Education Fund (NWEF) and the Center for the American Woman and Politics (CAWP) for a joint study of women's political campaigns in the bicentennial year. The two organizations and the Carnegie Corporation believed that the time had come to explore the important but neglected subject of women's experiences at the candidacy stage of electoral politics. While the mass media had begun to focus some attention on a handful of prominent women emerging in the political limelight during the early 1970s, little or nothing was known about what was happening to hundreds of women setting out on the campaign trail. A few studies had approached the subject of women serving in public office, but no one had examined the subject of women getting there.

In 1976 NWEF and CAWP worked with a group of journalists to gather information about races in which women were competing for a variety of public offices and where their participation in electoral politics would exemplify themes reflecting the collective experiences of today's pioneering female candidates. The two organizations sought to include races in which women were seeking higher offices than the ones they were holding as well as campaigns of first-time office seekers; campaigns for various types of offices in a variety of geographic areas of the country; candidates from both major political parties and from various ethnic and racial backgrounds; candidates from diverse educational and professional backgrounds; candidates of different ages, marital status, and parental status; particularly interesting or noteworthy candidates or campaign situations nationwide.

After determining which campaigns to observe, NWEF and CAWP located journalists who could follow women's races in ten targeted states —Arizona, California, Connecticut, Maryland, Minnesota, Missouri, New York, Ohio, Oregon, and Texas. Guided by the project's co-directors (myself and Betsey Wright, then Executive Director of NWEF), these journalists examined the candidates, the electorate, the political setting for each race, the structure and practices of campaign organizations, the issues raised by the candidates and their opponents, campaign finances, media coverage of the campaigns, and special areas of concern and interest in women's races. They conducted interviews with the female candidates, their staff members and supporters, and with opposing candidates and their staffs. The journalists also talked with local political leaders, influential citizens, representatives of women's organizations and other politically active groups, reporters, and sometimes individual voters. In addition, they observed campaign planning and strategy sessions, traveled the districts with candidates, examined campaign materials, and monitored campaign coverage by local media. Their work, supplemented with data collected by the staffs of NWEF and CAWP, resulted in a compilation of varying amounts of information about 102 female candidates.

Following the November 1976 elections, the journalists prepared three types of written reports based on their coverage of designated women's races. First, each journalist did profiles of the candidates she had observed. These were then shared among all the journalists. Next, selecting and integrating relevant material from her own state and from the other states included in the project, each journalist wrote a fifteen- to twenty-thousand-word report documenting a condition or a pattern of experiences or issues relevant to the campaigns under observation and illustrative of recurrent themes in women's candidacies across the country. Finally each journalist wrote brief descriptive narratives highlighting particularly interesting moments or situations she had observed in individual campaigns.

The journalists' work serves as a rich, varied, and basic resource for this book. Selections from their written materials have been incorporated throughout the chapters. The names of individual journalists are not identified on specific pages where their materials are used, but readers should refer to the list of contributing journalists following this preface for information about the states and themes assigned to each writer during the 1976 campaign season. While I take full responsibility for selecting among their writings and for the ways in which their work has been used, edited, and interpreted as well as for the overall framework and point of view articulated throughout these chapters, the book would not have existed without their contributions to the project. It is truly the product of a collective enterprise.

While the NWEF/CAWP project on women's campaigns in 1976 provided the solid foundation on which to build this book, its contents extend well beyond the states and races observed in that election year to give an overview of the whole decade. The material submitted by the journalists was revealing and suggestive enough to convince Avery Russell of the Carnegie Corporation, Betsey Wright of NWEF, a number of our colleagues, and me that we were looking at the embryo of a book about the circumstances under which contemporary women were struggling to establish a foothold in American political life. Firmly convinced of the importance of our subject and supported by the staffs of NWEF and CAWP as well as by a supplementary grant from the Carnegie Corporation, in the spring of 1977 I undertook the task of writing this book. For over three years, I have continued the research begun with the 1976 project to study women's experiences as political candidates. It has involved seeking further documentation and utilizing available data to test, substantiate, expand, and analyze our early discoveries. In some cases, I have followed the 1976 candidates into a later campaign season and have interviewed them for retrospective observations and additional assessments to expand the accounts of their experiences. The book also deals with the candidacies of other women running for various offices in other states and at other times during recent years. The information about their experiences is based primarily on direct contact with political women, especially on interviews I have conducted with the candidates and their staff members and associates as well as on formal and informal contact between CAWP, NWEF, and hundreds of female office seekers over almost a decade.

For aggregate data about candidates and public officials, the book draws most heavily on three sources: a national survey of women in municipal, county, state legislative, statewide, and congressional offices during 1975 conducted by the Center for the American Woman and Politics and reported by Marilyn Johnson and Kathy Stanwick in "Profile of Women Holding Office," in *Women in Public Office: A Biographical Directory and Statistical Analysis* (New York: R. R. Bowker, 1976); a national survey of women holding elective and appointive office in 1977, which included a comparison sample of male officeholders, conducted by the Center for the American Woman and Politics and reported by Marilyn Johnson and Susan J. Carroll in "Statistical Report: Profile of Women

Holding Office, 1977," in *Women in Public Office: A Biographical Directory and Statistical Analysis, Second Edition* (Metuchen, New Jersey: The Scarecrow Press, 1978); a national survey of female candidates running for the U.S. Senate, the U.S. House of Representatives, statewide offices, and state legislative seats in 1976 conducted by Susan J. Carroll for *Women as Candidates: Campaigns and Elections in American Politics,* a Ph.D. dissertation in the Department of Political Science, Indiana University, Bloomington, Indiana, 1980.

As author of *In the Running,* I am responsible for the views contained in it. The views expressed by me are not necessarily the views of the National Women's Education Fund or those of the Center for the American Woman and Politics, who co-sponsored the project which evolved into the manuscript.

Ruth B. Mandel
New Brunswick, N.J.
November 1980

Contributing Journalists

The following journalists and free-lance writers contributed research and insights to the study of women's campaigns in 1976 conducted by the National Women's Education Fund and the Center for the American Woman and Politics (see Preface). Edited and original sections of the written accounts of campaigns they observed and analyzed have been incorporated within the pages of this book. Their materials are related to the campaigns conducted during 1976 in those states identified next to their names below. In general, the information and observations shared by all journalists have proven invaluable in describing and assessing women's experiences as political candidates.

Nancy Boyarsky (California). Nancy Boyarsky is a free-lance writer based in Los Angeles, California. In addition to following eight women's races for state legislative and county offices during the 1976 election season in California, she prepared a thematic report on the subject of female candidates' personal lives and public roles.

Huntly Collins and Rosemary Maynard (Oregon). Huntly Collins, a reporter for *The Oregonian* published in Portland, Oregon, gathered information about fourteen women's campaigns for statewide, state legislative, and local offices during 1976. She also wrote an account of the political climate which female candidates are creating for other women seeking office. She was assisted in her work on the project by Rosemary Maynard, a fellow journalist at *The Oregonian.*

Jo Freeman (New York and Connecticut). Jo Freeman is a scholar, political analyst, and free-lance writer who was an assistant professor of political science at the State University of New York at the time she participated in this project. She covered Bella Abzug's and Gloria Schaffer's U.S. Senate races in New York and Connecticut, and she wrote an analysis of the ways in which image, style, and stereotypes affect women's political candidacies.

Betty Garrett (Ohio).   Betty Garrett, a free-lance writer based in Columbus, Ohio, followed six women's congressional and state legislative campaigns in Ohio during the election season of 1976. She is now Director of Communications for Ohio's Department of Mental Retardation and Developmental Disabilities. Her thematic report discussed the ways in which women running for office handled the experiences of victory and defeat.

Connie Koenenn (Arizona).   Connie Koenenn, formerly a reporter for *The Arizona Republic,* currently is an editor at *The Los Angeles Times.* In 1976 she covered eight female candidates running in Arizona for the U.S. Senate, the U.S. House of Representatives, and the upper and lower houses of Arizona's state legislature. She also wrote an account of how the organized women's political movement affected female candidates.

Carol Lacey (Minnesota).   A writer for the *St. Paul Pioneer Press* in St. Paul, Minnesota, and a political scientist, Carol Lacey examined the campaigns of eleven women running for congressional, state legislative, and county offices in Minnesota. In addition, she prepared a report on the backgrounds and motivations of female candidates in 1976.

Kay Mills (Maryland).   Formerly a reporter for the Newhouse News Service's Washington Bureau, and currently an editorial writer for *The Los Angeles Times,* Kay Mills followed nine women in Maryland who sought seats in the U. S. House of Representatives during the 1976 election season. Her thematic analysis focused on building clout and credibility in women's political campaigns.

Patricia Rice (Missouri).   Patricia Rice is a reporter for the *St. Louis Post Dispatch.* In 1976 she observed six female candidates running for congressional, statewide, and state legislative offices in Missouri, and she prepared a report describing the issue of sexism and the role played by antifeminism in women's campaign experiences.

Isabelle Shelton (Washington, D.C.).   Isabelle Shelton has reported for *The Washington Star* and has written many stories about women and women's issues during her years as a journalist. She participated in the 1976 campaign studies project as an advisor and resource person who attended the meetings of journalists and contributed her expertise and point of view about general issues facing female candidates as they compete for elective offices.

Saralee Tiede (Texas).   A reporter based in the Austin Bureau of the

Dallas Times Herald, Saralee Tiede followed eight women running for congressional, state legislative, and county offices in Texas during the 1976 campaign season. In addition, she wrote an analysis of the ways in which female candidates handled campaign organization, management, and techniques in 1976.

In the Running

Introduction
Participation

The stakes, the stakes are too high for government to be a spectator sport.
—Barbara Jordan
Harvard University Commencement Address, 1977

This book is about the women who have been changing the landscape of leadership in politics. The major breakthrough occurred in the 1970s, when more women than ever before competed for political office. Communities everywhere voted their "first woman" into office, sometimes as mayor, more often as town councilor, here and there as county commissioner, state representative, lieutenant governor, and even governor. Over a decade, elected women across the country more than doubled their numbers in state and local government. And while progress has been much slower in winning some prominent public offices—especially in the U.S. Senate and House—it is no longer unprecedented to encounter women eyeing political contests in even the most competitive corners of the electoral arena.

At the moment, among elected officials governing the United States, about 10 percent are female. Hardly a stunning figure. Indeed, the doubling (even tripling or quadrupling in some instances) has added up to only a small beginning for women's emergence among the ranks of public leaders. Yet the advances of recent years are both remarkable and important. Remarkable because for the first time significant numbers of women suddenly seem self-

3

assured about achieving success in politics, once considered far out of bounds, too "dirty" and too "tough" for women. Important chiefly because politics is the lifeblood of the system under which our society operates as a collective entity.

Rooted as it is in principles of participation and representation, our system of government relies on the electoral process for the practical application of those principles. The politics of the electoral process—the give and take, dealing and compromising, jockeying and competing—are as critical to the health and vitality of the body politic as is the flow of the circulatory system to the healthy human body. There are few places in society where individuals have as great a responsibility and as clear an opportunity for making a contribution to the general well-being.

During the early seventies, women began to recognize their own potential value to the larger society and to believe that as a nation we had been wasting half our human resources. The resulting influx of fresh talent from an underrepresented segment of the population has been an important event in American politics—particularly if it means that once the gates open, talented newcomers will continue to arrive in ever greater numbers.

At present, women's advancement in politics is important, too, for its immediate impact on the changing self-concept and aspirations of women in general. Of all the new roles women are playing, that on the political stage is among the most visible. Political people are well known. Often they are awarded celebrity status, even viewed as glamorous. Whereas corporate business is private, electoral business is public. Board meetings and labor negotiations are conducted behind closed doors, but campaigns, elections, policy debates, and legislative votes take place in the public view. The mass media bring politicians into our homes every day. Many more people can name such women as Barbara Jordan, Nancy Kassebaum, Jane Byrne, or Bella Abzug than would recognize influential businesswomen like Mary Wells or Jane Cahill Pfeiffer. Even more visible than political men, women in politics stand out and attract attention because they are still oddities. Relatively small increases in their numbers, therefore, can exert a disproportionately strong influence on other women's aspirations and sense of available options. As one alternative to the pervasive public images of actress or fashion model, the image of political woman—in general, that of a leader, an independent, self-confident, outspoken, and knowledgeable person—is a confirmation that women can venture into previously restricted areas, whether in politics, in professional life, or elsewhere.

What is behind this important surge forward on the political horizon? Literally, what is *behind* the women who are entering elective offices is a political campaign. Before anyone is an officeholder, he or she is an office *seeker*. Women are getting into office because they are going through the tests of pursuing nominations and organizing their races. Win or lose, on election day every office seeker has lived life as the candidate. It is that part of electoral politics—the experience of political candidacy for women—on which *In the Running* focuses.

Campaigning is a critical phase of political life which has received little scrutiny below the presidential level and no serious attention for its importance in facilitating or restricting women's access to leadership. As a candidate, the office seeker undergoes a test of personal performance and political strength required for everyone ambitious to govern in the electoral system. While men have passed this test for generations, women are just beginning to take it and earn high marks. Deciding to vie for votes, building acceptance as credible candidates for competitive ballot slots, developing political organizations, and hitting the campaign trail—here women face great personal challenges and confront formidable barriers to advancing as public leaders. Indeed, many talented women are barred from or knocked off the candidates' platform while pursuing nominations at the earliest stage of electioneering.

The process of campaigning for office as a political candidate is also a basic learning experience for preparing to function as a public official and to build a secure base in government. Candidacy does not cease on election day even for victorious political contestants. Campaign season begins yet again soon after the oath of office is administered. Officeholders anticipate reelection contests. They communicate with constituents, remain visible in their districts, invite opportunities to speak in public and attract media attention, appear at political gatherings, support other candidates—in effect, they behave as candidates while they are serving as public officials. This is neither strange nor inappropriate because elected officials'

public responsibilities and political interests are linked closely to
their ongoing status as candidates, first to seek and then consolidate
the support of the people they represent.

By implication, *In the Running* casts light on a broader canvas
than that of women as office seekers in the electoral system. Life as
a political candidate offers a concentrated, heightened encounter
with the larger community outside the home and family. In her role
as a candidate, a woman admits to being ambitious and willing to
compete in a public contest. She asks overtly for a new kind of
approval—not for good looks or domestic talents, but for good
ideas and leadership skills. She asks people to work for her, give
her their trust and loyalty, spend their money on her, and vote for
her. Rather than waiting to be wooed, she herself does the wooing.
Rather than keeping order behind the scenes, she takes to the
podium to deliver public speeches. She risks rejection and defeat
openly. She spends day and night in meetings, on public platforms,
on the road—away from home. These are uncommon—even frightening—experiences for most people, and they set campaigning
apart from most ordinary activities. Yet they are familiar types of
experiences to many more men than women. Outside politics—in
sports and in business and professional life—men have been expected to perform competitively in public view, but women have
not. Today, in trade unions, the religious establishment, educational institutions, private corporations—across the board—women
are saying they want to be in the running for leadership positions.
Almost nowhere does the shift in traditional values and patterns of
female behavior stand out in sharper relief than in the picture of
a woman stepping forward in the political arena to announce forth-
rightly, "I'm the candidate."

Because life on the campaign trail may well be a crucible for
women in change, the experiences and fate of the woman as political candidate are of uncommon interest. Who is this pioneer?
Where is she coming from? Why is she running for office now?
When she announces her candidacy, how is she received? What
barriers is she encountering on the campaign trail? Does entrée for
her carry its own unique advantages and disadvantages just because
she is female? Or are her experiences typical for candidates from
all underrepresented groups seeking political influence? How is she

going about the business of building credibility and strength in politics? Who is cheering her on and supporting her? Who isn't? What will it take for recent advances to continue? If they do, will women's presence in public leadership make a difference in the world?

These are the general questions about women as political candidates which this book addresses. It does so by looking at women who have been running for various elective offices across the country in the past ten years, and by analyzing selected aspects of their campaign experiences in the light of broad cultural, social, and political circumstances which have an impact on women's candidacies. What is new and central here always is that the political candidates are women. The book remains focused on how a situation, event, or point of view is related to the candidate's experience as a *woman* running for office. Thus, it does not attempt to deal with the complex interplay of shifting factors—economic, demographic, partisan—comprising the larger political context in which individual campaigns are played out. And it does not emphasize many obvious overlaps between women's and men's experiences as political candidates. Rather, this book isolates and highlights the ways in which a woman's sex affects her candidacy, her bid for leadership, at this moment in electoral history.

Chapter 1 reviews women's changing status in public leadership and then moves on to sketch today's female candidate and consider why she wants to run for political office. It explores the questions of whether there are similarities in motivation and outlook among diverse political women, and whether the women coming into public life bring with them a shared background which is different from that of political men.

On the campaign trail, women do share a challenge to disturb or bypass some settled obstacles in their own lives and in the world outside. Chapters 2, 3, and 4 examine the dimensions of a woman's public image, private life, and outsider status as related issues that pose special challenges, testing the strength and ingenuity of the female candidate.

Chapters 5 and 6 concentrate on the nuts and bolts of political candidacy and ask how women are utilizing the old resources and techniques of campaigning for their own purposes.

Chapters 7 and 8 look at feminism and other social forces

which are most directly related to women's campaigns and capable of influencing election results. In this larger context, also, the issue remains: what is helping and what is hindering women's drive forward in public life?

Women are in the running. The race is far from over. We have yet to see what will happen if at the other side of the finish line women and men stand in equal numbers as winners. Based on the experiences and attitudes of women seeking office today, we can locate some patterns and make some projections about where and how women in politics can make a difference and what it will take for women to stay in the running. These matters are raised in the Conclusion.

Most of all, this book is about participation. Women are not going to make a difference if they choose not to participate, not to seek positions of responsibility in the world at large. Until many, many more women see themselves as candidates, public leadership will remain one-sexed. Those running for office today are evidence that women can and should choose to be active participants in political life. The candidates described in this book know about the limited support, the formidable barriers, and the defeats women encounter in campaigns—but they believe strongly in the value of what they are doing. The experiences of these women can alert and prepare other women for the hard realities they will encounter on the campaign trail, while at the same time encourage more of them to move forward as candidates.

The example of these candidates should educate us all about the importance of widening opportunities for participation in public life. For its citizens to decide not to participate in the democratic process is the greatest threat democracy faces. Encouraging responsible, widespread participation should be one of our highest priorities. The women in this book are making a noteworthy contribution toward furthering that goal.

Chapter 1
The Advance Guard

I think one of my major uses is as an example to the women of our country, to show them that if a woman has ability, stamina, organizational skill, and a knowledge of the issues she can win public office.
—Shirley Chisholm
Unbought and Unbossed, 1970

A lady named Farenthold wants to be Vice President.
—Walter Cronkite during the Democratic Convention,
July 1972 (quoted in *The Decade of Women:
A Ms. History of the Seventies in Words and Pictures,* 1980)

The first female political candidates in the United States ran for office even before the federal Constitution granted suffrage to women in the nineteenth amendment (1920), and a handful of women served in elective and appointive capacities in government over the fifty-year period between 1920 and 1970.[1] Few and scattered, they were largely invisible, with merely a name or two like Margaret Chase Smith and Frances Perkins receiving any broad recognition. Only in the decade of the seventies did women as a group begin moving determinedly and in noticeable numbers into the public arena as candidates for positions at all levels of the political system. Even then, the pace of progress has been glacial enough that in 1979 Congresswoman Pat Schroeder of Colorado concluded, "We are still a novelty act."

An active decade did manage to bring a small but visible and, therefore, influential advance guard of political women to public attention and into contact with one another. In November 1977, for example, thousands of women gathered in Houston, Texas, for the historic National Women's Conference. Banners proclaimed, "Standing together women shall take their lives into their own keeping." Meeting to vote on a plan of action for women, they arrived from all over the United States as part of state delegations and as observers, speakers, and organizers. Elected women stood among them—congresswomen, state executives, state legislators, county commissioners, and city councilwomen. Nevada State Senator Jean Ford remembers the occasion in a way which speaks for many of the women who had tossed hats into the candidates' ring in recent years: "I found women I knew everywhere in the convention hall. It was the result of almost ten years of something happening. I realized I could pick up the phone and call women I knew all across the country. Every meeting I go to, I meet women and am inspired by them, and everywhere there's more networking. That didn't exist ten years ago."

Political women are becoming visible in an area where, except in rare individual cases, women have received virtually no attention. In the past, any given year's list of most admired women was likely to include a president's wife, but no woman who earned prominence in the political world in her own right. We are seeing the beginnings of a shift in patterns of admiration—from women whose public recognition depends on their husbands' political status to women who are themselves political practitioners. In 1979 the Sunday *New York Times Magazine* published a cover story about New York City Council President Carol Bellamy, and in early 1980 devoted its cover to Chicago's Mayor Jane Byrne. In the nine previous years, the magazine's cover stories had examined numerous political men but never had focused on an American woman seeking or holding elected office.

Women's changing perceptions about their own political participation have been affected by a combination of influences in recent decades, particularly by the social changes that have reshaped American life since World War II. Modern technology has reduced drastically the time and energy required for basic survival and household-maintenance tasks. Contemporary history has witnessed an expansion of women's opportunities for education, a continuous increase in women's labor-force participation, the control and reduction of family size, and the growth of social welfare programs which shift partial responsibility for family burdens to the public sector—all circumstances which contribute to drawing more and more women away from an exclusively private and domestic life for longer and longer periods of immersion in the world outside the home. In active relationship to environments outside the home, most people gain knowledge, build skills, and develop a sense of self which result in a more multi-faceted existence than is available behind one's front door.

During the same period of American history, social and political conditions have stimulated populist activism in segments of the public not traditionally considered part of the country's political elite. The civil rights and peace movements were followed by a proliferation of activities among consumers, welfare recipients, senior citizens, physically handicapped citizens, tax reformers, people concerned with the environment and energy, proponents and opponents of abortion rights, and a host of other special interests organized to bring their concerns to public attention and influence governmental policy. Some women who joined in support of grassroots efforts on behalf of specific issues moved into direct and sustained contact with the political system. They learned some of its inner workings, developed relationships with its practitioners, and evolved a continuing interest in influencing the shape of public policies. Citizen activism and running for elective office are very different kinds of political participation, with the first rarely causing the second. Yet in some instances, women who joined special-issue efforts to exert pressure on government from the outside came to view candidacy as one way to try for a say on the inside, where they might be able to shape laws and develop policies reflecting their views of public issues.

For example, some years before she presented herself as a candidate for elective office, Congresswoman Barbara Mikulski of Maryland made a personal commitment to take an active part in fighting for a humane and equitable society. She was employed as a social worker in 1963 when Martin Luther King led his march on Washington. Making her welfare-department calls that day, she came face to face with a conflict between her fears and principles. She had refrained from participating in the march on Washington because she was afraid of trouble and concerned that she would be ridiculed for making public her growing commitment to the under-privileged. As she went from home to home on the social worker's route for the welfare department, she walked into homes where, she recalls, "Everyone I visited was watching the march. I did something that day I had never done. I walked off the job." Mikul-ski went home to watch the rest of the march on television. Hearing Martin Luther King speak and watching the people, she says, "I swore I'd never be part of an audience again if I believed in some-thing." Mikulski went on to be a community organizer, helping to found the Southeast Community Organization in Baltimore in order to win better services for that section of the city. A social worker and community organizer, Mikulski knew the problems faced by people in working-class neighborhoods. She was also deeply concerned and frustrated at seeing working-class ethnic populations and racial minorities pitted against each other for social welfare crumbs. In 1971 her feeling that she could accomplish more as an elected official prompted her to campaign for a position on the Baltimore city council. In 1977 she moved up from the council to take a seat as one of eighteen women in the U.S. House of Representatives.

Increasingly negative public attitudes about politicians and government in general also have contributed to women's views of their own fitness for public life. Feeling alienated from govern-ment, more and more citizens judge it incapable of responding to the needs of individuals, and condemn it as soaking up in revenues far more than it returns in services. The specter of Watergate shrouded the country in a political era which has been marked by investigations of corruption among public officials at all levels. Renewed distrust of politicians and popular cynicism about politics-as-usual created a receptive atmosphere for new types of political candidates to emerge. Untainted by a history of shady deals and payoffs, stereotypically viewed as unsullied guardians of morality, and associated with no habitual need for personal power, some women running for public office began to think of themselves as representing a hope for positive change. Some voters saw them similarly.

WOMEN'S-RIGHTS MOVEMENT

Overriding all other immediate influences on women's changing perceptions about their place in the public world during the late sixties and through the seventies has been the broad and powerful impact of the contemporary women's-rights movement. The movement stimulated women everywhere to reexamine, sometimes reconfirm, and often reconstruct their self-images. It told individual women that they can plan for more in their adulthood than an exclusive focus on marriage and motherhood. Throughout the 1970s, feminists stressed the importance of political participation and power, insisting that women should take responsibility for the laws, policies, and institutions that regulate their lives.

Among the expanding numbers of women seeking public office for the first time, some candidates belong to feminist organizations and run as outspoken advocates of women's rights. A small number run as antifeminists in reaction against what they perceive as an ultraliberal, decadent threat to society posed by the women's movement. However, by far the largest group of political women is composed neither of card-carrying feminists nor antifeminists.

The woman who represents the greatest increase in numbers of female office seekers in recent years is someone who says she simply noticed that "my turn had come." She articulates no strong ideology regarding feminism, yet she is supportive of many public policy goals for equal rights and opportunities developed by the women's movement.[2] After devoting considerable time and energy to organizational life and civic activities, voluntary community service, or political party work, this woman sees it as only reasonable that she should be moving into elective or appointive positions of public responsibility. She may not even recognize that it was in fact the feminist concern with rigid sex-role stereotyping and the call for wider opportunities for women that focused her attention on the issue of whose turn it was. Yet without the women's movement she would not have come to believe she had a right to a turn.

"The women's movement and all the consciousness raising has caused women of all types to look at themselves anew and see broader opportunities open to them," says Illinois state legislator Eugenia Chapman. She and many other political women identify the movement as a direct source of inspiration and support for women's candidacies. When asked how she first got into politics, Vermont's Lieutenant Governor Madeleine Kunin states: "In 1972 a group of us started a women's political caucus. We formed a support group for one another and became active in local politics. One woman ran for the State Senate and I decided to run for the House. . . . I had always been interested in issues and had worked in campaigns. I thought I would run for office someday when my kids were older, but with the support of my women friends, I decided to go ahead."[3]

While the women's movement has had a direct influence on some candidates, most women in the political arena today identify less overtly with feminism, yet nonetheless have begun to view themselves as candidates because of the political climate it has created. "I'm not a women's libber, but I do think we should have more women in office." This combination of familiar assertions touches on a way in which the ambiance of feminism has propelled women into envisioning themselves as potential public leaders.

Indeed, most people feel positively about the idea of expanded opportunities for women outside the home. Public opinion polls indicate that the percentage of people favoring efforts to change and strengthen women's status in society grew steadily from 42 percent in 1970 to 64 percent in 1978.[4] On the issue of voting for a qualified woman for President of the United States, 57 percent of a national sample responded favorably in 1963, but by 1978 positive replies had risen to 80 percent of respondents.[5]

These issues were not being discussed widely in 1960. In the early 1970s women's political participation was one of many issues raised by the feminist movement, and it received widespread attention. The National Women's Political Caucus was founded in 1971, and the next year played an important role in promoting women's status and participation within the political parties and in raising women's issues at the Democratic and Republican presidential conventions. Also in 1972 Congresswoman Shirley Chisholm ran for the Democratic presidential nomination and was cheered on by many women across the country. Supported by feminists in coalition with other minority delegates, Yvonne Burke of California was selected vice-chairperson of the 1972 Democratic convention, and Frances "Sissy" Farenthold of Texas became a candidate for the vice-presidential nomination at that convention. The 1972 conventions made history in other ways as well. The Democratic convention attracted a record number of female delegates (40 percent), and it exhibited a show of common purpose among feminists who came to Miami willing to fight for improving women's status within the party. At the Republican convention, women comprised 30 percent of delegates, a large increase over their representation as 17 percent of delegates in 1968.[6] Jill Ruckelshaus, a member of the policy council of the National Women's Political Caucus, and other leading Republican feminists worked successfully for the adoption of a women's plank in the party's platform.[7] At both presidential nominating conventions in 1972 and thereafter, feminists and advocates of party reform expressed strong support for improving women's status within the political parties, increasing their numbers among convention delegates, appointing more women to public office, and encouraging more women to run for elective offices.

As the seventies continued, the idea that women should step up to the front and center of political life no longer seemed odd. A 1979 editorial in Georgia's *Macon Telegraph* is typical of the attitude prevailing a decade after the women's-rights movement advocated increased political participation for women. The editorial argued: "Talented women are wasted playing supportive roles only. . . . Developing leadership among women, both as party workers and as elected officials, is important. We need good people, of either sex, to run for office. And good people to influence party policies and to support good legislation. We need women in politics."[8] By 1980, feminist or not, a great many people agreed with the idea—at least in principle—and anticipated continued advances for women as political leaders.

NUMBERS COUNT

Across the board in federal, state, county, and local offices, women's total representation increased from well below 5 percent in the early seventies to about 10 percent of elected officials in 1980.[9]

In state politics, the nation has moved from never having elected a female to govern a state in her own right to electing two female governors—Ella Grasso, elected governor of Connecticut in 1974, reelected in 1978; and Dixy Lee Ray, elected governor of

Washington in 1976. In 1970 no state had a female lieutenant governor. By 1975 New York, Kentucky, and Mississippi had elected Mary Anne Krupsak, Thelma Stovall, and Evelyn Gandy, respectively, as their lieutenant governors. While all three women had served in more than one public office before seeking the second slot in their states, the time was right in the mid-seventies for them to move into an office to which only one woman ever had been elected.[10] Other women followed suit. By 1979 the number of women serving as lieutenant governors had doubled to six.[11]

The state legislature has been an interesting political arena to watch. At that mid-level of government the numbers of women seeking nominations and winning office in state senates and state houses have risen steadily. In eleven years, the total number of women state legislators increased from 305 in 1968 to 770 in 1979. Each major election day during the seventies brought women's overall representation in state legislatures up to above 10 percent by 1980. In 1981 it reached almost 12 percent.

The same general pattern emerges at more local levels in county and municipal government. Here also the gains are noteworthy; but here again women started from a position of virtual invisibility, working forward to the bare beginnings of representation. In the second half of the seventies women grew from 3 percent to 5 percent of county legislators, and from 4 percent to 10 percent of municipal elected officials across the country. In large urban areas, women moved into positions as mayors of five cities with over a half million population.[12] The largest among them is Chicago, which in 1979 elected Jane Byrne as the first woman to lead a major American city with a population of over three million.

Even with these advances, the proportions of women remain small at all levels of political life, and the rate of change is relatively slow. The snail's pace is remarkably apparent for the most competitive offices, particularly those at the federal level. A woman rarely acquires a nomination for the U.S. Senate or House in races where seats are open and where her party has traditionally held the district. While women have fared slightly better in competing for seats in the lower house, even there congresswomen have never achieved even 5 percent representation. For over twenty-five years between 1954 and 1981, the number of women in the U.S. House remained fairly static, never going below ten members and never rising above nineteen. Evidence of very modest progress, however, is apparent in the greater numbers of women winning major party nominations for House races beginning in 1972:[13]

Year	Number of Women Nominated
1958	27
1960	24
1962	21
1964	16
1966	25
1968	19
1970	25
1972	32
1974	45
1976	52
1978	45
1980	52

While the number of nominees has been rising, at the congressional level the rate of victory for women has been lower than at other levels in recent years. After watching women stalled before reaching Congress, political columnist David S. Broder remarked that the "gross imbalance in the makeup of Congress will not change until both parties start helping women candidates get nominated in races that are winnable—instead of putting obstacles in their way or forcing them to wait until they are widows."[14]

Few women are nominated in races that are winnable when it comes to prestigious competitive offices. Among races that are least winnable are those in which a candidate opposes an incumbent, since the vast majority of incumbents (regardless of sex) win their reelection races. In both 1976 and 1978 women received only 10 percent of the nominations in districts where U.S. House seats were open. With about 90 percent of female congressional candidates facing incumbents, it is easy to understand why the number of women in Congress has remained fairly static.[15] With incumbency the most critical variable in predicting a success for both primary and general election races, it is important to underscore the fact that most political women campaign for office in the unenviable position of challengers.

Indeed most political women are campaigning in the even more unenviable position of first-time office seekers. Among the

greatest challenges faced by political candidates in the United States
are those of finding supporters, attracting resources, and building
an organization for the first time. The majority of women holding
elective office during the 1970s were serving in their first term, and
since all women were occupying only one-tenth of all elective positions at the end of the decade, substantial increases in the ranks of
female officials necessarily will involve many first-time candidates.

The numbers from the seventies point out that change is occur-
ring. They suggest that what is significant is a pattern of slow and
steady advancement rather than a series of disconcertingly rapid,
dizzying gains. Newcomers in the 1980s enter a pool of female
candidates in which there is much room for growth, but which
exists and took shape because of advances in the preceding decade.
Still unknown is whether a long-term social trend has begun, or
whether women to whom the image of political leader is appealing
comprise only a very thin layer quickly peeled off the general
population of women. If women are to become a significant part of
the nation's public leadership for the future, the numbers willing
to take the first step and identify themselves as candidates for nomination must continue to mount.

MOTIVATIONS AND PERSPECTIVE

Counting the numbers casts some light on the where and when
of women's recent political activities. But why are women running
now? What are the discernible reasons for entering territory traditionally hostile to them? Within the context of some broad societal
and political conditions noted earlier which have helped to reshape
women's lives and have affected political attitudes and behavior,
women repeatedly identify particular motivations and perspectives
they appear to hold in common.

At one level, women are campaigning for many of the reasons
generations of men have sought office—public service, good government, attraction to politics, personal ambitions, power. The typical female candidate describes herself as an energetic, concerned,
and informed citizen who believes she can contribute to making
government more responsive to human needs and more efficient
and effective in its performance. She enjoys working with people
in teams, likes the excitement and give-and-take of electoral poli-

tics, and derives personal satisfaction from being in a position to represent people's interests and to influence the world at large. Particular circumstances and incentives range from the desire to shape the future of a given community's land use or housing policies, to a deep commitment to a specific agenda of social issues, to a concern with taxation and government spending, to a professional interest in government and personal ambitions for public careers. These are the explicit reasons political people have always been drawn to elective office.

At another level, some important motivational factors underlying their moves on elective officeholding are unique to women. Because of the women's-rights movement, women are looking at men *and* at one another differently. A good many women say they are running for office because they are not satisfied with the job men are doing and share a new confidence that women can do at least as well as men, and probably better in certain areas where they feel they can bring a fresh perspective to public affairs. Women also say they are motivated and emboldened by one another's example and the support they are receiving from other women.

Men "Motivate" Women

The feminist climate and political-reform efforts in recent years have affected the behavior and attitudes of women and men toward each other's candidacies. Men are more likely to see women as potential officeholders. Some male political leaders express genuine interest in bringing fresh talent into electoral politics, and they encourage women to take responsibility for public affairs, even to claim a fair share of political power. It is no longer unheard of for local leaders to see an advantage in recruiting female candidates as nominees on their tickets. One local councilwoman, recalling the circumstances which motivated her candidacy, describes a common occurrence nowadays: "I was involved in the League of Women Voters, but not really planning to run for office. Then the Democrats ran a woman who almost won in our very Republican town. So the next time, the Republicans decided they needed a woman on the ticket, and I put myself forward and got the nomination." Indeed the more women run for office, the more often male leaders seek out other women. This is particularly likely when a political party is facing a female candidate on the other party's ticket and is anxious to appear equally progressive or is concerned about losing potential crossover votes among women.

Ironically, however, the way men often motivate women to run for office today is negatively—by negative behavior on matters of public policy affecting women's interests, and especially by negative examples as corrupt, ineffective, or simply uninspiring public officials. "Many women have run because they have seen a need to have men take a second look before they think our concerns are frivolous," declares a state legislator who finds herself surrounded by male colleagues making light of the Equal Rights Amendment and other issues she takes seriously. More often, today's female candidates simply say they decided to run for office because they took a good look at male officials and concluded they could do the job better. The more confident they are about their own credentials for candidacy, the more they judge men's records as open to challenge.

Far from being radical ideologues, most women reaching for the reins of government express moderate positions on public issues and view themselves as political realists concerned that public officials meet reasonable standards for performance. Women like Democratic State Representative Harriet Keyserling of South Carolina have accumulated years of experience in civic activities and nongovernmental organizations before seeing themselves as candidates challenging men for elective offices. Keyserling recalls that she ran for her first office in county government in 1974 because "I was an observer for the League of Women Voters, and while observing County Council one day I thought—I can do that as well, or better, than some of them." After serving for two years in county office and then winning a seat in the state legislature, she offers advice to other women considering candidacies: "Don't subject yourself to finer scrutiny than you do male candidates. Just look around you. Can't you really do as well, or even better, than at least half the people now in office?"

In Maryland, Casey Hughes ran her first campaign for office in 1974. Losing a bid for the state senate by an agonizing ninety-four votes, she says the experience taught her a lesson in self-confidence. "The first time I was thinking about running—because you don't have backing and support and people are not coming to you to say you should run—I was petrified. Then you run and you find out you are so much better. If you think *you're* a dumb klutz, you see that man and say, 'Look at *that* dumb klutz.' You learn men candidates are not a bunch of superior beings."

Taking one's measure against incumbents is as common in politics as after-dinner speeches. Once women persuade themselves that the option exists for competing in politics, they articulate a variety of motivations for their individual candidacies. Running against politicians in power is not viewed as a contest between sexes (indeed, the politician in power is sometimes—although not often —another woman), but rather as a contest between issues, parties, ideologies, and competencies. However, there is a recurrent theme motivating many women's candidacies. Seeing themselves as representing an untapped source of talent, they run for office to bring new ideas and a fresh perspective to a tired political establishment. The theme is: we can improve government by making it more responsive to you, the people whose interests it exists to represent. Sometimes the "you" is specifically applied to women, with the female candidate speaking to voters as someone who understands women's needs.

Such was the case in Los Angeles in 1976 when Democrat Maxine Waters won nomination to a seat in the California state assembly. In a fierce primary race, Waters knew something about the women in her district whose votes she needed to win:

> California's 48th Assembly District includes the city-sized Watts slum, scene of the 1965 riots. Despite government programs and some efforts by private industry, little had changed in the ten years since Watts burned. Residents were still poor and unemployed at rates much higher than the national average for black Americans.
>
> Both Maxine Waters and her campaign manager, Leslie Winner, were veterans of other Southern California political campaigns. But they saw this district as different, and they felt the old inner-city problems should be approached in a new way. Since Waters herself is a black woman and a divorced mother, Winner explained, "We thought she had an advantage because so many women here are on their own. We were not sure of this because we had no money to poll. We just decided to gamble that it was true."
>
> Following their hunch and using their well-honed campaign expertise, Waters and Winner put the bulk of their primary campaign money into three mailers with positive stress on women's issues. In

targeting the women's mailers, the Waters campaign followed the practice of renting computerized voting rolls from the county clerk. The rolls were brought to a mail house in order to select names and addresses of those voters the literature was designed for. It had been decided that the mailer would not go to all women voters in the district, but only those who were single heads of households. The computer picked out names of registered women voters at addresses where no males were registered to vote. This single-women's list was so large that it even surprised the Waters' strategists. Out of thirty-five thousand Democratic households in the district, seventeen thousand had only women registered voters. While there may have been nonvoting males living at some of these addresses, Winner believed the bulk of the list represented women who were supporting families on their own.

The mailers prominently displayed the motto "Isn't it about time? Now let's get together and show them what a woman can do." Maxine Waters was referred to as "a woman and a mother with proven experience in government." The four-page brochure spread out into a large sheet showing a circle, which was divided into six sections containing tips about property tax, schools, and consumer fraud.

Waters' campaign manager says that a factor at work was an anger among voters at government and the men who traditionally run it: "We got a lot of feedback from the people, not only in the district but in other areas as well. Women were saying, 'If there's a woman running, I'll just vote for her because men have been running it long enough and it's a mess.' Even people I know who are not that liberal and who would say they're anti-women's lib—they would say to me, 'I'll vote for the women now, just to see what we can do.' "

If Maxine Waters' targeted mailings did in fact raise salient issues for her potential constituents more directly than men had in the past, then their feeling about voting for a woman may have been based on the best kind of evidence—the female candidate knew who they were, knew what they needed, and could speak on their behalf.

Women Motivate Women

On an increasing scale, indirectly by example as well as through direct support, women are stimulating other women to advance in political life. Following Margaret Thatcher's election as British Prime Minister in 1979, Midge Costanza declared, "I myself am a liberal and Margaret Thatcher is conservative. But we've all been run by men whose philosophy we don't agree with. Why not a woman?"[16] Acknowledging the obvious truth that women will hardly be monolithic in their political views, Costanza suggests the value of distinguishing between two dimensions of support for women—supporting a principle of leadership opportunities for women, and assessing individual women's political philosophies. On the first dimension—assent in principle to opening the political world to women—there is massive agreement. As a result, many women who might otherwise have remained on the political sidelines have felt encouraged to step forward. On the second dimension, there is predictable disagreement about individual political ideologies and candidates. Inevitably, all women cannot support each other's candidacies. They are as likely as men to engage in the healthy democratic process of campaigning in opposition to one another.

Diverse political philosophies notwithstanding, women who rise in public life bring other women up, too. Each time a woman makes a speech, appears on television, is quoted in newspapers, or greets crowds of voters, the image of women in politics becomes more familiar. The idea spreads to others. Winners inspire imitators. Losers demonstrate that resilience is a component of the political personality and that nothing can be won in politics without risking defeat. Win or lose, the example women are setting for other women is a major factor motivating more candidacies each year.

As a case in point, in Oregon female candidates acknowledge the impact on their campaigns of a woman whose statewide candidacies for governor and U. S. Senator, while unsuccessful, received a great deal of attention. Her accomplishments and defeats profoundly affected local political women:

> The pioneering role of State Senator Betty Roberts two years earlier played a part in the decisions and gains made by women on the 1976 ballot in Oregon. In 1974, Roberts, a liberal from Portland, surprised the oddsmakers by nearly winning the Democratic nomination for governor. In a field of three serious contenders, she lost to former State Treasurer Robert Straub by a thin 2 percent margin.

> Roberts herself called her statewide gubernatorial campaign "a

shock treatment for Oregonians." The shock was that "a woman had the gall to run against Straub, a household name, and come so close," she said. Two years later, the shock waves were still being felt, even by women of the opposing political party.

Republican Norma Paulus, a three-term state legislator, won her 1976 bid for secretary of state despite an overwhelming Democratic voter-registration edge in part because of Roberts' trailblazing role. "There is no question that Betty's races helped me," said Paulus, who became the first woman elected in her own right to a statewide office in Oregon. "She [Roberts] was the first one out of the chute. Two years later when I ran, it wasn't such a startling thing for a woman to be going after a statewide office." Paulus said she also believed that voters "felt guilty" that they hadn't elected Roberts and that some of the guilt spilled over to support for her own candidacy.

Democrat Jewel Lansing, another woman on the 1976 statewide ballot, also benefited from Roberts' earlier races. Although she was defeated in the general election, Lansing did upset a better-known male candidate to win the Democratic nomination for state treasurer. She acknowledges, "There's no doubt that the fact that Betty ran— and ran such a visible race statewide—made it easier for me and other women to run."

The case of Oregon illustrates a phenomenon of recent years which is not special to one state. It involved specific interactions among political women. In Oregon, Jewel Lansing's decision to enter the statewide race for treasurer in 1976 was made after she had been in the audience during the 1975 Oregon Women's Political Caucus state convention, where she heard speeches by Betty Roberts and Norma Paulus. At that meeting, Paulus announced her intention to run for secretary of state. As Lansing listened to Roberts and Paulus talk about the need for women to work together for their advancement, she was moved to reflect and act on her own political future. "It was the first time I had really considered running for state office," she recalled. "It was a very supportive dynamic."

While Lansing ultimately lost the general election in 1976, she believes that as someone who emerged to run for statewide office from relative obscurity, she made enormous progress in building a political profile. Ironically, losing at the polls gave her a new image of her own potential for victory: "Because I did lose," she said, "but came very close in a tough race, I plan to reassess my own view of my own potential in the next few years."

The lesson Lansing says she learned for the future is that "the most limiting factor on anyone's potential is in his or her own mind." This perception, coupled with the genuine politician's expectation that she will run again "not because I lost, but because I did so well," signifies a new attitude developing among women across the country who are watching each other and finding new opportunities for themselves in political life.

Beyond creating a general atmosphere of encouragement, women are motivating and supporting each other's candidacies in more concrete ways. It is common practice for well-known politicians to assist candidates within their own states and to travel the country on invitations to boost campaigns waged by members of their own political parties and ethnic and racial groups. But it is a development of recent years that with increasing frequency women have adopted this practice specifically to support other women's candidacies. Nowadays there are also signs that women are adopting another common practice traditional among men for motivating each other in a direct manner. That is, political women are urging other women to run for election, even grooming future candidates by providing opportunities to gain the right kind of experience and to make useful contacts. Women in politics have begun to play mentor roles for each other.

In some cases, candidacies are fostered when women work in other women's campaigns, thereby gaining expertise and confidence for a race themselves. Relatedly, women who have worked for female elected officials come forward as office seekers themselves. In 1976 two women from the office of former Texas state legislator Sarah Weddington ran for election. Billie Coopwood, legislative aide to Weddington, campaigned unsuccessfully for a seat in the state legislature. Ann Richards, who had worked as an aide and adviser in Weddington's office, won her campaign for a seat on the Travis County commissioners court. Weddington, about fifteen years younger than either Coopwood or Richards, believes strongly that women should encourage each other to consider candidacies. "While we never sit down in my office and decide that one person or the other will run," Weddington says, "I do tell them that they have the knowledge and capability to do it." In 1977 Weddington left the Texas house and moved to Washington, D.C., to join the Carter administration, first as general counsel to the Department of Agriculture, and later as the President's assistant, with particular responsibility for women's affairs.

SHE'S THE CANDIDATE

A profile of today's typical female candidate and officeholder at all levels of government would depict her as middle class in socioeconomic status, white, well educated relative to the general population, employed, married, and a mother of several children.[17] In 1976, among the women who conducted campaigns for federal and state offices, well over a majority were between 30 and 50 years old, about three-quarters were married at the time they sought office, and about 90 percent of candidates were mothers.[18]

As would seem inevitable given her willingness to conduct an active life outside the home, political woman is a joiner. She is concerned with civic affairs and belongs to more community organizations, professional groups, social clubs, and church groups than women in the general population. Of course, she also participates regularly in the activities of her political party.[19]

How does she compare with political men? A comparative survey of women and men in office reveals similarities in socioeconomic status, age, and patterns of domesticity.[20] The median age for both men and women serving in office is mid-to-late 40s, and the vast majority of elected officials of both sexes are married and parents.

The striking differences between political women and men crop up in their educational and occupational backgrounds. While women are as likely as men to be college graduates, women have far less education than men beyond the college level—in law schools, business schools, and other professional programs. Among officeholders in 1977, over twice as many men held one or more graduate degrees or had undertaken advanced studies. In their occupations, there is an even more conspicuous divergence between elected women and men. Men predominate in managerial and administrative occupations and are twice as likely to be lawyers. Employed women who hold public office are concentrated in traditional "female" occupations. Almost half of women officials in

1977 compared with a mere 8 percent of men reported employment in four occupational areas: secretarial/clerical, elementary/secondary teaching, nursing/health technical, and social work. While political women hold a substantially large proportion of high-status and better-paid jobs than the general population of working women, their overall occupational profile reflects patterns of sex segregation in the labor force as a whole.

Politically ambitious people seeking to hold office in the electoral system are not required to gain any specific educational or occupational credentials. Nonetheless, by custom and tradition, routes of access to political life have not coincided with the areas of educational background and employment where the general population of women has been concentrated. This helps to account for the low numbers of women in public office. Only the exceptional few secretaries, nurses, social workers, and schoolteachers have found a pathway into political territory. Women's relatively low income; their employment in clerical and service occupations; their absence from the ranks of high-level administrators, managers, and executives; their concentration in sex-segregated working situations and work-related social activities; and, consequently, their almost inevitable lack of contact with the important male political networks which operate in professional life and through business associations—these and other circumstances connected to women's labor-force participation have limited their access to the places where political leadership is encouraged and facilitated.

It is important to stress, however, that today's typical female candidates are not newcomers to the political process. While most are first-time office seekers and thus may be newcomers to candidacy itself, many are veteran political people who have built a record of participation in some phase of politics—as campaign workers, active party members, paid political staff, or appointed officials. What has occurred in the brief span of a decade is that many women who were already politically active now want to take the leading role—that of candidate.

For example, New Jersey's Anne Martindell had often contributed money to political candidates and had spent a number of years as an active party member, attaining a position of influence and leadership in the state Democratic Party. Suddenly in 1972 she became involved in a widely reported incident in which she vented her anger at state party leaders for excluding her from an important meeting because, as one man claimed, they were protecting her from hearing offensive, back-room language. "I don't give a shit what kind of language you use!" she remembers exclaiming in outrage. The following year, at age 59 and after years of supporting other people's campaigns, Martindell stepped forward as a candidate for office. "I didn't think I would win. It was just going to be practice for the next time," Martindell recalls. She did win, and in 1973 was sworn in as one of three women in New Jersey's state senate.

Four years after winning the senate seat in New Jersey, Martindell moved from elective office in state government to an appointive position in federal government, becoming the Director of Foreign Disaster Assistance for the Department of State. In 1979 Anne Martindell advanced further in her political career when President Carter selected her as U.S. Ambassador to New Zealand.

Whereas experienced political women like Anne Martindell are stepping into their first governmental offices in recent years, other practiced politicians who have already won elections have begun to climb higher on the officeholding ladder. Because she has attracted national attention, Governor Ella Grasso of Connecticut is a familiar and obvious example. Grasso had been politically active in party politics for over a quarter of a century before she became Connecticut's chief executive. As an elected official, she served in the state legislature during the 1950s, then gained statewide office as secretary of state in the 1960s. After spending over a decade in that office, she won a seat in the U.S. Congress and served for two terms before moving up to become the first woman to govern a state in her own right.

As each election season ushers in new female candidates, there is also less reluctance than in the past to talk about being motivated by the desire for power—even to mention the word. "Politics is social work with power!" declares Congresswoman Barbara Mikulski, pointing out the link between her earlier "female" occupation as a social worker and her growing political ambitions. "I think women have always been afraid to say they want power," remarks Oregon's Secretary of State Norma Paulus. "The colloquial interpretation of power is corruption. Women haven't wanted power. They've stuck to human problems. But if by power you mean having some control over the state's destiny," explains Paulus, "it doesn't bother me a bit to say that's what I aspire to." Still wary of the negative, even unsavory connotations associated with the word "power," many women cautiously qualify its meaning and its application to their situations. Yet increasingly, the typical candidate in today's advance guard of political women admits that in pursuing a mandate to govern, she cannot and should not shy away from the power it takes to do the job she seeks.

Obstacles

The biggest asset for a woman candidate is being a woman, and the biggest liability is not being a man.
  —Barbara Curran, former New Jersey Assemblywoman

Chapter 2
The Right Image

I'm not what a Senator looks like, but I am what a Senator should *look like.*
>—Bella Abzug, political advertisement for
>New York's 1976 U.S. Senate primary race

I am what I am, as Popeye said. . . . And until women know they can be who they are, act like they are and sound like they are, we're not going to make any progress.
>—Carol Bellamy, quoted in
>*The New York Times*, February 12, 1979

Who is the right woman for public leadership? Not this fat one. Not that loud one. She's just a housewife. No, she's too pushy. That gal's too pure. But she's too sexy. The seventies asked the country to begin recognizing that The Right Woman might be fiction. Many women were right for the job—and they were saying, "I'll take it."

By the end of the decade, however, still only a handful of women had acquired a political record and the political power to make their sex irrelevant either as a benefit or liability for creating a public image. Looking ahead to the 1980 election season, one writer asserted that "serious, direct, but nonabrasive women are gaining in popularity in and around politics these days."[1] That notion of the right image could be hung in the dressing rooms of female candidates next to prevalent assumptions that women are

33

especially honest, available, caring, and hardworking. Before she pastes and pins together an image to wear on the public platform, the woman running for office must come to terms at some level with the unsettling truth that many of the assumptions surrounding her are undergoing rapid change, and they are rife with contradictions. Among those contradictions and amidst change, she must move ahead—constructively utilizing how she is perceived by others, personally acknowledging who she sees herself to be, and thereby discovering the best ways to make a positive contribution in public life.

Standing in the campaign spotlight, men have image problems, too. There are limits on how far their appearance and demeanor can differ from what is expected at a given time in a given type of district. But these limits are less restrictive, with greater room for a variety of images because there is less doubt about men's basic suitability and competence as public leaders. Furthermore, since many men and few women have run for office, people are accustomed to a wider range of ages, sizes, and styles of behavior when it comes to males. One woman who took a race from her opponent was a 56-year-old Democrat who campaigned in 1976 against a 56-year-old Republican man for a seat in the New Hampshire state senate. He told a reporter for the *Concord Monitor* that he would make the better senator. "Why?" asked the reporter. The candidate responded jokingly, "Well, I'm a male and she's a female, for one." His wit may have been miscalculated for today's audience, and his reasoning may have been faulty for any day; but his basic assumption is supported by history and habit. The "right image" for a state senator or any other public official has been male.

Simply by virtue of announcing their political candidacies, women have been challenging that traditional image of who is appropriate to govern. Yet while the door to elective office did creak open during the seventies to make way for more members of the female sex than ever before, the passageway still seems narrow. Many a political woman has discovered a gulf between the self with whom she was familiar and other people's paper-cutout-doll image of a woman suited for candidacy. At issue are such items as her size, shape, manner of dress, facial features and expressions, tone and pitch of voice, and style of self-presentation, as well as the personal and professional history she brings to the podium.

The desirable image for political women seems to have been conceived as an idealized projection of womankind—a bit of everything that is pleasing, including many apparently contradictory characteristics. Emerging from the experiences of real women who collided with the platonic ideal is a long string of no-no's. They include: not too young, not too old; not too voluptuous, not too prissy; not too soft-spoken, not shrill; not too ambitious, not too retiring; not too independent, not too complaining about being excluded; not too smart, not uninformed. During the seventies one statewide candidate was urged to modify her "1950s college dean" image; a congressional candidate worked hard to counter a "suburban housewife" image; several women were advised to soften the "tough, hard old biddy" image; while others were advised to toughen up the "soft, sweet kitten" image. Bouncing between pillar and post with little space in between, women in politics found themselves pressed to mold and present an "I" who appealed to everyone's bias and offended no one, who approached a fantasy of "woman as candidate."

California legislative candidate Sabrina Schiller discovered that restrictions on what was acceptable were more rigid for women than for men. She reported: "I remember once walking a precinct and a woman said to me, 'I don't know if I want to vote for you. You're too young.' Then I realized I'm the same age as my opponent. Why am I too young and he's not? We're both 33." She was too young because, ideally, politicians are supposed to be "experienced" and "mature." At 33 he was and she was not, in the eyes of at least one district voter.

The age issue crops up often for the young female candidate, particularly in connection with related aspects of her nontraditional image. A candidate noted that her presence in the campaign was described repeatedly with references to her youth and stature—she being eight years younger and eight inches shorter than her male opponent. In an interview for television news, a woman campaigning in a special election for Congress in 1979 commented that among the problems she had encountered were her "youth and good looks." In contrast to the situation in everyday life, a woman's youthful looks are not often an asset on the campaign trail.

For women of any age, weight is a matter of concern because it frequently receives attention. In 1974, when she ran unsuccessfully for the Senate, Barbara Mikulski of Baltimore felt, "One of my problems is that I don't fit the image of a U.S. Senator. You know, an Ivy-League-looking male, over 50 and over six feet tall." Two years later, for her congressional campaign, Mikulski realized it would be impossible to turn a round, short, fuzzy-haired Polish woman from Southeast Baltimore into a Cary Grant overnight, so she did the next best thing: "I had to go on a seven-day fast, a vegetarian diet, and get an Italian boyfriend." Mikulski lost weight and drew on her diet for campaign material. "I told people it showed I could keep my mouth shut for a week. But it also showed them that when I make up my mind to do something, I can follow a goal."

In 1976 Bella Abzug dieted and lost forty pounds, but did not draw on that fact for campaign material. She treated the issue of appearance with a different twist, announcing that she did not fit the image of a U. S. Senator, but that she was what a Senator *should* look like.

One congressional candidate who lost weight specifically to avoid its use against her in the campaign was Pat Fullinwider of Arizona during her second challenge to House Minority Leader John J. Rhodes. When she first ran in 1974, she jokingly referred to herself as the "dumpy little housewife from Tempe." The press tagged her with that phrase, frequently describing her in print as "dumpy" while referring to her equally large opponent as "stoutish" or "solid." By 1976 she had lost weight and shed the "dumpy" tag, although at a candidates' night members of her own party introduced her as the one "who lost forty pounds and is beginning to look a lot better on television." An important aspect of the female candidate's credibility has to do with her appearance.

Most female candidates conscious about their physical images watch what they wear even more carefully than what they eat. Jewel Lansing experimented with wearing pants during her 1976 primary campaign for state treasurer of Oregon. She decided they were a liability after overhearing a bystander's comment during a parade in a blue-collar district of Portland. He looked her over and remarked, "Isn't it cute that this little girl is running for office." Cute little 46-year-old Lansing opted for matronly dresses after that experience. Another Oregonian who was even a decade older did wear pants during her legislative campaign, but deliberately chose to wear what she called "feminine colors" to avoid a "mannish image."

"You'd better not look too good," Texas candidate Nancy Judy said. Campaigning in a blue-collar district, she wore conservative clothes. "For six months I even wore turtlenecked evening dresses." At one contractors' meeting a builder told her she looked like "an uptight schoolmarm." "That was exactly the image I wanted to project to 99 percent of the people," Judy said. "You must be attractive enough so that men know there's a female there, but you can't make women feel threatened."

Handsome male candidates seem to benefit from their good looks in attracting campaign workers and voter support. For men seeking office, there hardly seems to be an issue of basic incompatibility between handsome looks and a fine mind. There certainly is no contradiction between the image of a striking masculine person and the image of a public leader. For the female candidate, on the other hand, it is problematic to be beautiful or glamorous; and there *is* a contradiction between the image of a striking feminine person and the image of a public leader. Oregon's Norma Paulus was 43 years old when she left the state legislature and won election as secretary of state. She had been fighting the "blond bombshell" image all of her political career. Her very first campaign brochure had proclaimed "NORMA PAULUS—Not just another pretty face!" Her advisors worried constantly about whether she was "too good-looking to get elected." As her campaign manager explained, "Being a blue-eyed blonde automatically means you don't have a brain in your head."

In a state legislative race in California in the mid-seventies a male incumbent was quoted as having said to an audience about himself and his female opponent, "Look, I lay it on the line to you. You can either elect a beautiful, young, attractive, energetic woman or you can elect a 60-year-old balding man." The implicit meaning of his irrelevant, self-denigrating remark, of course, was that glamorous young women are all well and good in their place, but not credible as candidates. On the other hand, outspoken and physically unattractive women often are hung with the other end of the rope. Overheard time and again among those reacting against women who stand up to speak up in public are remarks like, "She's too ugly to get a man, that's why she's out here doing this stuff." Motivations for behaving nontraditionally are suspect. Since women who can develop and fulfill their "proper" personhood do so on the basis of their physical appearance and in the context of private life with a man, those who behave otherwise must be compensating for their failures as true women by displacing their energies in inappropriate activities. Not too plain, not too pretty—women must find the perfect in-between in constructing a public image.

Age, height and weight, clothing, and physical attractiveness are related to the underlying issue of being taken seriously. Women running for office attempt to establish an image of credibility as serious adults who can be trusted with the electorate's confidence. To some extent they are still perceived as interlopers or as misfits who wish to displace themselves from their natural settings in the home or behind the scenes in politics. Even where they are welcome, women are highly visible on the campaign platform as a new population of office seekers entering a man's world. Thus they are subject to closer scrutiny than the familiar white male candidate. Age and looks have always been popular criteria for judging a woman's worth. With a different twist, these measures operate forcefully in political life as well.

Regardless of age and physical appearance, a candidate's image must emit a competence which is rooted and thrives in her self-assurance as a knowledgeable political person and also as a woman. All female candidates must deal with how they present themselves as women. Whatever the particular circumstances, their sex is part of women's campaign consciousness. This is a truth sometimes not recognized fully by women who, because they are women, expend effort on underplaying and drawing attention away from their sex—a task no man must undertake. Constituents' ideas regarding how women should behave set the limits of the candidates' own behavior and create many of the obstacles they must overcome. Women must appear strong and assertive at the same time that they look and sound feminine; they must be tough with the opposition, but avoid seeming strident. They must somehow convince the public that they are knowledgeable and prepared to assume public leadership, and that their experiences as homemakers, mothers, teachers, consumers, citizen lobbyists, and volunteers are political assets.

During the 1976 legislative races in rural Minnesota, one woman's unsuccessful campaign encountered a number of the difficulties faced by female candidates as they pinched, poked, stretched, and twisted the clay of their individual personalities into an idealized image of political woman.

The perplexities of how to show what you've got—without taking off your gloves—concerned Minnesota's women candidates in 1976. Sue Rockne, a woman with flair and flamboyance, ran for state senate from a rural southeastern Minnesota district. She was determined to be a serious candidate with an acceptable image.

"Wherever I go, I highlight my competence," she said, explaining her campaign strategy. A graduate of Vassar College with a master's degree from the University of Chicago, she observed, "They don't expect facts, figures . . . even in coffee parties. I have to show I know more than they do."

Her direct, robust, even aggressive approach to issues and constitutents drew mixed reviews.

One supporter wrote in a letter to the editor in the *Cannon Falls Beacon:* "Those who know her best have observed her qualities of leadership, the knowledge and seriousness with which she approaches each issue, and her enthusiasm and vitality, qualities not commonly found in today's political world." The letter concluded, "Her academic training, her teaching experience, her years on the Zumbrota school board, and the positions she has held on numerous public boards and councils have, in my opinion, prepared her well for the office of state senator." Another fan wrote in the *Lake City Gazette:* "Sue Rockne is not only educated, articulate, and respected by state government officials and the voters of this area, Sue Rockne is experienced."

Her education and her experience did not help with those who disliked her aggressive style. Ken Pariseau, campaign manager for Steve Engler, her opponent, couched his criticism of her style this way: "She acts too much like a man . . . for a woman." He said, "Biologically, there's still a difference that's acceptable in the average mind. One expects a woman to be a little more refined."

Rockne concentrated on building her image as competent and experienced. But she tried not to overdo it, concerned about appearing "too" competent. She emphasized other, more conventional aspects of her life. Any mention of Vassar or the University of Chicago, any chronicling of her years of community service were usually buried after emphasis on such details of her life as "daughter of an Episcopalian minister . . . Sunday school superintendent and teacher for fifteen years . . . DFL* party worker for eighteen years.''

Early in the campaign the *Rochester Post-Bulletin* carried her quip that she offered a ''clear-cut alternative to that young, inexperienced gentleman.'' However, after noting similarities in stands on most issues (except abortion) between Rockne and Engler, the *Post-Bulletin's* columnist observed that ''age and sex may be the only differences between the two.''

When she lost—and lost heavily—she and the media did not see eye to eye on the reasons for her defeat. She herself outlined some reasons: ''One is being a woman. Two is being a DFLer, and number three is the abortion issue.'' As a woman, she said, she discovered that ''very definitely, the people of this district are not ready to be represented by a woman. They may want to work with a woman, but not be represented by one.''

The *Red Wing Republican Eagle* took issue with this. In an editorial on 4 November 1976, it asked, ''Why did Zumbrotan Sue Rockne fare so poorly against Engler, she who has been so active in public affairs, who carries a well-known political name and has such obvious ability?''

''Not we think because of Mrs. Rockne's sex by itself. . . . Our surmise,'' the editorial concluded, ''is that, with Engler an attractive alternative, voters didn't want this particular woman. . . . Perhaps,'' it observed, ''Sue's personality is a little strong, at least in contrast with the less vocal, easier going Steve.''

Would it have been otherwise if Sue Rockne's opponent, Steve Engler, had been the one with the ''strong'' personality, and she had been quieter and more easygoing? Had she won, it seems unlikely that his defeat would have been attributed in part to a ''personality'' that ''is a little strong.''

The classic problem of the ambitious woman is how to be assertive enough to get what she wants without being charged as aggressive or unfeminine and thereby dismissed as abnormal. In politicians, the public favors those who will fight for their constituents. But a ''fighting woman'' is perceived as a contradiction in terms. Female candidates spend a good deal of time worrying about stepping over the fine line that separates the image of an acceptably assertive woman from that of an unacceptably aggressive woman.

*Democratic-Farmer-Labor: Minnesota's Democratic Party.

Most agree with Minnesota's Sue Rockne that aggressiveness in a woman is not perceived as an asset, yet all are conscious that the public likes a fighter who will champion the causes considered worthy by constituents. In rare instances a fighting woman does find an angry public willing to support her as a crusader. More often, however, women's experiences on the campaign trail have confirmed Bella Abzug's view that were she a man, those who dismiss her as "abrasive" and "aggressive" would instead describe her as a leader possessed with strength and courage.

It has been rumored that women are weaker than men and require masculine protection. Certainly differences between females and males in physical strength have shaped attitudes about weakness and strength in other human endeavors. Direct competition between females and males for high stakes has been virtually unknown. Therefore, very rarely have men been placed in the conflicting position of responding in public to challenges from women and at the same time restraining themselves from attacking the "weaker sex." On the women's side the dilemma is equally difficult. To assume a posture as challenger, confronter, attacker, she must adopt a mode of behavior she was brought up to consider inappropriate for members of her sex. Furthermore, when those whom she challenges are men, she is not only behaving counter to the ways acceptable for women, but she is doing so against the very human beings she has been told are stronger than she is and can defeat her in any direct competition.

In political campaigns these dilemmas are virtually unavoidable. Two or more candidates desire the same prize—a victory on election day. Whether opposing candidates are members of the same sex or members of opposite sexes, they are positioned during the campaign in direct competition with each other. They play out the struggle to win in public view. One of the biggest dilemmas any candidate with serious opposition must face is how much, how sharply, and how personally to cut down a rival. This is more of a problem for a challenger than an incumbent, as an incumbent usually runs on his or her record, and a challenger runs by denouncing that record. It is a problem because the public appreciates a fighter, but not a dirty fighter. In politics, what is and is not too dirty is a matter of opinion.

Opinions vary with time, place, and sex of candidate. Women are more immune from attack than men partly because of the fear which still exists in many parts of the country that the public will react adversely to attacks on women. A campaign manager whose male candidate was facing a female opponent said that his candidate was placed in a difficult position because "It's three times harder to run against a woman—we're halfway between liberation and old chauvinist standards." Women are supposed to be treated as equals; but, he said, "You can't go out and take her on. If you attack her, you're attacking a woman—and that won't go." In the mid-seventies, male opponents of Congresswomen Marjorie Holt and Gladys Spellman of Maryland felt that "attacking is a less desirable approach to take against a woman." As they perceived the situations, Holt's image as a "conservative white-gloves lady" and Spellman's ability to play "the hurt-female role" created a strategic problem for opponents. Holt herself has never felt protected, claiming that her opponents have not refrained from being abusive and from attempting to malign her personally. Both Spellman and Holt feel that as more women move into politics, if they are losing the protection of an imaginary pedestal, they are gaining the credibility properly accorded to serious political people.

A woman's major problem, however, is not in being attacked but in attacking. Attacks on an incumbent's record are frequently the only way in which an incumbent can be dislodged. Unless given a reason to alter their public officials, voters return incumbents to office because they prefer stability over change. Since women are far more likely to be challengers than incumbents, the double standard on attacks hurts them more than it helps.

In this case the double standard is one which says, "Men are acceptably aggressive, women are unacceptably shrill." Time and again women who went on the attack found their charges described in the press as "vicious," "mudslinging," and "negative." Other women avoided launching attacks because, as one candidate put it, "I'm just afraid that I'll come off as 'Superbitch' if I try."

The issue of whether a double standard operates in political life to reward men and punish women for similar behavior was discussed with greater frequency as the seventies wore on and more female candidates pondered how to win victories without losing votes for seeming too aggressive. They knew that one does not campaign successfully by sitting indoors and smiling, but rather by stepping outside and speaking up. They knew that competitive play is sometimes not polite. In a February 1979 *New York Times* article, a number of well-known political women spoke about the "double bind," with Gloria Steinem pointing out: "If you are assertive and aggressive enough to do the job, you're unfeminine and therefore unacceptable; if you're not aggressive, you can't do the job—and in either case, good-bye." New York City Council President Carol Bellamy noted, "Women are not supposed to be loud, and to some extent they are supposed to be deferential. . . . We are expected to be seen but not heard—and if heard, then in rather a limited way. There has to be much more measurement of a woman's personality —suppression, to a certain extent." Expressing a similar point of view, Bess Myerson, former Commissioner of Consumer Affairs for New York City, stated that the word "aggressive" is "one of the highest compliments you can pay a man . . . but with a woman it's a putdown. And ambitious: with a woman it becomes 'pushy,' and takes away her femininity."

If enmity is directed de facto against women who run hard to win, and if that enmity worries female candidates and their staffs to the extent that it ties their campaigns in knots, it is unlikely that even a small number of women will manage to win powerful leadership positions. "This power business" is something "men have been practicing for years, and the ones who succeed have got it down cold," observed New Jersey's Congresswoman Millicent Fenwick in the same *New York Times* article. She believes that women have to "keep [their] eyes and ears open" in order to avoid being "offensive" and to develop "the habit of limited aggression, which men have perfected: the good-humored, effective ways they've developed with such skill."

Commenting on the discussion about a double standard for women and men in public life, political consultant David Garth calls the issue a "cop-out" and says there is a "vast difference between being forceful and dynamic and being abrasive and obnoxious." He stresses that in order to survive in politics, any woman or man has to develop an acceptable style.[2] Nonetheless, women's campaign experiences during the seventies suggest that in political personalities there seems to be a larger margin of tolerance for overpowering males than for bold and demanding females.

In 1976, the issue of attack strategies caused problems for women in Texas. Nancy Judy's congressional opponent, Jim Mattox, projected a feisty, street-fighter image. He emphasized this image by using words like "tough" and "fighter" in his campaign literature. "The public wants someone mean enough to say 'I don't like what you're doing,' and hit him in the mouth," is the way Mattox described the ideal candidate. Yet every time Nancy Judy attacked him for his voting record or campaign spending practices, he retaliated by saying she was "unladylike" or "vicious." In the meantime, he painted her as a suburban fatcat and a country-club Republican. Judy's family income was a modest $18,000, less than Mattox's. Nonetheless, she was unable to use his substantial salary and stock holdings to her advantage. Instead the overriding image of their 1976 campaign was that she was being negative.

Texas legislative candidate Billie Coopwood had the same problem. When a poll showed her behind 25 percent to her opponent's 75 percent, she went on the attack. The strategy boomeranged, and her media aide said later, "At the last, we couldn't turn around and be positive. Billie came off as strident and shrill." Her opponent, Gerald Hill, who did his attacking early so he could "take the high road" later, agreed with this estimate: "Attacking took away her natural advantage as a woman." Even the local newspaper, which did not endorse in this race, spoke positively of Hill and noted of Coopwood, "Her shrillness gives us pause." "Shrill" is a term rarely applied to men.

Republican Leon Richardson shared Coopwood's problem but to a lesser degree because she was armed with a great fear of "looking like a shrewish woman." Nonetheless, she felt she had to attack, and even her opponent's supporters viewed the charges as emanating not so much from her as from the Republican hierarchy. This perspective did not prevent incumbent state legislator Pike Powers from commenting later, "She was full of cheap shots. It hurt her. It sounded too shrill coming from a woman." He made it a point to stay aloof, emphasizing his performance, record, and seniority, and was the only one of three incumbents in his county to return to the legislature in Austin. One newspaper reporter speculated that Richardson's tough-talking manner might have unsettled people in the working-class part of the district: "She just isn't like the women in her district. They wouldn't consider running for office."

While cumulative experience strongly indicates that women lose favor—and perhaps elections—when they attack, at least some candidates feel they lose because they hold back. When two male opponents of Oregon's Caroline Wilkins were involved in a widely publicized mudslinging dispute during the primary, Wilkins refrained from criticizing them, and lost press publicity as a result. She said she refrained from commenting because, as former chairperson of the state's Democratic Party, she has always preached that Democrats should not go after their own. In retrospect she believes she could have won some political points and visibility by attacking them as "two turkeys."

Another Oregon candidate, Republican Virginia Vogel, had established a record as a city council member which her opponent for a state legislative seat constantly attacked. "I didn't retaliate," Vogel said. "That's just not my way of conducting a campaign." In retrospect Vogel believes her reluctance to strike back may have cost her the 1976 election, which she lost by only 365 votes.

Reports from campaigns also indicate that women aspiring to political careers encounter yet another tangle in the process of weaving an acceptable style. It appears when women holding lower-level positions set their sights on advancing to higher office. A nonaggressive, conventionally female image may be an asset in local races and even in contests for selected positions that have developed a tradition as "women's offices," but in running for highly competitive, powerful offices, a more aggressive stance may be required in order to create an image of forceful leadership.

Drastic changes in anyone's public image are difficult to fashion and, when accomplished, often produce problems of credibility. As one of Gloria Schaffer's supporters described the reaction to the "toughening" of her image during the 1976 U.S. Senate race in Connecticut: "Her image has been of a sweet, young, very personable, outgoing woman. When her literature came out with a tough image it was disorienting to those who knew her." It took several weeks for people to believe this is what the candidate would look like. Yet this toughening was also seen to be necessary. As another supporter explained, "Gloria's being pretty opens doors at the bottom, but closes them at the top."

Schaffer's image was "toughened" very deliberately. For the preceding eighteen years of her political career as state legislator and secretary of state she had always run as "Gloria," and her campaign color had been a bright pink. Her outside paid political advisors told her that if she wanted to be taken seriously as a candidate for the U.S. Senate, she would have to get rid of the "fluff." Therefore her Senate literature proclaimed in bold red and orange, "Schaffer for Senate." Her campaign photographs were shot to counter the "pretty blond lady" image. In fact, the photo used in her first leaflet made her look "so much like a bulldog" Schaffer made them do it over.

Bella Abzug did not need to toughen her image when leaving the House of Representatives to run for the Senate. In fact, many people thought she should tone it down. According to her campaign staff, Abzug did not consciously change her image, but ironically, many people thought she was trying to do so. More than one newspaper reporter wrote about the "new" Bella, who had "softened her often contentious manner." One of her chief congressional assistants, Harold Holzer, said these apparent changes were because "Bella is a person of many moods." In his view, all that the press remembers in between campaigns are her strongest statements and actions. As Abzug herself has pointed out, she "is an outspoken person and says things when they aren't in vogue." But in every campaign, Holzer said, the press is again exposed to a multi-faceted person and interprets this to mean Bella is deliberately changing her image.

Throughout her Democratic primary campaign for the Senate, Abzug aimed her specific attacks at her Republican opponent, incumbent Senator James Buckley, even though she was appalled that her main Democratic opponent, Patrick Moynihan, had been a staunch supporter of the Nixon administration. Two weeks before the primary, a reporter asked her if she would support Moynihan if he won. Firmly believing that she would be the winner, she replied that she could not support him unless he clarified his position on Richard Nixon. The press only reported her refusal to support, not the condition on which it was premised, and the party regulars who opposed her chortled that she had finally shown her true colors. *The New York Times* reported that "the nearly unanimous reaction of Democratic politicians" was that "after a year of the 'new' Bella biting her tongue and being nice, the 'old' Bella emerged . . . and got the 'new' Bella in trouble." It was not much of an attack that she was accused of making, and male politicians had made similar ones previously. Nonetheless, it gave her opponents in New York's Democratic Party just the occasion they sought to say that "battling Bella" would attack anyone who got in her way.

The press's stress on the tough side of her personality did have an unexpected dividend during 1976 in upstate New York, where Abzug was not personally known. Precisely because she had such a negative advance image, she came across well in person when people could see there was more to her than her press portrayal.

The following year, during the 1977 New York City mayoral primary, Abzug's television advertising played with some humor on several aspects of her personality. She appeared on screen announcing with a smile that she knew how to be "soft," then changed her facial expression and tone to state that she also knew how to be "tough." A male narrator spoke over the visual image to end the advertisement with a statement that New York City needed a "fighter." Defeated between 1976 and 1978 in senatorial, mayoralty, and congressional races by three men who could hardly be termed "soft-spoken," Bella Abzug more than any other female candidate has been seen as a warning about what happens when a woman cannot escape a negative image after having been labeled as "too ambitious" and "too aggressive."

In fact, guilt by association has plagued female candidates on a large scale in relation to what has become a negative image of political woman based on a caricature of Bella Abzug. An outspoken forerunner for women seeking public office and a pioneer for women's rights, Abzug's aggressive style has been held up as a symbol of bad behavior, and her image as a fighter has caused some backlash for other women candidates. When Oregon's Rosemary Batori, a 62-year-old widow, took to wearing hats in the early weeks of her unsuccessful general election campaign for the state legislature in 1976, friends advised her that it might appear she was trying to imitate Abzug. After that, she left the hats at home. In 1979, Nevada State Senator Jean Ford attended a businessman's political-action breakfast wearing a white straw hat because "my hair looked absolutely awful." She encountered "several comments about 'Bella' being at breakfast," and concluded, "it would have been a better decision to forego the hat because it attracted too much attention."

Missouri's Mildred Huffman, a candidate in 1976 for secretary of state, overheard this remark while campaigning at a senior-citizen luncheon in a St. Louis suburb: an approving elderly citizen leaned over the table and commented to friends, "And she's not like Bella Abzug." Even a politician as well known locally as Maryland's Gladys Spellman, who served for twelve years on the Prince Georges county council before being elected to Congress in 1974, found herself confronted with Abzug's image. "In 1974, I was a Bella Abzug. It was in those voters' minds a negative image I had to fight in Prince Georges County. The enmity was not at me personally, but at the image of women politicians."

In an article analyzing New York's primary races for the 1978 elections, a writer made the following observation about the candidacy of Brenda Feigen Fasteau for a state senate seat: "For her part, Feigen Fasteau's problem is the major hardship of most women candidates—trying to convince the voters she isn't another Bella Abzug."[3] While it is true that no male politician would wish to be compared with Richard Nixon, the former President is associated with misuse of his office and criminal behavior. Abzug has been guilty of no abuses of power, and carries a record as an effective and courageous public official. It is difficult to call to mind an individual political man whose public image *alone* has been used so epidemically as a warning and a weapon as Abzug's.

Women have become well aware of the warning. Because they are sensitive to the fact that a demure image is still required of them, and those who cross over the fine line into what is perceived as "unladylike" behavior are punished, female candidates expend great effort to avoid "sins" such as those attributed to Bella Abzug and to some of the other women who have preceded them on the campaign trail. In Oregon, where Betty Roberts served as a great inspiration for encouraging other women's candidacies, she has also taught another lesson. Women running for office in 1976 learned from what they perceived to be Roberts' mistakes. Whether true or not, Oregon women seeking both statewide and legislative seats believed that Roberts had muffed her U.S. Senate race by becoming "too strident" in the closing weeks of the hard-fought campaign. With women required to walk the line between appearing too soft or too tough, candidates in 1976 believed that Roberts had crossed over into unacceptable criticism of her opponent and had, as one put it, "turned witch." It was a perception that had a profound effect on how her successors ran their campaigns.

"Betty was too strident," said Caroline Wilkins. "She tried to be all business and never smiled. That's something I tried to avoid." Jewel Lansing said the subject of attacking her opponent came up at virtually every campaign steering-committee meeting. "Always the advice was that you don't want to end up sounding shrill like Betty did at the end of her U.S. Senate campaign," Lansing said. "People kept saying that they had wished Betty had smiled more. Maybe it had all become just folklore, but I tried to make myself more relaxed." When Lansing did step outside the bounds of "acceptable" criticism, questioning her opponent's constitutional right to be on the ballot, she was slammed in the press.

Norma Paulus perceived the flaw in Roberts' style. She determined to keep her cool and, above all, to smile. Her opponent, State Senator Blaine Whipple, repeatedly directed personal attacks at Paulus, but "no matter what he said, I smiled," she said. "Most of the time I could stick it to him with a lot of humor." One of her favorite lines, taken from a television commercial, was "Don't let Mr. Whipple put the squeeze on you." When Paulus changed her posture, even to deliver reasoned replies to Whipple's attacks, she received negative press coverage. Following a major debate with Whipple at the influential Portland City Club, Paulus was described as "emotionally upset" by *The Oregon Journal,* the state's second largest daily newspaper. *The Oregonian,* the state's biggest daily, said Paulus had "behaved like a perfect lady," implying either that she was courteous or that she did what women always do—threw a fit. *Oregonian* reporter Early Deane, who filed the story, had originally written that Paulus acted like "a perfect gentleman," implying that she was diplomatic in her criticism of Whipple. But the story had been edited and the lead changed. Deane, a long-time supporter of women candidates, was furious. To point out the connotations of the edited version of his story, he wrote a mock lead and gave it to his editor: "An obviously premenopausal Norma Paulus Friday debated Blaine Whipple, a man.''

While many people were made nervous by Jimmy Carter's ever-present smile during the 1976 presidential campaign, many more seem to feel uncomfortable in the presence of an unsmiling woman. The idealized image of political woman calls for a smiling face.

Women acknowledge the tactical value in staying cool and smiling. In addition, some women seeking votes have plucked the sting from negative images by confronting them directly, and even using them to make other people smile. For those candidates with the talent and flair to employ it, humor serves as a powerful tool for dealing with stereotypes. It was a valuable asset for Barbara Sigmund, a county commissioner in New Jersey, when a political opponent referred to her in public as a "witch." Shunning a direct counterattack, Sigmund donned a tall, black, pointed hat and carried a broomstick when she appeared in the state capital the next day. In a statement to a bevy of journalists, she laughed and noted that it was October and her opponent apparently was celebrating Halloween a bit early in the month. Sigmund's press coverage on that occasion more than compensated for any negative publicity his remark had generated.

In Maryland's 1976 congressional campaign Barbara Mikulski chose a direct, good-humored approach for undercutting potential negative reactions to her image as an outspoken woman. Mikulski specifically aimed her door-to-door campaigning at areas of the congressional district she ran in which were not part of the district she served on the Baltimore city council. The people in her council district liked her and knew her personally. But in the rest of the congressional district she felt she had to prove she was not a "loud-mouthed broad" or a "six-foot, two-hundred-pound truck driver." When such epithets were hurled at her specifically, she turned them to her advantage by using a talent for public speaking. During her campaign she told the Civic Democratic Club: "My opponent is going around calling me a big mouth. Well, when they call me a big mouth, they're right. When I fought against putting massage parlors to keep the sleazos off Eastern Avenue, I was a big mouth. When I fought to keep the prison ship off our neighborhood, I was a big mouth. . . . And when I go to Congress and tell the President of the United States not turn his back on the MIA's, they can call me a big mouth. That's okay, I'm proud of it.''

Barbara Sigmund and Barbara Mikulski eschewed defensive responses to attacks on their public personalities. Since an angry reaction is more likely to confirm rather than to counteract a negative image, astute women like these are discovering other means for winning votes short of shaping their personal identities to fit an idealized cardboard cutout of political woman. They keep cool; they use humor to reverse a stereotype to their advantage; and most of all, they strive to make personal contact with the greatest possible number of voters because they are confident that once people know them, negative stereotypes will fade in the light of a more complex and more positive reality.

Yet sometimes it does seem as if women searching out the right posture for public life confront a choice between the pit and the pendulum. While finding good-humored ways to avoid being judged as offensive or stamped a "Bella Abzug," a "witch," or a "loudmouth," women cannot afford reticence. They must appear confident and outspoken to disabuse the public of another negative image—a widespread notion that women are political novices, thus unqualified for public leadership. In addition to deciding how feminine to look and sound, how assertive and outspoken to appear, and whether or not to move on the opponent with an attacking stance, women more than men must convince people that they know what public business is all about and that they are equipped to conduct it. Because she is assumed to be ill experienced outside the domestic sphere and her circle of personal relationships, a woman must consciously construct a public image which exudes competence. Female candidates for all levels of office feel pressure to prove themselves by spending a good deal of campaign time discussing complicated issues and asserting their ability to handle difficult problems. Despite the fact that election analyses have shown the public rarely deciding on the basis of issue expertise, female candidates are selecting competency as the most critical tool to hone for their success. It is gospel among them that a woman has to be twice as good and work twice as hard as a man to go half as far.

"Image is always an issue, even when not played up," says Vermont's Madeleine Kunin. In her 1978 race for lieutenant governor, Kunin felt a great sense of confidence because she had spent six years in the state legislature and especially because she had served as chairperson of the powerful appropriations committee.

The legislative experience not only gave her confidence in debates with her opponent, but also was invaluable in creating her image of competence for holding statewide office. In building her candidacy, "a woman must make clear first that she's knowledgeable," Kunin observed.

Even when it is not explicitly asked, the question about competency is one almost every female candidate feels bound to answer. In her legislative race, Minnesota's Sue Rockne tried to strike the right balance between seeming experienced and competent and not appearing "too competent"—the old problem that no one likes a woman who is too smart. Most female candidates do choose to stress their knowledge and competence for handling public affairs because the image of the "dumb woman" worries them more than that of the "too smart" woman. Even Bella Abzug, whose professional and political career paralleled that of any suitable male candidate, found it necessary to make her abilities, not her ideas, the main issue of her Senate campaign. The focus of the entire campaign was to portray her "as an effective legislator and not a crazed peacenik feminist" by emphasizing what her public works committee had done for New York.

The women who feel most concerned about displaying their basic competency are those whose images fit the traditional feminine stereotypes—the ones with a striking physical appearance, or those whose primary career has been as a housewife.

Former actress Sabrina Schiller found that when she spoke at Rotarian lunches, "There was a certain lack of respect when you first got started. There was tittering, not taking me seriously—joking or ridicule." As a woman of striking appearance, she had to prove that her attractive body housed a functioning brain. During her campaign she felt confident about handling the problem because it was a familiar one: "I'd had experiences like that in the legislature." As a consumer-affairs activist in the California capital, she found, "I'd be testifying when somebody would say, 'The chairman of the committee would like to have a little private lobbying after the sessions.' You'd just be furious. But you hold your anger in check, shut your mouth, and coolly and quietly steer your best course. You talk about subjects which will impress them—basic economics, legislation which most people know nothing of, voting records. You ask them a question and then you make Swiss cheese of their arguments. You do it in such a manner that's not alienating, that has a positive note. It removes the stigma of being a sex object."

During Pat Fullinwider's congressional campaigns in Arizona, she dealt with skepticism about her competence and the derisive responses to her image as a housewife in a manner similar to that utilized by Schiller. "I have to be three times as competent as my opponent," she reported. "I can't be flippant. They'll think I'm not serious. In speeches, I cite statistics right down to the decimal point. This is an old debate trick and is much more effective than rounding off the figures. You need all kinds of little gimmicks to establish credibility, because the basic assumption is that as a woman, you are frivolous and not competent. You can get away once, and only once, in any given meeting by saying, 'I don't know, but I'll get the answer,' when someone asks a question." Fullinwider managed to turn the latter handicap to her advantage. "One reason I should be elected," she told a local television interviewer, "is that I'm not afraid to ask hard questions. People say, 'Oh, another dumb question from a female!' I say that's all right. 'Why?' isn't such a dumb question to be asking. Children ask it and they get answers. I think a few more people in Washington should be asking 'Why?' "

Despite her ability to turn the "dumb female" stereotype on its head, Fullinwider still resents "the fact that I'm held to a higher standard. If I talk about tax reforms, closing loopholes and saving $107 billion, the press wants to know my source. They wouldn't ask a man that." Perhaps male candidates should indeed be held to the same high standard which Fullinwider describes women as having to meet. At the moment, however, the assumption frequently seems to be that men know about what they speak, or that it is less appropriate to challenge a man's basic understanding of issues and grasp of facts.

A state legislator recalled that when she first entered politics in the early seventies, she sought a position on a planning board. After being told by local officials that the town was not yet ready to put a woman on that board, she presented herself as a candidate for appointment to the zoning board. In preparation for the interview, she spent days studying and memorizing the zoning code. She was one of six candidates, and the only woman. Each of the men was interviewed for approximately fifteen minutes. As she describes her interview, "I was grilled for over two hours" by a group of men who "had a hard time convincing themselves that I knew what I was talking about."

More recently the same woman decided to move up from the state assembly by seeking her party's nomination for a state senate seat. After the party passed her over for the senate nomination, she was shown to another room on the assumption that she wanted to be alone to cry. Instead, she turned around and rushed back into the screening-committee meeting room to make sure that she got her assembly nomination. Bemused by these experiences, she concluded that men like to imagine women as "frail and dumb. Or maybe," she added, "we scare them because they don't know what we're all about."

Even when a woman has a proven record of effective action, she still has to overcome some classic stereotypes, especially that of being competent only for certain positions (usually the one she currently occupies) and being suspect if she is ambitious for advancement. Female candidates who have run for offices higher than the ones they hold have encountered comments to the effect that while they were good public servants at local levels, they might be unequipped to handle state or national affairs. Furthermore, there have been interesting cases of an ironic reversal on the issue of competence. Many female local officeholders have encountered praise for their effective performances as public officials but have discovered that those who praise them may be reluctant to extend support for efforts to move up to higher office, claiming that a move to higher office would be a loss to the community. It is a situation similar to that encountered by secretaries whose bosses, reluctant to promote them to management positions, argue that the office could not function without them. The women are urged to remain where they are and keep up the good work. Expressions of this attitude were overheard frequently in New York with regard to Bella Abzug's Senate race. In one discussion of the Democratic primary candidates, Abzug's name was not mentioned at all until the only woman in the group said, "Why isn't anyone discussing Abzug?" and a man replied, "I have nothing against her. She's done a good job in Congress, so why doesn't she stay where she is?"

Women are supported for their achievements and encouraged to stay put, asked to do even better at what it is they have proven their capabilities for accomplishing. Men are supported for their achievements, too, but they are encouraged to take on the next challenge and keep moving up. The issue is simply that female candidates often experience a reaction to their competence and to the direction of their public careers that is based on assumptions—probably unconscious assumptions—usually not applied to male candidates. Those assumptions derive from stereotypes with which political women must contend, and against which they work very hard to construct alternate images for public consumption.

In her Senate race, despite her eighteen years in public office, Gloria Schaffer anticipated skepticism about her attempt to move up a rung of the political ladder. To preclude it she spent two years prior to the 1976 election educating herself intensively on national issues that were important to Connecticut. While she did succeed in making people listen to her, at least one veteran political observer who felt it was the wrong approach said, "Instead, she should have played upon her intimate, personal, provincial knowledge of Connecticut. Showing how oriented she was to the state would have been a woman's approach."

The point is not that in any given race a woman's decision to be aggressive or wear pants, or appear competent by studying one set of issues rather than another, is *the* decisive factor affecting the election outcome. While in Schaffer's 1976 race the fact that she was challenging the popular and highly respected Senator Lowell Weicker was likely the decisive factor in her defeat, it is interesting to notice, nonetheless, the ways in which she shared with other female candidates the need to construct an image that attempted to mitigate the presumed disadvantages of being a woman running for high office. It is also interesting to note that no matter what strategy women decide upon, some political observers will assess mistakes with regard to what should have been "a woman's approach." That sort of observation in itself is a problem for the female candidate. When she sits down to look over the list of "shoulds" and "should nots" drawn up by friends and advisors to help her compensate for the disadvantages of her gender, she finds that almost every "should" on one person's list will show up as a "should not" on someone else's list.

The political observer who felt that Schaffer should have focused more on her intimate knowledge of Connecticut and should have led from her provincial strengths did hit upon an issue that arises with variations in other women's races—the issue of whether and how women should present themselves with regard to some of the expertise they have acquired while leading their lives playing traditional female roles. Ann Richards, successful candidate for county commissioner in Austin, Texas, prepared her television spots to show a nice-looking woman in a big house who was concerned about utility bills and taxes. In another Texas race, Congressman Jim Mattox said that his opponent Nancy Judy "was a fool not to make use of her housewife's expertise on bill paying, the high cost of living, and the problems created by inflation." His television spots showed him pushing a shopping cart around a market. "It was a stupid mistake," Mattox said. "She was paranoid about her credentials. She had no job experience. So she kept trying to show off her sophistication and knowledge on issues. She should have played up a woman's familiarity with grocery prices, utility costs, that sort of thing." The other side of that "should/should not" coin, of course, is that when women play up their knowledge of grocery prices, they are told to stay home and do the shopping because the price of cereals and soaps bears no relationship to voting on federal expenditures for the defense budget or social welfare programs.

Thus for good reasons many women are ambivalent about identifying themselves primarily as homemakers when vying for positions as elected officials. Some female candidates find themselves labeled "housewife" even when other activities they perform and their other credentials are far more relevant. For two legislative races in Minnesota during the mid-seventies the male and female candidates who opposed each other on the ballot essentially were unemployed. In one race a young man lived with his parents on their farm. He was called a farmer even though he seemed to be doing little farming and spent most of his time campaigning. In the other race the incumbent male candidate had won his first election at age 21 and had no occupational or career history to speak of; nonetheless, he was described with regard to an occupational label. On the other side of the ballot, both female opponents of these male candidates were community activists—one a school-board member, and the other a party leader and former nurse. Yet both were called "housewives" by the press.

In Missouri, Democrat Jean Berg encountered similar difficulties in her 1976 congressional race. Despite the fact that she worked as an administrator of hospital services, she was depicted primarily as a housewife zealous about social causes. In a 1978 congressional race, Republican nominee Claudine Schneider of Rhode Island opposed a male incumbent who was quoted as having announced at a campaign appearance that candidate Schneider would "soon be back keeping house and scrubbing floors." He succumbed to using this image of a housemaid despite the fact that Schneider was the organizer and first executive director of the Conservation Law Foundation, and the Federal Coordinator for the Rhode Island State Coastal Zone Management Program. Schneider was defeated in 1978, but has not been deterred from pursuing her political ambitions. A wife and homemaker as well as an environmental planner, she ran again in 1980 and added the title of "Congresswoman" to her image.

Some women running for office have deliberately used the "housewife" label to their advantage. Mae Yih of Oregon—elected in 1976 to her first term in the legislature, reelected in 1978 and 1980—emphasized that as a housewife she would have more time to spend with the electorate. She promised to establish a constituents' office in her home town. Sandra Richards won another Oregon legislative seat using a similar strategy. When a local newspaper editorialized, "If she can squeeze in the time away from her home and family, she'd be an effective legislator," Richards countered by claiming that as a housewife she had more time than a man with a full-time job. Pointing to her long record of community activity, she argued that being in the legislature would take no more time than being a citizen lobbyist.

Even women who were not primarily housewives found it to their advantage to emphasize their availability. Ironically, accessibility is a traditional stereotype that works in favor of female candidates. Professional women have complained for years that their families, friends, and colleagues would interrupt their work under the assumption that women were always available to meet others' needs, whereas such people would realize that a male professional needed to be alone to get his work done and were loath to interrupt him.

In politics this assumption of availability makes women attractive candidates. People more readily believe women when they say they will conscientiously attend to constituents' problems and be on the spot when needed. "Women are seen as more willing to go the extra step to provide service for people," says New Jersey's Barbara Sigmund. Female candidates sometimes use campaign gimmicks to emphasize their opponents' unavailability without worrying that voters will think they would be equally unavailable if elected. In her county race, Ann Richards used a radio spot with a phone ringing, unanswered: "For $22,500 a year, you'd expect your employee to answer the phone," a voice said. Chris Miller, running in Texas for state representative in 1972 against an incumbent who was both "ineffective and nearly invisible," found that even voters who did not agree with her views appreciated her willingness to discuss issues with them. In one case Miller refused to support an antibusing resolution drafted by her opponent. She told this to the leader of a community antibusing group and was pleased at his reaction: "He said he had tried to reach my opponent by phone and registered mail for two years without success. He ended up sending out four thousand cards supporting me."

Creating an image that takes advantage of the stereotype of woman's availability and responsiveness to the needs of individuals may be more useful in local races than for election to statewide or national office. It is part of the picture of a woman staying close to home, nurturing those immediately around her. It may also result in other kinds of problems, especially when the candidate has become an officeholder and finds herself very busy and very much in demand. Not only do constituents seem to feel more comfortable making direct contact with a busy woman than a busy man in the first place, but many a busy woman who has encouraged that attitude among constituents finds herself inundated with requests for assistance from citizens who do not even reside in her electoral district, but who telephone her in the office or at home, write to her, and visit her seeking advice.

Former Mayor Ann Crichton of Decatur, Georgia, was often called upon to serve people far beyond the twenty-two thousand residents in her community's densely populated four square miles. "I am asked to speak about women's issues around the state; I get calls from women whose husbands are in jail and from people who have been evicted and don't have a place to spend the night. They may live anywhere in metropolitan Atlanta, and may not even know my name, but they know there's a woman mayor in Decatur." Responding to frequent calls from people who were not her constituents and who lived outside her city, Crichton observed that she had additional responsibilities because "the perception is that women care."

A woman elected to local office says she has received calls from all around the western half of her state with requests to arrange visits to Washington for classes of students, to facilitate the processing of citizenship papers for aliens, to find funds for establishing shelters for battered women in other localities. The voices on the phone tell her, "Everybody says you'll do it" and "You have a reputation for getting things done for the people." In addition to requests for aid about issues beyond her jurisdiction, she frequently receives calls about nongovernmental matters. "People call me about their personal problems after they've seen my picture in the newspapers," she says. "They want to talk, they're lonely, and many times they want me to intercede with someone in their lives." She believes that men get fewer calls and are more likely to brush them off. She quotes her male colleagues as warning, "You can't let them get you so involved in their lives." After presenting an inviting image, political woman often must look for reserves of energy, time, and patience to live up to her implied promises and to the electorate's preconceptions about her caring nature.

Another very familiar stereotype which so far has operated in women's favor sees the female of the species as less corruptible than her male counterpart. "Women are viewed as more idealistic, not as easily bought off," said one Texas county GOP chairman. "If they make up their minds, no amount of money will change them." That familiar assumption about women is sometimes articulated in admiration, although often it is charged with condescension and a Hobbesian cynicism which implies that given half a chance women will be equal to men even in corruptibility.

Corruption is a particularly potent issue in Texas, where voters during the seventies saw their governor, lieutenant governor, and speaker of the house implicated in scandals which involved insider stock deals exchanged for legislative favors. If the men have made a mess of it, why not let the women try—this appeared to be the attitude in areas where honesty was not the long suit of office-holders. It is an attitude which boosted the successful campaigns of Irma Rangel and Ernestine Glossbrenner for state house seats against male incumbents in 1976. Rangel's race against Greg Montoya contrasted his reputation as arrogant and inaccessible with her personal warmth and concern for the plight of the poor. She took long walks in sweltering barrios to underscore that concern. "Issues were not important at all in Irma's case," said the South Texas coordinator for the Texas Women's Political Caucus. "People wanted to know about her and her family. She does not represent the power structure; she really cares about people."

Ernestine Glossbrenner's opponent had not been indicted (as Montoya had), but he was tainted by his association with the Parr machine. Glossbrenner took advantage of assumptions without actually making charges of corruption. She focused on her opponent's voting pattern, which showed more concern for special interests than for his poverty-stricken constituency. If elected, she argued, the office would serve the interests of the district by representing the real needs of the people who lived there.

Street wisdom has claimed that power corrupts. People are fond of asking: if the day dawns when large numbers of women control large centers of power, will the image of the virtuous female appear only to illustrate the quaint mythology of a bygone time? The situation is hardly likely to develop in simple either/or extremes between virtue and corruption, but more predictably to be ambiguous and reflect the multiplicity of diverse individuals. In 1974, when Ella Grasso campaigned to become the governor of Connecticut, *The New York Times* reported, "Connecticut loves Ella Grasso," and continued, "the reason, it is generally agreed, has less to do with the issues than it has to do with the image of virtue that she projects. . . ."[4] Four years later the situation had changed considerably after a difficult first term in office marked by controversy, although certainly not corruption. Standing on her record and projecting herself as a strong leader who had made tough decisions, she managed to win reelection—but not on the basis of an "image of virtue." Her image as a woman and politician had grown far more complex.

If increasing numbers of women continue to enter public life and remain to be judged on their records of performance, the issue of sex-related advantages and disadvantages in the candidate's image undoubtedly will diminish in importance. Yet, as Colorado Congresswoman Pat Schroeder reminded us in 1979, "we are still novelty acts." As such, political women in the seventies felt the weight of stereotyped preconceptions about their behavior, but they also benefited from their visibility and from the rewards of being perceived as fresh, untainted by "politics as usual." In an effort to explain Nancy Kassebaum's unexpected victory in Kansas's 1978 U.S. Senate race, a political observer reported that as election day approached, the candidates increased their emphasis on personal images: "Bill Roy's campaign laid heavy stress on his public service and his Congressional experience. Nancy's produced a new theme, that of a 'fresh voice' that would be heard in Washington because it would belong to the only woman in the Senate. Senator Bob Dole trumpeted this theme around the state. He assured audiences that Nancy would become an instant celebrity and have immediate clout in the Senate, unlike other freshman senators." Successfully appealing to a desire among Kansans for visibility, recognition, and respect on the national scene, local newspaper editorials and Kassebaum's political advertisements promoted the idea that her victory would create a new and positive symbol for the state. The observer's postelection analysis explained that the "desire to make history in a respectably dramatic fashion and develop a new image may well explain the apparently successful projection of Nancy's womanhood and inexperience as assets."[5]

For Nancy Kassebaum and others like her who announce candidacies at a time when women remain a largely untested element in the equation for political leadership, the present moment offers an extraordinary opportunity to take advantage of their novelty. At the current rate of increase in their numbers, female candidates can utilize their visibility and freshness as well as other positive attributes of an image which derives from their status as rarities on the public platform. If she is seen as honest and incorruptible, political woman can seize the moment to reassert standards of behavior no one should disapprove. If she is perceived as more humane, available, and responsive in serving human needs, political woman has an unusual opportunity to encourage in the political arena a set of values which may have suffered from neglect. If she is viewed as a creature newly emerging from the domestic hearth, she can bring into the public world the experience accrued from intimate knowledge of people's daily lives. In effect, when women review their assets and liabilities for political candidacy, theirs is the opportunity to select, utilize, and reinforce those stereotypical aspects of a collective image which will serve them in promoting excellence, service, and sensitivity as standards for public performance.

Yet the female candidate is bound to continue encountering difficult problems in shaping a public image because traditional stereotypes about women and conventional expectations about political leaders do not blend together smoothly. Change will occur slowly as more women permeate political life and the image of women in leadership positions is assimilated in the public consciousness. The immediate challenge is for a woman to recognize and then to capitalize on those traits of her appearance, personality, and background that can be used to advantage on the campaign trail. The time does seem favorable for women with flexibility and humor as well as some ingenuity to design the "right image" for their individual situations—even using inherited materials that were cut to an ideal shape no real person ever fit. Many impressive candidates are doing just that.

Chapter 3
Private Life/
Public World

A woman's place is in the House . . . and in the Senate.
                                                 —1970s feminist slogan

Regardless of whether a woman running for office is young or middle-aged, unmarried or married, childless or like the old lady who lived in the shoe, her experiences as a public person are likely to be affected by the contours of her private life as a female. Political women contend with curiosity and scrutiny in a society not yet comfortable with the idea that women might be able to arrange their life patterns so as to function as public leaders. Centuries of history and custom have taught that women belong in the private sphere. Rather than seeking elective office, a single woman is still thought to be better off seeking a good husband; instead of serving in office, a married woman is expected to be serving her husband's and children's needs first. In either case, if her life as a private person is not receiving top priority, a woman is suspect.

The absolute rigidity of dicta like these for measuring success or failure in women's lives has softened considerably in recent years. But the values they represent are still in force. Archaic as they may sound in some quarters, and despite the fact that for many people they no longer carry decisive weight, traditional standards of judgment have been internalized by women and men and continue to influence attitudes and behavior in a variety of ways. A woman's private life is not only an issue for the people looking at her political candidacy from the outside; very often it is a real and serious problem for her and for her family as well. A woman candidate is expected to appear beyond reproach by traditional standards and to exhibit the reserves of energy and emotional fortitude of a superwoman as she coordinates campaign activities with her private life. She demands as much of herself.

Several areas of women's private lives are apt to crop up as issues in their political careers. These range from sexuality per se to concerns about women's primary social roles as historically defined by their gender. Because the act of competing in the public world still represents a deviation from time-honored norms, the female candidate is liable to encounter questions and innuendos suggesting that she might be an "unnatural" woman in either her sexual behavior or her domestic arrangements. Frequently she feels obliged, or is asked, to give evidence that her mode of living is feminine and stable—that her sexual life is conventionally acceptable, that she does not shun domesticity, that she has not abandoned a husband or neglected children who want her at home. In order to cope with the stress of campaign life, she must also come to terms with her own ingrained conflicts about these and related matters. The effort and strains involved in dealing with these concerns exact a toll from diverse women running for all levels of office.

According to female candidates across the country, political opponents frequently succumb to exploiting the public's latent fears and suspicions about the personal life of a woman who has chosen to behave unconventionally by spending her time away from home in a man's world. This situation persists despite increases in numbers of women running for office, striking changes in social relationships between the sexes, and often in disregard of the actual facts. Happily married and the mother of three children, Congresswoman Geraldine Ferraro of New York observed that during the 1978 campaign she faced it all—allegations that her marriage was in trouble, rumors that she was having sexual affairs with several men, and accusations that she was a lesbian. Insinuations about lesbianism arose repeatedly during women's campaigns in recent years. As in Ferraro's case, they were not targeted solely on unmarried female candidates. In Texas, for example, the issue came up in Ann Richards' race for county office despite the presence of a husband and four children. "I told David when we started that he would hear that I was sleeping with every man in Travis County," Richards said. "What he heard was that I was sweet on Sarah Weddington."

With a shorter history of being exposed on the public platform, women may be especially sensitive about skepticism and innuendoes regarding personal matters. As victims of double standards, women are also more vulnerable than men to curiosity about the conduct of their private lives. The same behavior that goes unnoticed or is tolerated in male candidates may be considered a useful weapon against women. For instance, it is common knowledge that many political men engage in extramarital sexual activity, yet it rarely becomes an issue used against male candidates in election season. On the other hand, female candidates often report taking special precautions about where they go, how they travel, and with whom they are seen. Protecting their private reputations becomes a serious issue because suspicions and harsh judgments are more easily aroused against women.

It is also common knowledge that political men have little time to devote to routine family life, yet that too is rarely an issue within a man's campaign or used against him by opponents and the public. By contrast, female candidates are expected to explain satisfactorily how they can manage to fulfill all their domestic, spousal, and maternal duties while at the same time taking on the arduous demands of candidacy and officeholding. "When you're a woman running for office, people think it's because you're running *away* from something wrong at home," laments a woman campaigning in 1979 for a municipal council seat in New Jersey. Everywhere she goes in the district, people ask, "Where's your husband?" She says that her male running mate is never asked, "Where's your wife?"

On most counts, the issue of personal life is generally less troublesome for men simply because they are expected to make fewer explanations to counter skepticism and fewer adjustments to minimize built-in conflicts between their private and public identities. When he runs for public office, a man does not exhibit behavior unusual for his sex. Because he is performing in an arena where men have always been active, he is playing a role consistent with established social patterns. Since women have been regarded for centuries as symbols of private virtue and keepers of the hearth, when they move into the rough and tumble of the public world they may seem to be violating an innate natural order. Thus they are automatically suspect—burdened by their historical status to demonstrate that in choosing to enter public life they have not renounced femininity and that ancient values can be reconciled with newer modes of behavior and broader responsibilities. In proving her case, political woman faces a number of challenges. She must be sensitive to the public's concern that a woman's private life and a political career seem incompatible, and she must discover ways to short-circuit that anxiety. She must deal with her own internal tensions and come to terms with her own identity as a woman and a political person. She must juggle practical necessities both at home and in the campaign to avoid jeopardizing either. Except for a lucky few who face no conflicts between private and public life, the women who do compete in elections and remain in politics are those for whom the public world holds so much appeal that they are willing to pay the high costs of participation.

THE UNMARRIED CANDIDATE

The Double Standard Again

There are some differences between the sexes in the way single status is viewed and even used by opponents. The public assumption about a young single male who runs for office may be that he is an ambitious go-getter whose personal agenda ranks domesticity and family life below other priorities. But the young single woman seeking office frequently is asked to answer for or made to feel defensive about her unmarried status. Twice defeated in races for the state assembly, Cindy Wear of California ran in 1976 at age 27, and then again in 1978, against a male incumbent a quarter of a century older than she. He attempted to use her age and single status against her. In the 1976 race Wear's opponent produced a chart comparing their qualifications. He listed age and marital status at the top, emphasizing that he had the ripeness as well as the traditional long-term marriage with children, while she was young and divorced. Only further down the list were the candidates compared on the basis of qualifications such as familiarity with the district and government experience.

Male candidates are by no means immune from rumors about

their single status and their sexual habits, but the sexes have been viewed differently regarding these matters. Traditionally it was assumed that he had a choice in the matter of his marital status, and she did not. Marriage has been her primary goal, wifehood her primary role. They have been secondary in his life. Thus, when a woman chose not to marry and then to flaunt her deviation from the norm by presenting herself in public view as a single person, she was doing something more unusual than a man who followed a similar course in life. These habitual ways of perceiving the sexes still persist.

Maryland's Congresswoman Barbara Mikulski has even used male escorts in a campaign. She had faced problems about her single status in 1971, when she first ran for the Baltimore city council. At that time she was the target of a whisper campaign. Her amazed campaign manager told a newspaper reporter, "They said she was sleeping with the Black Panthers—*all* of them." During the campaign, people were always asking why she was not married. Mikulski said, "So once I was asked to my face and I said, ''Cause nobody ever asked me.' " Mikulski may be single, but she does have a family whose members are very much part of her campaign strategy and public image. Her parents, aunts, uncles, sisters, brother-in-law, cousins—all of them campaign for Mikulski. She advises women to get everyone in the family into the campaign no matter how young or old. She notes that her nephew was a thoroughly "political kid" by the time he was 8 years old.

Looking back in 1979 on nearly a decade of successful candidacies—first for the Cleveland city council in 1972 and then for the U.S. House of Representatives in 1976 and 1978—Congresswoman Mary Rose Oakar of Ohio observed that as a single woman she was "much more vulnerable to dirty tricks and whispering campaigns." In Oakar's view, single status was an advantage insofar as it allowed the candidate mobility and freedom to pursue office, but a disadvantage for a woman whose opposition decided that a young, unprotected, unmarried "nice girl would run scared and was not used to playing hardball."

Congresswoman Oakar is a strong candidate who has been elected to office by a constituency confident she can serve them in public life and unaffected by rumors concerning her private life. Nonetheless, while campaigning is arduous for anyone, it is even more difficult and draining when one is the object of the "dirty tricks" Oakar feels are played consciously and frequently on a single woman and are often targeted on her sexuality. "When you're single, they try to make you seem promiscuous or a lesbian," she said.

One female candidate who is divorced firmly believes that women cannot ignore public interest in their private lives. In her view a woman candidate who is single and still relatively young is "perceived as either a whore or a lesbian. I decided it was politically more acceptable to be on the whore side." She chose to joke about her divorce during the campaign in order to counter in advance any lesbian rumors, convinced that "women must analyze what image they want to portray. Then go on the offensive. People are going to classify you anyway, so you should play into it. Your personal life is always an issue." Because sexuality is used often in attempts to discredit women and an acknowledged double standard in political life tends to protect men and threaten women, the female candidate is cautious. She has to present an impeccable personal life which can withstand severe public scrutiny.

Single Is Easier, but . . .

Despite their vulnerability to rumors and public curiosity, single women do encounter fewer problems than married women in integrating their private and public lives. Frequently that is because private life becomes virtually nonexistent for the active unmarried woman. In a lengthy profile of New York City Council President Carol Bellamy published in *The New York Times Magazine* in early 1979, Francis X. Clines observed repeatedly—and with some chagrin—that there was no private Carol Bellamy. There was simply the career politican whose "real life is public, not private." Minnesota state legislator Mary Murphy believes that for a woman like herself who sometimes feels displaced in married-land, there is "more of a place in politics for single women." Believing that Congresswoman Elizabeth Holtzman's single status had no negative effects on her political candidacies, a member of her congressional staff noted that because she is single, Holtzman did not have to face conflicts between a sick child and a grueling campaign schedule or a crisis in the office.

California Assemblywoman Teresa Hughes, who is divorced,

says that it is easier for her to have a political career as a single person because she is free of emotional conflicts when officeholding responsibilities keep her away from home, which is frequently. Hughes also feels, however, that it has been more difficult for successful political women to remarry or find men with whom to socialize because of reactions to the women's high status. Hughes says that men will not approach her "because they think I have a better job than they do. All I can say is that well-educated politicians need love and affection, too." In contrast, single males in office do not seem to have a similar problem in attracting female companionship. Powerful men have always been perceived as sexy, whereas powerful women have not.

While they may have less anxiety about contorting themselves to satisfy conflicting demands of wifehood, motherhood, and candidacy, single women without young children are still responsible for managing a domestic establishment and completing household chores. One campaign manager reported that because his female candidate was single, the campaign schedule benefited from the fact that there was no pressure on her from a family, "but we forget in scheduling her twenty hours a day that she doesn't have anyone to do the laundry or cooking." A female state senator described a similar problem. A divorcée with two grown children, she kept a busy schedule combining a legislative career with a teaching job. One afternoon close to a November election she dashed home from school to meet a reporter for an interview. After she threw the dirty clothes in the washer, she was ready to answer questions. She talked while she sipped a drink and browned some pork chops for dinner. "Being single does make a difference," she observed. "I don't have the problem of a husband being jealous of my outside activity or job or interest. I don't have to schedule time for anybody." Nonetheless, she must handle domestic responsibilities. "There's nobody to do my laundry, to keep up the house, or to buy the groceries." There is a further disadvantage in living alone, she feels: "There's nobody to tell things to. That's what I miss the most —after a speech or something, when I want to come home and tell somebody how it went, there's no one here."

Sometimes friends and campaign staff have become, in effect, substitute homemakers and family to provide personal support for the unmarried female candidate. Irene Lyons, campaign manager for Madelene Van Arsdell's state senate campaign in Arizona during 1976, recognized the advantages as well as the loneliness and other problems faced by her candidate as a single woman. Lyons, a former state coordinator of the Arizona Women's Political Caucus, was herself so committed to Van Arsdell's candidacy and the liberal issues the candidate represented that she enlarged the campaign to an extent that is unusual for a legislative race in Arizona. She knew that someone should be available to provide personal support and that the role could be filled by someone other than a husband or relative. In the Van Arsdell campaign, support came from the campaign manager herself as well as from a group of volunteers. They were all headquartered in the candidate's home, where the living room had been stripped almost bare except for books and campaign material. "Madelene is in a unique position to be a candidate right now," observed Lyons. "She is a widow with four children, and they're grown. She can, and does, spend all her time on her own activities. She does only what she wants to do, which is politics. That means I can schedule her for three meetings in one day and not mess up her personal life. She has no personal life. She's the candidate. I'm the mechanic and technician."

Lyons was demanding of her candidate, but also of herself. "I do a lot of things for her," said Lyons. "If I'm going to demand as much of her as I *am* going to demand, I have to provide this support." Support from a campaign manager or campaign staff members who become, in effect, the candidate's temporary family includes being available to talk over disappointments and frustrations, serving as companions at social events, acting as escorts so that the candidate does not have to travel alone, and even taking over household chores such as buying the groceries. The relationship between Lyons and Van Arsdell illustrates a way in which the candidate who is alone and does not have the involvement of a family to help during the campaign may find alternatives for personal and professional support.

CANDIDACY AND MARRIAGE—
AND SPOUSAL SUPPORT

Although in the 1970s a visible minority of single women entered the circle of candidates and became officeholders, the large majority of political women are married and living with their husbands.[1] For many of them the problems of private life are more complex than for their single counterparts.

In 1976 Texas state legislator Irma Rangel finished defending her single status by telling her audience at a candidate's coffee that she had been engaged, but an "act of God" prevented her marriage; she went on to joke, "and if I were married now, I would be divorced in a minute because I'm never home." She raised an interesting and difficult issue. It is true that she would almost never be at home during campaign season. It does not follow that she would be divorced. The women who announce candidacies and the women who hold office do not have a higher divorce rate than other women in the population. Their divorce rates are about the same. Nonetheless, the strains and stresses on marriage are severe during campaign season; and they hardly disappear during the time one of the marriage partners is serving in office.

Almost all couples in which one partner seeks office—regardless of whether it is the husband or wife—experience similar problems. While the difficulties may increase the higher the level of office being sought, they exist even when a candidate is vying for a seat on the local borough council. She or he becomes responsive, by necessity, to a demanding schedule of activities away from home (including, if not especially, evenings and weekends). The pace of activity is often frantic. The candidate belongs to a team of people who work together closely, provide each other with mutual support, and share an intense interest in the outcome of the team's efforts to win a public contest. Sometimes the candidate's spouse is part of that team; but often he or she is outside the circle of activity, standing by at home and catching brief glimpses of the candidate, who may check in during rare moments between speeches, meetings, campaign coffees, and neighborhood canvassing. If home is not being used as campaign headquarters, it is also not a sanctuary during election season. When the candidate arrives there after a hectic day on the road, there are telephone calls to make and to receive. One does not establish "office hours" as a candidate; any hour of any day is a fair time for campaign business.

Ideally, the spouse's role in all of this is to be supportive, encouraging, actively helpful in the campaign, totally nondemanding of personal attention from the candidate, and willing to be alone most of the time during the campaign. The level of intensity drops after election day; but for the candidate who wins and is sworn into public office, many of the campaign season's demands become conditions of life with which the spouse has to contend.

Traditionally wives have been expected to accept agreeably the role of spouse to a husband's candidacy. The political wife smiling and standing at the side of the male candidate remains a familiar image in American public life. A partner in a political public relations firm noted that the role of wives in many campaigns doubles the candidates' efforts: "In 1976 Rosalynn Carter became the standard of excellence for political wives on the campaign trail. Wherever she went, on her own separate campaign schedule and on behalf of her husband, she impressed people and aided the campaign."

After her 1978 reelection race, Colorado's Congresswoman Pat Schroeder pointed out that her campaigns always are difficult, and she is always perceived as vulnerable. Many of her male colleagues in the Congress are married to women who have the time to serve as an enormous campaign resource for their husbands. "In June, when school is out for the children," Schroeder notes, "the wives leave Washington and go campaigning for their husbands in the home districts." She says that she would not ask that of her husband. Trying to get back home to the district every weekend during campaign season, she sees herself "competing in a world where people take it for granted that campaigning is done by a two-person team"—a male candidate and his campaign–partner wife.

Many political wives have not enjoyed their roles in campaigns, but most have kept silent because it has been in their own interest to support advances in their husbands' public careers, and because an uncooperative wife is a political liability to her husband. Social disapproval has fallen heavily on a politician's wife who voices dissatisfaction and places her own personal needs before her husband's career. Recently the situation has begun to change. As more and more political wives pursue their own business and professional interests, there is less time to spend participating in their husbands' campaigns. Yet it is still not considered too much to ask that they exhibit patience and, if necessary, behave self-sacrificingly. Their husbands' political ambitions are assumed to reflect the mutual goals of both husband and wife.

Can these assumptions be made in the case of political husbands? To expect such behavior from a man is viewed as inappropriate both psychologically and pragmatically. From a pragmatic perspective, most men have no time to be political husbands because their jobs demand their full attention. From a psychological viewpoint, men who participate actively in their wives' campaigns are often perceived as subordinating themselves and playing a secondary role—hence they contend with raised eyebrows and even ridicule. Sometimes the husband is assumed to be the *real* politician, with his wife acting as a surrogate candidate for him. Notwithstanding these strains and confusions, the wife in a marriage needs her spouse's understanding and help when she runs for office. In fact, without spousal support, a woman is not likely to become a candidate.[2]

While a male candidate is campaigning, his wife's role is to be even more of a wife—a stereotype of the perfect wife. The nature of her traditional role in the marriage (to provide domestic services, encourage his ambitions, assist in their attainment) remains constant. It merely intensifies. In contrast, while a female candidate is campaigning, her husband presumably continues to do what it is he has been doing professionally for years, but with a difference: she is not there to run the household for him; she is not there as the human companion he is accustomed to finding at home; and to add insult to injury, there is a need for him (or someone) to provide *her* with domestic services and to appear at public events as her smiling, unthreatened, supportive spouse. These reversals of conventional marital patterns are disconcerting for most adult males; and they are equally uncomfortable for most women who reached adulthood viewing their positions in the marriage from a traditional perspective. Granted, these rigid sex-role patterns and judgments appear to be changing, but for the moment the female candidate and her husband must be flexible enough to let each other play unconventional roles.

When Carolyn Warner, Arizona's Superintendent of Public Instruction, ran unsuccessfully for the U.S. Senate nomination in the 1976 Democratic primary, her husband conceded that not every man was capable of doing what he did. Working hard in her campaign, he had major responsibility for fund raising. He was conscious that people did not understand how he could surrender the spotlight to his wife. "A lot of men," he said, "including some of my close friends, find it difficult to understand how I can support Carolyn in this role. My response is that Carolyn played a secondary role in our business career. She was willing to let me have what you might call the romantic part—the design, the advertising, the selling. She did the dirty work—operations, budgets, arranging of credit, hiring, firing, the complete financial and operational work. She did that for twenty-five years; so in a sense, we're switching roles.

"If she is elected to the Senate," he observed during the campaign, "she will have the lead role, and I often say there can be only one star in any political arena—one person has to be willing to do the things that don't give a lot of glory."

While campaign experts are wary of a candidate's spouse who is emotionally involved in the campaign and may want to take a controlling role without being accountable to management, most women running for office are very grateful for their husbands' contributions. Wisconsin State Representative Susan Shannon Engeleiter considered her husband a tremendous asset during the 1978 congressional primary, in which she drew on his earlier experience as a campaign manager in another congressional race. Other women draw on their husband's expertise and network of contacts. In March 1976, for example, Ron Lansing, a law professor, wrote a letter of solicitation to fellow lawyers in Oregon asking them to contribute money to support his wife Jewel in her campaign to become state treasurer of Oregon.

There is virtual unanimity among married women running for office that having a supportive husband is most important to their candidacies. The point is raised spontaneously by women whenever they speak about their lives as political practitioners. By citing a supportive husband, a woman running for office usually is referring to his pride in her political activities and his enthusiasm about her candidacy, not necessarily any direct contributions of time and other resources her husband might make to the campaign. In Arizona, Diane McCarthy acknowledges she could not handle her hectic life as a political candidate and officeholder without the help of her husband Tom. Beyond his emotional support, she appreciates whatever direct work he contributes to her campaigns. "He campaigns, but I let him do the things he wants to. He loves to go out and put up signs." Diane and Tom McCarthy have discussed her political ambitions as well as the way they will affect his life. In her view, "Tom has enough feeling of personal well-being that he doesn't need me to add to it. He's been called 'Mr. Diane McCarthy' as a joke, and it doesn't bother him. We have talked seriously about whether he could be 'First Lady' of Arizona."

Everyone agrees that "a wife who is a candidate needs a husband who has a very strong sense of personal identity." So said Renee Simon, who lost her 1976 race for a seat in California's state senate. Then a local city councilwoman, in her fifties, and the mother of grown children, Simon was married to a man who provided strong support that helped sustain her through a difficult campaign and a disappointing defeat. In his work as a trial attorney, she said, "He's always been in the spotlight. I think that's why trial lawyers become trial lawyers." But he was well able to accept the idea that it was all right for her to be in the spotlight as well. She considered her husband's support essential, saying that she would not have run without it. "It's difficult to feel that you're not involved in a role reversal," she noted. "Most men who are married to candidates are enormously proud of their wives. But there are some men who refuse to cooperate. I don't know what I'd do—yes, I do. I wouldn't run. But I'd be resentful. What it takes is a husband and wife who have their own individual interests and a respect for each other's desire to pursue those personal goals."

Going Public with Spousal Support

While a wife's candidacy does not require that a husband abandon his occupation and ignore his own urgencies to give his life over to her campaign, it does seem to require more than personal support delivered in private communication between husband and wife. It often requires a public expression of support— because when a wife becomes the candidate, she is asked to exhibit proof positive that all is well at home. Often her own word is not good enough. She is asked to produce her husband in the flesh, smiling and enthusiastic in cheering on her candidacy. If she is not requested explicitly to produce a cheerful husband, the female candidate often feels she ought to provide other evidence that will dispel prejudicial assumptions about the state of her marriage.

Norma Paulus' race for secretary of state of Oregon emphasized that she was a happily married woman candidate. In Portland,

Oregon, legislative candidate Sandy Richards had her husband write a form letter to many of her potential constituents explaining why he supported her candidacy. During her campaign, Caroline Wilkins brought her husband home to Oregon from his temporary job in Washington, D.C., in order to prevent rumors that their marriage was on the rocks. And many candidates follow the example of Bella Abzug, who took her husband on campaign trips to show she had one. Abzug emphasized pointedly in speeches and campaign literature during her candidacies between 1976 and 1978 that Martin Abzug had been her partner in a happy marriage for over three decades, and that he continued to be a critical source of support and strength for her political career. She was fond of saying that he looked forward to an invitation to accompany her to dinner at the White House so that he could check over the rooms in anticipation of the day when he would live there as 'First Man.'

Voters often seem incredulous that a candidate's husband would cheerfully accept the prospect of his wife and the mother of his children being away from home a great deal of the time. When she ran for the California state legislature in 1976, Marilyn Ryan, a Republican, was considered the front-runner in a four-way primary. But voters expressed concern about Ryan's family—a minor but recurrent theme in the campaign. At countless small coffees held on Ryan's behalf during the primary, the question would come up. Ryan recalls, "Sometimes people would ask, 'What does your husband think of all this?' You know they're really saying, 'Does your husband give his permission?' . . . It would frequently come up as 'How's your family going to manage when you go to Sacramento?' " She pointed out that her daughters were 17 and 19— too old to need her full-time supervision—but often she had the feeling, whether they asked about it or not, that other women wondered how she was going to manage as a woman with a family.

Occasionally she brought her husband along to meetings. This helped Ryan to deal with the voters' concerns about her private life. Toward the end of a presentation, she would invite her husband to make a few remarks. "Then Jim would give this very positive statement about how he'd figured it out and how they would manage very well. Afterward women would come up and say how relieved they were to hear my husband."

In knowing that their husbands are extremely cooperative and supportive of their candidacies, few female candidates seem to mind when their husbands skip candidates' nights and other political functions. In fact, women with husbands who are not temperamentally suited for campaigning prefer going alone than to being accompanied by a husband who feels forced to sit through a boring evening, is subjected to the perceived indignity of taking a secondary role, and must spend the evening dealing with embarrassing remarks or jokes about his role as the political husband.

Sabrina Schiller, a California senate candidate, remembers, "One time I went to a dinner out in the Valley and supporters of mine said to me, 'Where's your husband?' I said, 'He's working tonight.' They said, 'You shouldn't come to these things alone. You ought to come with your husband.' " Schiller disagreed, but she did mention the comment to her husband. "It looks bad," he agreed. "All right," she said, "please come with me." He replied, "I'm not going to those things."

Schiller explains, "My husband is unwilling to attend these kinds of functions because they bore him. And he was very busy. He resented the intrusion of my activities on his free time. And secondly, I don't mind going to those things alone. I felt I didn't have to worry about another person."

Schiller continued, "There's the old saying, 'One reason that women aren't successful is that they don't have good wives to stand behind them.' Rosalynn Carter was out there shaking sixty thousand hands while Carter himself was shaking another sixty thousand hands. But I have no reason to be resentful against my husband. He really did a terrific amount for me. But he couldn't do much compared to that [i.e., Rosalynn Carter's performance]. I'm not sure he would have. It wasn't his campaign."

The observation that "it wasn't his campaign" tells volumes about the attitudes of many candidates and their husbands to "her campaign." "His campaign" is more often perceived as "their campaign" because the outcome of his candidacy and the prospects for their family—its social status, economic prospects, geographic location—merge into one direction for the future. In the mid-1970s "her campaign" was still more likely to be seen as an unanticipated offshoot away from the direction in which the family was established to go. Her campaign tended to seem like something interesting to observe, something to be tolerated with equanimity, a game without any heavy bets or anyone's future success really riding on it. Thus, a husband might decide to help, but it was highly unlikely that he would neglect his own occupation, risk his own future, or redirect his own interests for "her campaign." Indeed, women understand and contribute toward this assessment of where their campaigns rank in the family priorities.

Spousal Nonsupport

Madelene Van Arsdell's husband had objected to her interest in political activism; she withdrew from politics and office seeking. In the 1960s, she had tried once to run for city council in Phoenix, Arizona. "Our slate was defeated," she recalls. "It was probably just as well. My husband hated what I was doing. He didn't think nice women got their names in the newspaper. So after that, I sort of subsided into my usual housewife-mother role." Years later, when she was 56 and a widow, she did leave the house to run for the legislature and won a seat in the state senate.

Van Arsdell's legislative colleague Betty Morrison ran a half-hearted 1976 reelection campaign. After she lost the election, she admitted she was not sorry. One reason was her dislike of campaigning; but the pressure of her home life was what really sapped the vitality of her campaign. Morrison said, "My family's rather happy I lost—the kids and my husband."

There is little doubt that men who are unenthusiastic political husbands or who explicitly oppose their wives' officeholding aspirations do have a marked impact on the shape of women's political careers. Jane Tolmach, a woman in her fifties who was married and the mother of grown children, had served on the Oxnard city council in California since 1970. She had been very active in local politics for well over a decade before moving on to the council. In the early seventies she had made a choice between family and political advancement. She notes that her husband had "always been opposed to me running for anything out of the area." But in 1973 there were rumors of a vacancy in a congressional race. Tolmach says, "I talked to my husband to see if he would agree that I could run for Congress, and he just about blew a fuse. He said that I must be wanting a divorce or something like that. It would be pretty unworkable, I think, to run for Congress. You can't come home every weekend. And to have any kind of marriage you need to be together a few days of each week. I think I'd had in my mind that maybe he'd want to take off from his practice as a pediatrician and take a job or do research in the Washington area; I'd had some dreamy idea like that. He said, 'No,' that he just wanted to practice in Oxnard.

"Then, later on, I told him I'd really like to run for some office —the assembly—if an opening came up. He agreed that the assembly would probably be not so bad." In 1976 Tolmach was defeated in her bid for the state legislature. She felt that if she had won she could become one of many state legislators who commute home every week to their districts. She would have spent Monday until Thursday in Sacramento, which is about a two-hour trip from her home by plane and automobile. Her husband adapted to the idea and even "got pretty enthusiastic as the race went on," she said. "He was really looking forward to my winning it and getting something that I was working for. He was very disappointed when I lost, but I noticed he wrote on our Christmas cards, 'Jane lost the election, but I won a wife.' There was always that mixed feeling. Also, I knew it was a little bit risky to do that. It could break up a marriage."

The possibility does exist that in marriages where a wife is the partner with political aspirations, the rhythms of electoral politics and the domestic patterns of traditional marital relationships are fundamentally incompatible. Such an incompatibility is likely a major reason that large numbers of women have not pursued elective office, or public leadership in general.

THE PROBLEM OF SEPARATION

Those special few women who have managed to toss hats into the candidates' ring and take oaths of office while keeping their marriages intact are a great subject of interest among a much larger group of people who think it cannot be done or who are very curious about what kinds of extraordinary arrangements married political women make with their husbands in order to "do it all." Most people imagine or fear that in exchange for winning public office, a wife must lose her husband. Fascination with this issue played a large part in the popularity of a series of situation comedies shown on national television in the mid-seventies.

When television's Maude began to think of herself as a political candidate, she did what many married women do before making an important decision. She waited until the end of the day to try the idea out on her husband. She began cautiously: "I've just had the most incredible honor bestowed on me." Maude was not planning to ask Walter's permission to run for the state senate. She knew of men who denied permission for their wives to enter politics. But Walter was different. He would support whatever decision she made. As she told him, "I am so lucky you're the most sympathetic, compassionate, supportive, woman-oriented. . . ."

Walter listened quietly for a while. Then he spoke: "I have one question," he said. "While you're in Albany, who's going to take care of me?" A tantrum followed. After shouting and breaking her best dinner plates, he walked out. Maude was left with a choice—Walter and marriage, or public life alone.

The struggle over Maude's candidacy entertained evening television audiences for five weeks. It was a high point in the series, drawing twenty million viewers. Walter took up life as a separated husband. Maude followed her candidacy. The result? The script took the easy way out—Walter came home, and Maude lost the election.

A major ingredient of the show's success was its solid base in reality, in more ways than one. Maude's flirtation with politics was based on real life, inspired by Sabrina Schiller's candidacy for the California state senate. The candidate's husband, Robert Schiller, was a writer for the "Maude" television series. Like Walter, he was upset at the notion of finding himself married to a politician. While the Schillers were going through a painful crisis over this, they taped their discussions to be used as source material for the "Maude" series.

Sabrina Schiller enjoys talking about the parallel between her experiences and Maude's. Although the shows were made months before the November election, they turned out to be prophetic. Sabrina Schiller, like Maude, eventually lost by a narrow margin. The similarities went deeper. "There was a line of Walter's that was Bob's," said Schiller. "'I have an uncommon need not to be alone.' That really summed up his fears. He didn't want to be alone. He didn't want to take second place." Schiller's husband did not walk out. "With Bob I suppose that was a possibility, except that we had a tremendously strong bond. We really need each other very much. He was, of course, opposed to it at first, because it was strange, and frightening, and new, and threatening."

Schiller had never considered living apart from her husband and

4-year-old daughter if she were elected. "I wouldn't have done that.
You see, I have an advantage. Bob is ready to retire. He's been a
writer for twenty-seven years. He's working too hard as is. He would
have changed his work pattern. He would have gone into developing
projects [new television programs]. . . . He would have moved up
there with me. I would not have done it if it meant being away from
my family."

Eventually, Bob Schiller, like Maude's Walter, capitulated and
supported his wife's candidacy. His initial reaction to becoming a
political husband is not uncommon. Sabrina Schiller's insistence
that she would not have begun to consider candidacy if it meant
leaving her family is also familiar. The issue of a husband's support
for a campaign which might result in his wife's departure for a state
capital or Washington, D.C., is part and parcel of the difficulties
faced by women seeking office.

A traditional political wife stays home and tends the household
while her husband is away from home serving in the local county
building or in the state capital; or she may move the household and
follow him wherever his political career leads. A political husband
only very rarely relocates. In one well-known case, Congresswoman Pat Schroeder moved to Washington from Colorado in
1972 accompanied by her husband and two young children. He
had been willing to move his law practice to Washington, where the
family has remained in residence as Congresswoman Schroeder
won reelection throughout the seventies. While their example has
been cited often as an instance of innovation heralding new types
of family arrangements, it is still so unusual as to be more like the
exception which proves the rule. As more wives make politics a
career, the situation may change.

When an elective office takes the officeholder far from home
on a regular basis, the alternative to relocating the household is
maintaining two households, and living with varying periods of
separation. That was the choice made by Congresswoman Geraldine Ferraro when she moved to Washington, D.C., early in 1979
to live for part of each week, first in a hotel, and then in an efficiency
apartment, without her husband and three children. Her husband
continued his professional life and maintained their family home in
Queens, New York.

Establishing two residences is difficult on each spouse, even when they have been used to leading independent professional lives. When Bella Abzug went to Congress, it was understood that her husband, Martin, would remain at his job and in their apartment in New York. She commented, "I'm a family person. Living apart from my husband was the only part I didn't like." After the first year in Congress, Abzug moved out of her Washington apartment into a hotel because she felt lonely. As she worked late and had an insignificant social life, she only wanted a place to sleep while she was away from her husband and their New York apartment.

The choice of separation is one which many people are unwilling to make, with the result for politically ambitious people that the level of office sought and the shape of a political career are determined by compromises with the demands of private life. During the years she represented California in the U.S. House of Representatives, Yvonne Brathwaite Burke and her husband divided their time between coasts. Burke told *The New York Times,* "It's expensive, but my husband and I try to avoid separation as much as possible. . . ." As parents of a small child, they kept duplicate baby equipment on both coasts, from cribs to strollers and sandboxes. In 1978, Yvonne Burke left the Congress to run for attorney general of California, a campaign which she lost. It was widely understood that her bid for the state-based office was motivated in large part by her desire to continue building a political career, but to stop commuting between Washington, D.C., and the West Coast.

Most candidates who are not seeking congressional office need not contemplate the kinds of arrangements undertaken by Schroeder, Ferraro, Abzug, Burke, and the other married women who have served in the nation's capital. Nonetheless, the problem of separation exists for political people at all levels. State legislators in large states often live beyond commuting distance of the capital. Even those officeholders who serve at local levels are out of the house at meetings and political events so often as to make it all but essential for a married couple to live together separately, maintaining independent patterns of activity. In the past this type of arrangement has been unspoken and understood when the husband has been called to one type of civic or professional duty and the wife has remained behind to tend the symbolic hearth. In reversed situations, nothing of the sort can be taken for granted, and very specific understandings must be reached between the candidate or officeholding wife and her husband.

For California Assemblywoman Marilyn Ryan, it took a long time to come to grips with the prospect of running for an office that required she spend four or five days a week in Sacramento without her husband and daughters. Her husband is a school administrator in Palos Verdes, south of Los Angeles. While she still was serving as a local officeholder in Palos Verdes during 1973, Ryan remarked in a newspaper interview that she was doubtful about any woman holding an office that would take her out of town: "I really don't know how a woman could be a legislator in Sacramento if she were married," she told a reporter for the *South Bay Daily Breeze*. "I'm sure people who are more into women's lib say there's no problem. But I think that depends upon your attitude toward your family and your children, and how you're going to resolve all or some of the issues. I look at Yvonne [former Congresswoman Burke], who was married and divorced and married again. But her current husband married her knowing she was a politician. That's a lot different from having been married for ten years and deciding to run for Congress. I would think that maybe women reach a point after children have grown and they are older when they feel that they could assimilate that into their personal life. And yet I just don't know if the rewards are that great to make the sacrifice. That's the issue."

After much soul searching, Ryan did run for the legislature three years later. Her family backed her enthusiastically, insisting they could manage the four days a week she would be away. Ryan said her thinking had not really changed since the newspaper interview. "I don't think that I feel that much different. I think that I really meant it more in terms of a question. I was saying I don't know if a woman can—I don't know what the answer is. And I'm not sure I even know today. In fact, I don't know how it's going to affect my personal life. Jim and I were talking about it yesterday. I said, 'It's a very exciting time for both of us.' But I can't say it isn't going to affect us. It could have a good or bad effect on our lives."

Two years and one legislative session later, Ryan ran successfully for reelection. In 1979, she moved into a position of influence by acquiring an appointment as chairperson of the California Assembly's Elections and Reapportionment Committee. After a first term in the legislature and facing her next two years in Sacramento, Ryan described her life as a "juggling act." To keep it working well required a sharing of responsibilities at home and the ability to work out new arrangements when relationships among family members changed. Ryan's older daughter had lived with her in Sacramento during part of her first term in office. Ryan's husband occasionally visited her in the capital. Her schedule involved flying the 350-mile distance home for weekends. Noting that the speaker of the California assembly flew home from Sacramento to San Francisco to be with his family every night no matter when the session ended, she stressed that political life puts tremendous pressures on marriage regardless of the politician's sex. "Politics probably is easier for any single person, male or female," she observed. The strains are especially difficult in dual-career families when the wife or husband cannot pick up and follow a spouse. In 1979, having worked out a manageable arrangement for her situation, Marilyn Ryan was looking forward to her twenty-eighth wedding anniversary. "Everything is fine at the moment," she said, and added, "I am not about to predict the future."

CANDIDACY AND MOTHERHOOD

If arranging politics and marriage within the same life space challenges a woman's ingenuity and tolerance for flexibility, the presence of children—especially young children—increases the challenge considerably. When the candidate is not only a wife but also a mother, the campaign inevitably becomes a family issue. In the great majority of political families, children are affected by a mother's campaign far more than by a father's political activities. He is away from home a little more, a little less. The difference regarding the candidate father's presence at home is often quantitative. His schedule is minimally worked into the arrangement for children. It is lived independently, and taken into account for his needs, but not often with special regard to children's comings and goings. The children's daily way of life in most families has depended on the mother's presence, or on the way in which she has made arrangements for the minutes and hours during her absence.

If she is a full-time homemaker, her absences have been timed to coincide with children's absences—at school, at day-care centers, at team practice.

Women who bear primary responsibility for their children's daily lives and who also work outside the home strive to schedule their jobs and their children's lives to interlock as well as possible. The mother arrives home from a part-time job to meet children dropped off by the school bus. The mother arranges for a sitter, or play group, or after-school activity when her work schedule and the end of the school day do not coincide. The mother arranges pickups and deliveries with other mothers. The school telephones the mother, whether she is at home or at her job, to announce sore throats or suspicious rashes and to request that the child be picked up and taken home. When snow closes the schools, mothers are expected to make emergency arrangements for the children's day. Mothers accompany children to shop for clothes during hours when stores are open and schools are closed.

With some difficulty and by negotiating a compromise between occupational goals and maternal responsibilities, a working woman may be able to arrange the location and schedule of her job outside the home to dovetail with her children's schedules and needs. Most jobs offer stable hours in a routine weekly schedule. Domestic arrangements can be geared to a fixed timetable. Snow-storms and measles notwithstanding, it is possible that without insuperable difficulty a woman can manage to be reasonably available as a mother, a homemaker, and an employee. Figures released by the U.S. Department of Labor's Women's Bureau in 1978 revealed that a majority (51 percent) of all mothers with children under 18 years worked in the paid labor force during 1977, indicating that whether easily or with hardship, women are managing to juggle obligations as mothers, wives, housekeepers, and employees.

The political candidate who is a mother of young children confronts a challenge of a different magnitude from that encountered by a working mother who has a set routine. On the issue of schedule alone there is an inherent conflict between candidacy and mothering. The single most predictable element in a candidate's calendar is election day, when the campaign is over and there is a breathing spell for a few weeks before the onset of officeholding schedules for winners. The other predictable element in a political schedule is its appetite for a daily 6:00 A.M. to midnight (or later) availability on the part of the candidate. The appetite fluctuates depending on a number of variables, and it is affected by the level of office being sought.

Even more to the point: whether one is a current candidate, an officeholder, or a party leader, what one *cannot* expect of political schedules is regularity. Meetings take longer than expected; hearings run late; people stay behind to talk with the candidate or officeholder after a speech; a party leader phones to request that one appear at a political dinner, a testimonial banquet, a club picnic, a last-minute gathering to greet an important visitor arriving from out of town. The political world does not work on the steady, weekly routine of an office, factory, or retail business schedule. Mothering requires predictable scheduling, whereas politicking requires availability for erratic scheduling. The demands of each are intense enough that when they conflict, a woman experiences the worst kind of emotional turmoil.

Many political women are overheard wishing for a "wife" who can run the household while they are running for office. Various surrogates have been utilized by candidates faced with the difficulties inherent in campaigning on the one hand and maternal and housekeeping responsibilities on the other. A California candidate —wife of a working husband and mother of a preschool-aged child —asked her sister to move into the house for the campaign's duration. Her sister obliged, and the candidate was relieved of all domestic duties during election season. In Oregon a state legislative candidate imported her mother from South Dakota to take charge of cooking for the family during the last weeks of campaigning. Husbands help out in the same manner by offering their domestic talents for the good of the campaign. Relatively affluent candidates hire housekeepers to handle chores and watch over children. In many areas of the country, special support systems have included teams of volunteers assigned to chauffeur a candidate's children from school to dentist, to music lessons, to gymnastics classes, or to baseball practice. While some campaign workers drive the car pools and direct the traffic of children, other volunteers pick up the dry cleaning, wash the laundry, and vacuum-clean the candidate's house. In the meantime, two volunteers take turns stocking the larder, baking meatloaf, and preparing casseroles to slip into the candidate's freezer for the next few days' family meals.

Devising a workable arrangement for supporting her political career and also for providing her children with a warm, stable family life is a challenge which has confronted Polly Baca Barragan in the years since she first ran for the Colorado legislature in 1974. The only Mexican-American woman in the legislature, she was the mother of an infant girl and the wife in a strained marriage. Two years later, after she had been reelected to the state house of representatives, Baca Barragan was the mother of an infant boy and her marriage had ended in divorce. She needed a way to support life as a single parent with two babies and a legislative schedule made even more demanding when she assumed a leadership role as chairperson of the House Democratic Caucus in 1976.

Working out a mutually beneficial arrangement with her parents, who lived one mile from her home, Polly Baca Barragan began to pay her mother a monthly retainer for babysitting services. She established two stable family homes for the children and provided her parents with additional income which helped their financial status during retirement. In 1979, having moved up to a seat in the state senate, Baca Barragan noted that the arrangement with her parents was working beautifully. "My mother gives me less hassle than a husband would when meetings run past schedule and I call to say I'll be late," she observed.

In addition, Baca Barragan has included the children in her political life. After the legislature adjourned at 7:00 P.M. on July 1, 1975, she went to the hospital and the next day gave birth to her son. When he was nine days old, her son attended his first meeting with the governor, and he was present at legislative committee meetings regularly during the seven months while she nursed him. "There were lots of jokes about Mikey sleeping through the committee meetings," she recalls. In the 1978 senate race, she and her daughter walked precincts to distribute campaign literature, and both children were accompanying her to political barbeques, local parades, and weekend Hispanic-American Democratic meetings. In an essay written for a second-grade class, her daughter stated, "When I grow up, I want to be a state representative, and I will go to meetings and come home with work to do."

Rather than creating a distance between political candidacy and family life, many candidates have experimented with ways to

integrate rearing their children and running their campaigns. It is
not unusual for women to express strong convictions about the
benefits to children from being in contact with what mothers (and
fathers) do out in the world beyond the family's front door.

One young political mother, Ronnie Brooks of St. Paul, Minnesota, made sure her children were not left out of the excitement.
A candidate for the state senate in 1976, Brooks handled child care
and political education for her children in one sweep of women's
campaign logistics.

Despite the heavy time and energy demands of campaigning, and
despite the help she could count on from her husband to take care
of the children, candidate Brooks wanted very much to share this
experience with her offspring. She wanted them to feel as if they
were part of what was going on, not just spectators watching from
the sidelines. Brooks did not press her children into active campaigning—avoiding the kitsch of sending a toddler marching house to
house asking someone to vote for her mommy. Nonetheless, the
Brooks children and the children of her campaign workers became
a regular part of the political troupe.

It helped that her campaign headquarters were located in the
basement of the Brooks home. Campaign workers, election-season
excitement, and political activities were brought right into the house.
Headquarters at home also brought political friends for the children.
Most little kids make their friends at the playground or across the
backyard fence. The Brooks children have found some of their play-
mates through a preschool political network.

Every Tuesday night was door-knocking night. While some campaigns did door-knocking out of a storefront office, the Brooks'
brigade started as a family affair from the candidate's living room.
Each week at least two or three dozen people—a good number of
them parents—met there late in the afternoon. They would go off for
a couple of hours working the streets, knocking on doors, distributing campaign literature. Meanwhile, the children played with their
new "political pals." Later, the volunteer workers returned to share
supper, children, and campaign talk before calling it quits after a
night of electioneering.

The Brooks strategy can benefit the children as well as relieve
a candidate's anxiety about abandoning them. It also serves the
campaign by offering a way for parents of young children to handle

their babysitting needs while doing volunteer work for the candidate. Conceiving unusual personal arrangements and making them work is the usual pattern for active political women.

Creative solutions notwithstanding, every office seeker acknowledges the difficulty of keeping motherhood and candidacy together, and also the pain in pulling them apart. "A candidate must be willing to divorce her family for the duration of the campaign," says Ann Richards, Travis County Commissioner in Texas, the mother of four children, and the wife of a supportive and helpful spouse. Richards is no stereotyped image of the chocolate-chip-cookie mother. She is an outspoken, tough, experienced, knowledgeable, successful, very impressive public person. Even with her family's full encouragement and a well-organized support system to relieve her from being on duty during the campaign, she identifies as her most "severe drawback" her inability to be there for the family and be available in her mothering role. On the other side of the same conflict, a female candidate who lost a congressional race says that after the election, her campaign manager told her that if she were to do it again, she would have to work at it full-time instead of spending almost half her time on family duties. The mother of two children, she tried to combine responsibilities at home with campaign duties: "I got help once a week in August, but until then I did all my own housework and cooking. It does make a difference because if everything's all huffed up at home you can't go out and make a bang-up speech." Furthermore, her campaign staff somewhat resented the noninvolvement of the family in her campaign. "I finally had to tell them to lay off. I said, 'I'm running. My family is not.' " With pressures and conflicting demands from all directions, and vulnerable to the enormous guilt easily aroused when women worry about neglecting the family, a person must either be emotionally numb or a superwoman to handle the strain.

Not only do political women who are mothers contend with the grinding difficulties of coordinating politics and motherhood, but they have to answer to the public for their solutions. Well-advised candidates anticipate queries about child-care arrangements. For example, Sandy Smoley, a county supervisor in Sacramento, California, assumed that voters would be concerned about whether "I'm shirking my duty as a family woman" when she ran as the Republican nominee for Congress in 1978. To forestall inquiries and ease voters' minds, she mentioned in every campaign speech that her children were grown.

The opposition is apt to probe and see whether the female candidate's vulnerability and the public's concern about neglecting the district or neglecting the children can cause the candidate embarrassment and cost her votes. Georgia's Virginia Shapard believes that this was a critical issue in her unsuccessful 1978 congressional race against Republican Newt Gingrich. She describes her attempt to move up from a seat in the state senate and run for Congress in Georgia's sixth district as a "family decision." With the help of a very supportive husband who had always driven the car pool, done the shopping, and shared other child-care and domestic chores, her campaign was launched with "no problem inside the family." Outside the family, however, Shapard's opponent called attention indirectly to an issue the voters might consider a problem. The Gingrich campaign issued a piece of literature—entitled "This Time You Have a Choice"—which lined up two columns of comparisons between Shapard and Gingrich designed to depict Shapard as an outsider to Georgia, an elitist, a spendthrift, and a woman who apparently cared little about family unity. The comparison between the candidates on the issue entitled "Family" read as follows:

Newt Gingrich has been married to the former Jackie Battley of Columbus for 16 years. The Gingrichs have two daughters, Jackie Sue, 11, and Kathy, 15. When elected, Newt will keep his family together.

Virginia Shapard is married to Robert Shapard, III. The Shapards have four children, Virginia, 13, Robert 11, Christy, 9, and Loyd, 7. If elected, Virginia will move to Washington, but her children and husband will remain in Griffin.

Hitting a note similar to that sounded in Gingrich's campaign literature, a local newspaper article raised suspicions simultaneously about the sins of affluence and of neglectful motherhood in Virginia Shapard's 1978 candidacy. Writer Jasper Dorsey commented: "Most damaging . . . is the fact that if elected, she will be apparently leaving her four young children at home to be reared by the servants and a husband who has a full-time job running the family textile business."[3] Shapard views her district as a microcosm, feeling that a response to the traditional role of motherhood lies dormant, ready to be activated by an opponent who has only to hint that a woman is neglecting her duties.

THE PROBLEM OF GUILT

Whether or not there is a cost in votes, the price in guilt often taxes women running for office while raising children, especially when their children are preadolescent. Indeed few mothers of young children present themselves as candidates for elective office anywhere in the country.[4] Geraldine Ferraro says that had her children been younger than they were in 1978 when she ran for Congress, she would not have considered a candidacy. Congresswoman Marjorie Holt says, "I don't think I'd do it if I had small children." Many other political women echo this view.

Endemic to women, guilt about some aspect of private life often exists even when no small children are in the picture. There is the guilt associated with not being home for adolescent children; with neglecting a husband; with exposing the family to the glare of publicity, or the expectation they will pitch in and help, or the discomfort of adjusting their own lives to the homemaker's absence. There is guilt about neglecting or assigning low priority to all the daily tasks of running a household. Even among single women there is often a kind of guilt about not keeping an attractive house or not cooking meals and entertaining guests. In many cases women react to the guilt by trying to do everything—by being supermom, superwife, supercook-hostess-cleaner-laundress. And supercandidate. Since one body cannot occupy two different spaces at the same time, many human superwomen are forced to adjust the demands they make upon themselves, and come to accept living with guilt. Or else they judge themselves harshly for a series of self-perceived failures, and try to satisfy unrealistic, internalized expectations that they be capable simultaneously of superb performance in mutually exclusive areas of activity.

Rationally women know that it is all right not to be available for sewing patches, or even tending bruised and bloody knees . . . temporarily. Not so rationally, women are plagued by a self-perceived distance between what they manage to accomplish and what they "should" be capable of achieving. The culturally inscribed list of "shoulds" is often different for the two sexes. High up on woman's list are myriad commandments about private and domestic life—the "should do" tasks for the household manager, hostess, wife, mother. After all these tasks have been accomplished and checked off the list, a woman sometimes grants herself permission to step outside and hit the campaign trail.

While television's Maude may not have experienced guilt even though her husband's unhappiness about her candidacy resulted in a separation, the woman whose situation inspired the television series sees guilt as one of women's special problems. "We are culturally programmed to feel guilt and to accept the responsibility unquestioningly," says Sabrina Schiller. "It's hard for me to determine how much of it is my own natural desire to be with my family and how much of it is my conditioned responsibility to be with my family. I know that Bob is a terrific parent and would be completely competent to run the household if I were gone. He would be as much of a help to Abbe as I would were I the only parent. Yet he feels no qualms about working to midnight night after night when it comes to the crunch. But I can't do it without feeling tremendous guilt. I just can't do it." Schiller's point is echoed by women everywhere. While some men may not enjoy working late regularly or even intermittently, very few women allow themselves to remain away from home and unavailable for children or husbands in a late-night-after-late-night schedule.

The qualms and guilt described by Sabrina Schiller underlay her decision that, even on a temporary basis, some family commitments simply could not be sacrificed for her campaign. It was a decision that cut into campaigning time. "For our own family sanity," she said, "we agreed on one rule—that I would come home for dinner. I would avoid dinner-time meetings unless it was absolutely necessary. It was something I wanted to do because I have a very young child. I felt it was important to keep the stability of the family going, and I did it. There were times, for example, when I was out in the Simi Valley, which is an hour's drive from my home, and I would drive home for dinner and then back out and home again in the evening. I don't think any male candidate would do that. I did it many, many times."

She admits that the "home for dinner" rule absorbed campaign time. She experienced "a lot of guilt" when she broke the rule: "The best time to walk precincts was when other people were home. I would start at 4:30, and after the daylight-savings-time change, I could go until 8:45. Yet it was a tremendous burden for me . . . I just drove myself crazy thinking I was out walking a precinct and not home with my family."

Another state legislative candidate said that despite all the help she had in handling domestic duties, she would not run for office again until her children are grown and out of school. "We managed. My friend drives the car pool. My mother and mother-in-law help out. One of my friends had the children for dinner almost every night." But there were times when a mother substitute was not acceptable: "I did get to every baseball game and pet show. I was aware it would be a negative factor if I didn't."

California's Assemblywoman Marilyn Ryan told of similar conflicts in her 1976 campaign. However, a single incident early in the primary convinced her to make a choice between the campaign and family duties.

It was a busy day for the candidate. Her daughter was returning from a camping trip, and Ryan had promised to pick her up at a drop point in Hollywood, forty miles from home. At 4:30 in the afternoon Ryan was battling freeway congestion on her way home to fix dinner and prepare for a campaign appearance at 7:00. "The traffic was horrible," she recalled. "But I had my speech outlined. Jim came home early so we could eat at 6:00, and I would leave at 6:45. Just before dinner I said to him, 'I want you to listen to my speech.' He listened. Then he said, 'I don't think that's a good beginning.' It was the first candidates' meeting, with twenty-four candidates running. So he felt I had to get my message across in the first few sentences. So I had to redo my speech. When I got into the car, I knew we'd just barely get there in time. We were about half way there when I realized I had the wrong manila folder with the old speech. I had forgotten my introduction and everything. Then I started crying.

"I said, 'I just can't go through this. I can't do everything. I can't go pick Cindy up and fix dinner and go to a candidates' meeting. I can't be superwoman.'

"Jim said, 'You're really right. You can't. You don't have to cook dinner when you have a candidates' meeting. You have to go and do your best.'

"So I did less. There was less pressure on me. I'd sleep late and the rest of the family would get up and fix their own breakfast after I'd come in at midnight all wound up."

Like most women, Ryan had been in charge of managing the house for the family, from their meals to their laundry. When she decided that getting elected was her first priority, her husband and two daughters sustained a dramatic change in their daily lives. She remembers, "It was kind of a traumatic thing. Everyone complained, and we just struggled through. We all lived this kind of wild existence. But I don't feel guilty about that." Handling guilt had been part of the experience. What happened to the household chores? "Sometimes they didn't get done." The children took over more responsibility for their own lives, Ryan letting go inch by inch with some pain. Later she saw the experience as beneficial for everyone, good for her "in helping me work through my own role with my family. . . . Supermom is going to go away. Really, I think it's more destructive in the long run to be doing all of these things for your family."

Congresswoman Pat Schroeder believes that during almost a decade of public life she has made all of the difficult decisions. She recalls one evening—after a long political day—spending hours stirring, shaping, and frosting the perfect cake for a bake sale at her son's school. He told her after the event that her cake was "okay," but "the rich kids brought money." Sending money would have saved an evening she needed badly. By the time Schroeder's first congressional campaign lay behind her, she had decided to pack the guilt away with old campaign brochures, to accomplish whatever had to be done without worrying about how to satisfy traditional images of the way things *ought* to be done. Thus, she and her husband bought their home in Washington by telephone. They ordered the house, the carpets, the draperies, and other furnishings in telephone calls from Colorado so that all would be ready to use when the family of four arrived in Washington. Schroeder knew that everything would be less than perfect. She decided that would be fine.

Schroeder also learned to avoid adopting other people's worries about her children's mental health and her success as a mother. Students of child psychology requested permission to interview the Schroeder children to examine how they were coping with a mother who is a political candidate and a member of Congress, and with a father who moved his professional life to Washington following his wife's election. When the children turned out to be "normal," the psychologists "were almost angry," Schroeder noted. Pleased that her children are "independent and mature," she is certain they have benefited from not being raised as "hothouse plants" under her constant gaze. While Schroeder does recall a time when she had to convince herself it was all right not to bake cakes or to appear in person to select the perfect shade of carpet, and that she had to remind herself she was not a terrible parent, by 1979, when she returned to Washington after her fourth congressional campaign, the Congresswoman from Colorado claimed to have left guilt far behind. She remembers, "I had all sorts of apprehensions," but today, "as I look back, I wonder how I ever got saddled with them."

DOMESTIC SUPPORT SYSTEMS

Just as it is necessary to find a replacement when someone resigns or is absent for a long time from a set of professional responsibilities, it is necessary to make plans and conscious decisions about how to handle the absence of the woman responsible for directing a household. Everything can be handled with proper support, agreement, and a plan for sharing household chores. Nonetheless, one congressional primary candidate noticed that even when a woman does get family support, her male opponent is still likely to get some services she cannot expect. She remembers looking at other candidates and noticing that they seemed to be better organized than she was. "I knew somebody else ironed their clothes and made sure their socks matched," she said. "How in the hell can you think full-time about campaigning? You're driving home and instead of thinking about issues, you have to think about what to wear. It's a hell of a drag." Her husband, a sign manufacturer, participated in her campaign by making all her signs. "But he did complain about stuff that didn't get done," she said. "Like his clothes. There is no way you can do it all."

Ranking the family priorities, adjusting standards to satisfy basic family needs, and sharing responsibilities for what has been known as "woman's work" may sound reasonable, even mild as social issues. Yet their accomplishment on a broad scale depends on rather profound changes in individual personality as well as shifts in conventional expectations and social patterns. A shift away from placing the entire weight of responsibility for the family's domestic needs on one individual, and full responsibility for the family's financial support on another individual, means spreading burdens and rewards, fostering the development of diverse capabilities among members of a family unit, and decreasing dependence on an individual member's specialized skills. One woman, a candidate in her fifties, remembered feeling very guilty when she had no time to spend with her husband. He spent his evenings alone, and since he was unable to cook, he depended on restaurant meals and dinner invitations from friends. She believes the upcoming generation of women politicians will not share her guilt about neglecting traditional roles. "This may be the last generation that we have in this situation," she says. "Our children are in their twenties. Their attitudes are different. We were brought up in an era when a woman knew what her role was, and it was basically a home-oriented role. A man's role was to be out in front." At the very least, a loosening of rigid role divisions would result in encouraging this man to be more independent. He would know how to feed himself, thus being able to choose freely to eat in restaurants or with friends rather than thinking he is dependent on them for survival. A woman who believes she cannot survive without her husband's paycheck, or a man who believes he cannot survive without his wife's steak and salad, is victimized by a rigid system of specialization that stunts individual growth in adulthood.

Families can be resilient. They accommodate constantly to changes in number of members, in economic status, in social conditions, in geographic location, in the health of family members, and especially in the members' ages. It is not unreasonable, therefore, to assume a family capable of elasticity in the way it handles domestic support systems. Those systems can be arranged so that the family unit nurtures its members instead of assigning to one person (usually the wife/mother) total responsibility for serving as nurturer to everyone else. But new assumptions about who is responsible for managing a household and nurturing its members will mean questioning and dislodging old, deeply rooted attitudes. To make the family capable of serving the needs of its individual members without exploiting the time and energy of a particular individual, alternative ways to operate family units will have to develop. During a time of transition from old habits to new patterns of behavior, family members may be coping with guilt because they are flying in the face of time-honored traditions. They may experience the misgivings and insecurity predictable in any situation where familiar values are exchanged for benefits not yet tested on a large scale over a long period of time. They will also reap the rewards enjoyed by families which give an individual member room to stretch her or his capabilities and capacity for growth.

Chapter 4
Outsiders

"Dear Senator-Elect Vuich:
   Congratulations on your election. You have successfully crashed the
last publicly-funded gentlemen's club in California."
                    —Open letter from David Roberti,
                       Majority Leader, California Senate,
                       to Senator-Elect Rose Ann Vuich,
                       The Los Angeles Times, December 5, 1976

In numerical reality women constitute more than half the voting population of the country. In political reality women are outsiders, exerting very little power or direct influence on the conduct of
public affairs at any level of government. By virtue of where they
are positioned, outsiders seeking nomination and election to public
offices encounter situations peculiar to their status.

At times candidates who appear to be outsiders benefit from
their position. As curiosities, they may attract attention and thus
achieve the high visibility so valuable to aspiring politicians. As
unfamiliar faces, they are untainted by records of ineffective performance or long association with suspect political machines and
established interests.

More often, however, women's status as outsiders is a liability
for political candidacy. Some problems women face as outsiders
overlap with those already discussed—namely, issues related to
image, and to the conflict between private roles and public life. But

other obstacles require separate attention. First, since women often do not hold membership in prestigious fraternities and established political networks, their passage into office is rarely eased by the people, money, and organizations ready to support accepted insiders. Second, because women stand out as anomalies in campaign politics and are noticed *as women* rather than simply as political people, a small minority of female candidates may give the appearance of a large influx of women into politics. The misconception arises that if "all" these women are running for office, there are no barriers and no special efforts need be undertaken to make room for more women in politics. Third, female candidates are still apt to encounter a blatant antiwoman bias from political leaders and the electorate. And, finally, the isolated and rare political woman bears a burden of being judged as a symbol for all women's behavior and competence, thus unintentionally affecting other women's opportunities for advancement. These are some of the common issues mentioned by political women who believe that their position as outsiders makes it very difficult to increase their numbers as elected officials.

It would be naïve for any outsider fantasizing political success to stand around waiting for an invitation into the informal networks, private clubs, party structures, or the established institutions. Entering the political world depends in part on demonstrating to insiders that if they make room to include someone new in their ranks, the change will prove beneficial. Men who are accustomed to dealing with women as dependents and subordinates, but not as competitors or colleagues, cannot be expected to foresee apparent benefits in making space for women in their domain. Thus contemporary political woman confronts some closed doors that are particularly difficult to unlatch. To open them and invite herself in, she must possess knowledge, resilience, clarity of purpose, determination, and a will to win.

OUTSIDE THE MAGIC CIRCLE

People do not win elective office in isolation. From time to time, a candidate who deliberately maintains a distance from traditional circles of political power manages to organize a successful campaign without support from the interrelated communities of local business people, labor organizations, civic associations, religious groups, and party leaders. But the great majority of aspiring officeholders know that without the endorsements and material support that come from access to established political networks, life as a candidate is lonely and defeating. It is simply a fact of history that established political networks are dominated by men. Men rarely serve as mentors or sponsors for women, and as yet very few women are "inside" the political world, able to sponsor other women seeking entrance.

Congresswoman Pat Schroeder of Colorado sees no significant change during recent years in women's acceptance within male circles. "We're not in the same networks," she comments, "men don't have women as friends and vice versa." Schroeder does not feel that attracting campaign support from established networks gets much easier for women in tough races even through successive candidacies as an incumbent. "Because you're a woman, you're a lot more vulnerable. Most women in Congress come from one-sided districts where the Boston Strangler could win if he had the right party."

Yet the incumbent—even in a tough district—comes closer to being an insider than does any challenger. Incumbency generally brings with it the combined benefits of people support, financial support, and party support. Challengers cannot count on similar automatic benefits from established political circles. They must find the levers which open the way to support for building a viable campaign. When women are challengers—as they are proportionately more often than male candidates—those levers are even more difficult to find. Being both a challenger and a woman—that is a double whammy.

Most newcomers, both women and men, lose elections because they cannot unseat entrenched incumbents. The difference between women and men aspiring to first or higher office is that women stand farther outside the inner circles, and are less often invited to become insiders. Furthermore, the higher the office a woman seeks, the more difficulty she has in finding a welcome as she attempts to join those on the inside who operate the informal networks, exert influence, and write out checks. It is the same in electoral politics as in all areas of activity where opportunities and advancement depend far less on formal credentials than on informal relationships. What you know counts little; whom you know matters more. And how you are perceived matters most. Men are perceived as likely to fit in with current members of political clubs; and women are perceived as strangers, even intruders. Understandably, clubhouse leaders are more comfortable about placing their bets and calling out their troops for candidates who look and behave like one of them.

This situation does not make it impossible for women to win nominations and elections—just more difficult, especially in raising money. Women are not members of influential circles in the financial community and have little experience raising large sums of money for themselves. In running for high-level offices, where hefty campaign treasuries are a necessity, women sometimes develop fund-raising strategies to circumvent the disadvantages they encounter in seeking contributions from large donors. Although a woman may have achieved candidacy for a statewide office, she is still sometimes seen as the wrong person to make contacts for campaign contributions in the world of high finance.

Both of Oregon's female candidates for statewide office in 1976 hired male fund raisers who brought to the campaigns their contacts in the business and professional communities. Republican Norma Paulus, in addition, hired a woman whose job it was to contact women for campaign contributions. The Paulus staff decided that the male fund raiser should accompany Paulus when she made visits to businessmen, which she did on approximately fifty occasions. "The time is not yet right for two women to go around to talk to businessmen and say they're running a statewide campaign," said a member of Paulus' staff.

Campaign money comes from sources which have a special stake in political issues. It goes to candidates who look like winners and who, seemingly, can be trusted to remember the interests of those who have been good to them. At this point in history, traditional sources of large campaign contributions view men as better bets than women and are more confident that men have been schooled to understand the *quid pro quo* world. Most female office seekers stand outside established financial networks, and they lack sponsorship for entrée. Even when they find a way in, their candidacies are greeted with less seriousness and viewed as higher risks than those of comparable male office seekers. Thus, women have a harder time locating and raising political dollars for themselves.

A similar situation exists with regard to endorsements and campaign support from political parties. Here women are not strangers because they have always populated the political parties in large numbers. But they have occupied low-status positions within the hierarchy. Men have been the influential party leaders and the endorsed party candidates, whereas women have been positioned outside the proverbial back rooms where the power was located.

In a period when political parties are losing strength and influence over voters in many areas of the country, some people believe that party support holds less significance than in the past. But political realities still suggest otherwise. "The party can't elect you, but the party can defeat you," says one woman who lost a congressional race in 1978. In the Ninety-sixth Congress four women served in Maryland's delegation to the House of Representatives, as many women as have ever been represented in a state's congressional delegation at one time. Noting that three of the congresswomen had started out with little or no party support, an aide on Representative Marjorie Holt's staff once observed, "If they had allowed the process to get into the back room, none of them would have gotten nominated." The fourth female Representative from Maryland was nominated by her party when her congressman husband died suddenly during the 1978 campaign season—a familiar courtesy granted political widows.

Nonetheless, once women succeed in establishing their own constituencies and bases of power—as did the congresswomen from Maryland and many of the women who manage to break into politics and demonstrate longevity—the political parties, special-interest political-action groups, and other traditional sources of support eventually do assist them, albeit sometimes grudgingly. Those women who put together successful campaigns learn how to build a type of strength people on the inside cannot risk ignoring. Ohio's Congresswoman Mary Rose Oakar, a Democrat reelected to her second term in 1978, recalls that when she first ran for the Congress in 1976 the party "didn't expect me to win, and when I did win, there was silence." She says, "The reality was too overwhelming for anyone to digest. They come around, but you're never really catered to. When I say 'they,' I mean the establishment." In Oakar's view, "Parties are usually not enthusiastic about women candidates."

New Jersey's Marge Roukema recalls that after she announced her candidacy for a congressional nomination in 1978, "Party people came to me and said, 'Why don't you run for freeholder [a county-level elective office], not Congress?' " That is a piece of advice many women hear—stay near home, and don't reach too high. Roukema remained in the congressional race and put together "an independent organization of people not meshed in party battles." When she proved her strength and won the Republican primary, the national party targeted her district and did come through with financial contributions and political campaign services in an unsuccessful effort to unseat incumbent Congressman Andrew Maguire. Two years later, with substantial support from the national party, Roukema did defeat Maguire.

Of course there are situations in which a woman's candidacy is encouraged by her party, such as when she is willing to run in a district so strongly held by the opposite party that the race is more symbolic than competitive, or when she is owed the nomination for outstanding party service and loyalty, or when special circumstances make her candidacy useful or appealing in a changing political climate. Now, more often than at any time in the past, ambitious women are consciously utilizing special circumstances which can enhance their positions and advance their political careers. Like good politicians anywhere, they assess their strengths and take advantage of resources available to them.

A good example is Joanne Collins of Kansas City, Missouri, who had to judge how to handle a difficult situation in her own political arena. A Republican in a Democratic area, a black in a white congressional district, a woman in a man's political world, and a challenger against an incumbent so entrenched as to be a local institution—Collins ran with virtually every handicap in the book of candidates. With a minuscule campaign treasury and a great deal of energy, she was determined to take whatever advantage she could of a political opportunity.

All three television networks focused on Congresswoman Barbara Jordan. The Democratic National Convention hushed to listen to her. And the sound of her standing ovation echoed all the way to Kansas City.

It was only natural that a few Republicans would look at the starring role of the magnetic Jordan and think of Joanne Collins. The

Republican Party has been seen by its progressive members as too white. They believe that to win, even to survive, the party must reach the black voter.

Republican Joanne Collins is black, bright, feisty, and was serving her second term as a Kansas City councilwoman. Kansas City was the site of the 1976 Republican National Convention, to be held just weeks after Barbara Jordan's keynote speech had been televised from coast to coast. Collins had filed for a no-win spot on the Republican ticket in the August Missouri primary. Her Republican opponent in the primary fight was John McDonough, a conservative who ran and lost constantly. Whoever won the primary election would face U.S. Representative Richard Bolling, the Democrat from Missouri who was practically an institution after twenty years in Congress.

But just two and one-half weeks before the Republican National Convention in her home town, the White House gave Councilwoman Collins an unexpected and unusual boost. White House Deputy Assistant Arthur A. Fletcher arrived to endorse her and help her raise funds. He talked issues with her, gave her advice, and appeared at a benefit dinner in her honor.

"My presence here in Kansas City breaks every rule in the books," Fletcher (President Gerald Ford's Deputy Assistant for Urban Affairs) said at the dinner for Collins. "The White House is not supposed to meddle in congressional races until after the primaries. But I don't care."

He told guests at the dinner that he works frequently with the Republican Caucus in the House and that he, a black man, was tired of it being a "lily white" organization. Senator Edward Brooke of Massachusetts was the only black Republican in Congress at the time.

"It is time for us to send forth somebody to integrate that Republican Caucus, and Joanne Collins is that somebody."

The audience of more than a hundred persons applauded enthusiastically. Fletcher explained to Collins' supporters that five major pieces of civil rights legislation passed in the 1960s were political decisions and that future political decisions could be made that would negate civil rights gains unless more blacks are elected to Congress, where they can protect the interests of black Americans.

Joanne Collins could create the kind of excitement for Republicans that Barbara Jordan of Texas had created for her party in New York at its convention, he said. Kansas City Mayor Pro-Tem Richard Berkley, also a speaker at the dinner, praised Collins as "our Barbara Jordan." Missouri's Lieutenant Governor William Phelps went farther, saying that Collins would be better than Barbara Jordan once she was elected to Congress.

Joanne Collins has been a Republican since her teenage years. She ran in the district knowing that only one-fourth of the population of approximately half a million is black. Congressman Bolling had carried the district by nearly 63 percent in 1972, while President Richard Nixon won 53 percent of the vote.

Collins admitted she ran the race with the future in mind. "At first I had planned to wait until next time," she says. "But Republicans urged me to run." Washington scandals surrounding Wayne Hays and the voters' general dissatisfaction with incumbents were persuasive arguments other Republicans made in urging her to run. She acknowledged that the race would give her visibility for a later attempt.

Collins was pleased with the endorsement of the White House deputy assistant, but she was clear about whether and to what extent she would allow her token status to be used. There was mention that she might be asked to make a speech at the Republican National Convention. "I have convention passes I can give to people," she said repeatedly over the phone to members of the black community, "but I won't talk. I don't want to be used as a token because of Barbara Jordan. No, I won't do that."

During the convention, research and advisory staff for the national campaigns told Collins she should raise $80,000. She laughed and said she hoped to run on $2,000 to $10,000. In the Republican primary, Collins defeated McDonough narrowly.

In mid-October during the general election campaign, Republican vice-presidential nominee Robert Dole arrived in Missouri to help raise funds for GOP nominees from the Fourth and Sixth Congressional Districts in the Kansas City area. But not for Collins. Unlike the other two Republicans, she faced a Democratic incumbent. Her race was not targeted by the Republican National Committee since it was not considered to be a race in which a Republican had a chance to win.

Collins expressed her displeasure to the press. "A very cold, hard decision has been made by top-echelon political planners that there is no way under the sun that the incumbent in the Fifth Congressional District can be defeated," she said. "They have a right to their opinion. It is the opinion others have had every time I have run for political office; and each time, when the votes were counted, I had won."

A spokesman for Dole said that Collins was not meant to be excluded from the Dole stop but that she would not benefit from attending a farm meeting with him. Unlike the other two Republican congressional nominees, she had no rural vote. Dole's staff attempted to mollify Collins by inviting her to greet Dole when he arrived in her district at the Crown Center Hotel. Her appearance was put on his official schedule, but she did not arrive. She kept to her previous schedule—visiting a black sorority and a church.

In November, Collins lost to the incumbent Congressman Bolling. Her decisions about why, when, and how to run for a higher office than the one she holds were made carefully, with an eye toward present possibilities and future opportunities. Knowing she was likely to be defeated by the incumbent in the general election, Collins used her strengths to win a primary and to acquire her party's congressional nomination, thus gaining status and attention within the local political culture. Locally her position is still firm, gaining her reelection to the Kansas City city council in the 1979 campaign. When the circumstances seemed opportune, Collins took advantage of unusual support from Washington to the extent that the support was available and helpful to her. She articulated a position of refusing either to be used or to be overlooked. To the extent that the party's interests and her aspirations intersected, she was able to derive some benefits from the double burden of her outsider status as a black and a woman in a white male political establishment. Although they are few and far between, circumstances sometimes operate favorably for the outsider who is willing to take a risk and who is intent on building support for tenure in public life.

THE PERILS OF "PLENTY"

Political reality teaches the simple lesson that outsiders are unlikely to be perceived as winners, and that supporting winners serves the purposes of established interests. It also teaches that clubs which protect the high status of members do not willingly risk losing their exclusivity by expanding membership to include strangers. Thus women can anticipate a cool welcome or even resistance when they announce intentions to occupy seats in the political establishment. Traditional gallantry notwithstanding, no political insider can be expected to rise and relinquish his seat to an ambitious female.

Before 1977, the California state senate was an exclusively male political institution. Insiders operated to keep its membership closed, with those already there assisting and protecting each other from losing one of the nation's best paying, best staffed, most prestigious and powerful state legislative positions. At least that was the lesson taught to one of the women who lost her general election race in 1976, a campaign season in which four women won primaries to gain major party nominations for senate races.

In the process of building her campaign, Renee Simon learned about the difficulties of breaking into the upper house of the state legislature. A 50-year-old councilwoman from Long Beach, Simon won the Democratic primary and was given good odds for a November victory. Before and during the primary campaign, Simon traveled to Sacramento to gather support among officeholders. But she met a cool reception from fellow Democrats in the senate. In pursuing an endorsement from one senate leader, she was informed that his lack of support was final, but not personal. "Here at the club," he explained, senators in both parties operated under an agreement that no candidate who was challenging a senate incumbent would get money from the political funds of any other senator regardless of party allegiance.

The gentleman's agreement to refrain from helping nonincumbent challenges to the senate was not directed specifically against women, of course. Yet the situation points up one of the challenges women face in breaking into politics. In California's senate there had never been a female incumbent for the senators to support, a situation mirrored across the country in the countless clubs, caucuses, institutions, associations, and informal networks which have had no female members. Ambitious political women approach doors closed by generations of tradition and habit. Shoving them open is possible, as two women did prove in taking aim on California's senate to win elections in 1976 and 1978. But no such outsider can expect inside support to ease the way.

"The pity of it is," writes Harold J. Wiegand, contributing editor for *The Philadelphia Inquirer,* "there is a vast reservoir of talent at hand which has been virtually untapped for almost any governmental office you can mention: a large number of women who are invariably pushed aside when it comes to picking someone for elective office." Wiegand notes that "party leaders act as though the women were invisible, or dim-witted, and unfit to hold offices which men have consistently disgraced." He describes politicians as "clinging to their monopoly," insiders who "consent grudgingly only to an occasional job for women, and rarely a top one. It is a policy of unmasked tokenism."[1] That is the way Wiegand viewed the situation in Philadelphia and elsewhere in 1979, a year by which women had made significant advances as candidates and officeholders but were still by and large political outsiders.

Many women are highly sensitive to what they perceive as subtle or unconscious sexism. "If I hear anyone else say he's in favor of supporting 'qualified' women for office, I'll explode!" exclaims someone at every meeting of political women these days. It is no longer safe to assume that a woman will not take offense at the types of jokes she has smiled at benignly through generations of comic routines which have made fun of her sex. On a more subtle level, verbal signals are important for understanding how men and women view each other and for revealing the distance between public rhetoric about equal opportunity and personal sensitivity to the issue of women's status. Insiders and outsiders so often operate with different definitions of the same words—a truth apparent to anyone who has been through the conversation about the meaning of the word "equal." What appears to be shared vocabulary articulating identical goals may be fostering only the illusion of agreement.

A man examining the titles in a bookcase exclaimed, "My god, these books are all written by women!" In response to being asked whether he had not realized that women wrote books, he said, "Sure, but there are so many here." "Many" is a relative term. Like some other words connoting quantity, its application is often imprecise and depends on an individual's sense of what constitutes magnitude in a given situation. This particular man is someone who could be counted among those favoring women's equality, and would express willingness to cast a ballot for a female political candidate. While he lends verbal support to a more balanced picture of females and males participating in all activities, he is accustomed to a world in which men dominate most publicly visible activities. It comes as a shock and makes him a mite uncomfortable to discover even three shelves of women's writings.

Recent public opinion surveys consistently document a high

level of support for women's passage toward full equality. But notwithstanding support given to the concept of equality, the question remains whether men and women do not construe the meaning and application of equality in different ways. Perhaps no issue in casual conversation about sex differences stirs so much controversy and ignites tempers so readily as whether, all else being equal (rights, opportunities, responsibilities), women and men would view the world differently, make different choices, champion different causes, and assign different priorities in the game of life. Gross and crude measures of difference such as public opinion polls may be relatively useless and even misleading as indicators of fine but crucially significant distinctions.

In 1977 *Good Housekeeping* magazine sponsored a conference to stimulate a dialogue between prominent women and men about issues concerning women's passage toward full equality in public and professional life. In the course of contributing his observations about women and public office, former Congressman Bruce Caputo of New York stated that the world of today is much better for women than ever before, pointing out that he may represent a "new wave of elected people" who are "used to seeing women in positions of responsibility" and who see nothing unusual in that. His remarks focused on several areas of activity with which he had firsthand contact. During his military service, he said, there were "plenty of female lieutenants" in the Army. At law school he found "a crowd of women." He could not remember a time when women were not active "in public office, the law, the military, in Albany, in Washington. . . ." Praising former New York state legislator Constance Cook, he attributed to her an observation with which he agreed—"that there are plenty of influential women in the Congress."

Caputo favors equality and is genuinely pleased at progress in its direction. But what is his sense of the term "plenty"? Elected state assemblyman in New York in 1972 and reelected in 1974, Caputo served in a legislature with a total of 210 members, including seven women during his first term and nine women during his second term. Women comprised approximately 4 percent of legislators in Albany during his tenure as a state legislator. In Washington in the Ninety-fifth Congress, of which he was a member, there were 535 House and Senate members, eighteen of whom were women

—less than 4 percent of total membership. Obviously his "plenty" and the "plenty" understood by women speaking out for social changes promoting equality would not seem to share a common definition.

These are the perils of "plenty." There is no question that by and large public leaders do favor equality, expressing honest pleasure that women's representation in the public world seems to be improving. Were they called by interviewers surveying attitudes about women in politics, their responses would indicate widespread approval of equal opportunity for women. Surveys suggest that the public world today is open to seeing women as candidates, office-holders, leaders. Nonetheless, a gap appears to exist between what insiders perceive as "equality" or "plenty" and the experiences of those whose aim it is to raise the proportions of women in state legislatures from the 1980 figure of 10 percent nationally, and in Congress from about 4 percent, to a figure more closely represent-ing the proportions of women in the labor force, the voting booths, and the population.

Also, if notions of "plenty" with regard to gender are vastly different between insiders and outsiders, can it be assumed that shared definitions operate for the word "qualified" in this typical poll question: "Would you vote for a qualified woman for mayor, senator, or governor?" Furthermore, can it be assumed that willing-ness to support one "qualified" woman means willingness to sup-port women candidates in the plural?

Observations from recent elections indicate that the former congressman from New York is by no means expressing an idiosyn-cratic or unique point of view. His choice of words reveals a type of attitude voiced by officeholders, party leaders, influential citi-zens, and voters around the country. Even exceptional women who have managed to win acceptance for themselves in political inner circles sometimes interpret their individual success as a sign of general receptivity to the female sex when that is not necessarily a reality.

UNWRITTEN QUOTAS

As women begin to gain entrance to a public world dominated by men, a few women may seem like a large number. They may even appear ominous. Some voters feel they have paid their dues to equal rights by casting a ballot for a woman in the last election and, therefore, are disinclined to view the next female candidate as deserving serious consideration in the voting booth. One is fine. Two are acceptable. After that, things get a little crowded.

This is a problem long familiar to outsiders—quotas. These quotas are not ones prescribed by law, but by custom. The custom is that only so many women are welcome as public officials, with the magic number varying, depending on the particular political context.

When Billie Coopwood decided to run for the Texas legislature in 1976, she walked into what appeared to be a political climate favorable to women. Two of the four house seats in surrounding Travis County, for example, were occupied by women. Another was held by a Mexican-American. In addition, there were three women on the Austin city council and two on the local school board. A woman also served as county clerk, and another was elected that year to the Travis County commissioners court.

Despite the record, Coopwood, a legislative aide, lost her runoff election against Gerald Hill, an Austin appliance-store owner. In her affluent and largely conservative district, some observers of the race suggested that Coopwood was hurt by the fact that two women legislators already served Travis County. "The fact that there were two women in the legislature already did not help Billie," said her opponent after his victory. Coopwood's media aide comments, "No one ever said she couldn't be in the legislature because she is a woman, but the feeling was you can't have three women." It is hard to imagine the same comment being made about three men. Overheard among some local citizens during the campaign was the line that if Coopwood were elected, Austin would be represented by "three chicks and a spic."

The possibility that a quota mentality might affect women seeking high-level positions concerned both women who were running for statewide office in Oregon in the 1976 general elections. Despite the fact that they were candidates for different offices, both Republican Norma Paulus and Democrat Jewel Lansing commissioned polls to test the "two-woman" issue. Paulus' poll, based on personal interviews with 626 respondents around the state, found that 51 percent approved of two women serving in statewide office, 34 percent said it did not matter, and 15 percent said the idea would "not appeal" to them. Lansing's poll, based on 856 face-to-face interviews, showed that 38 percent approved, 53 percent said it did not matter, 8 percent disapproved, and 1 percent was not sure. The candidates' fears were allayed by the voters' attitudes. However, poll results which show that 15 or 8 percent of voters are biased against two women in statewide office deserve some attention. In a close race, such a bias may hurt.

In general, however, the issue of how many women can fit on a ballot appears to be less of a problem for voters in the general public than for political leaders who influence the selection of candidates for nomination and who regulate access to the support a candidate needs in order to build a strong campaign. During the 1977 municipal elections in New York City, for example, two of the most visible and popular women in the metropolitan area were seeking nomination in heavily contested primaries—Bella Abzug for mayor, and Carol Bellamy for president of the city council. In the middle of May, four months before primary election day, political insiders were deciding whether to endorse only one woman for consideration by the voters. A newspaper article analyzing the overall political situation for announced municipal candidates made this observation about candidates' chances at an upcoming New Democratic Coalition endorsement meeting: "In the council president race, State Senator Carol Bellamy has a clear lead over incumbent Paul O'Dwyer and Assemblyman Leonard Stavisky. An Abzug victory [for endorsement in the mayoralty race] could change this, however. No one wants to talk about it, but some delegates feel that two women at the top of the ticket might smack of gilding the ballot box."[2]

No one wants to talk about it, but a quota system seems to be operating to protect the traditional political establishment from "too many" women. Women holding local offices report that on a given school board, municipal council, or county legislature the number of female officials remains constant because screening committees, local bosses, and party officials view women as a special category of officeholders and operate on the basis of unwritten quota systems. If a woman does not seek reelection or is defeated, another woman can be considered in her place.

There are indications that on the issue of tokenism and the perils of "plenty" some women join men in an unconscious symbiotic relationship to maintain a status quo which limits the numbers of women in public office. It is a matter of differing expectations and patterns of experience converging on the same result. Men may be quite satisfied when the magic number of women has been reached. Feeling they have done their share to promote equality, they may view any dissatisfaction or demands beyond that point as unreasonable, asking the classic question "What do women want?" Some women behave as if they have come to the same conclusion when they dismiss the idea of seeking a nomination or vying for an office higher than the one they currently hold—their reasoning being that because a woman already serves at that level, no one is going to support another female's bid for office. It is the mentality of accepting crumbs because the loaf is owned and sliced by someone else. But the situation will not change until there are so many women running for so many offices at the same time that the issue of a candidate's sex becomes as irrelevant as the candidate's eye color in decisions about campaign support.

"I'm here to serve the people and to act on behalf of my district's interests" is a remark repeated by political women at all levels. It is often followed by "I do not consider myself a woman, but rather a candidate concerned with the public welfare." While this view of one's role and responsibilities is appropriate and strategically sensible for anyone in public life, it is also important not to delude oneself about those elements of one's identity that are never overlooked by the rest of the world. One of the prices exacted for such self-deception may be confusion and despair. A nomination or a winning vote count may not be obtainable despite one's assumption that gender is irrelevant to political candidacy. If gentleman's agreements are operating to keep women in the position of the outsider by controlling access, by limiting the numbers of women passing through screening committees, receiving endorsements, and appearing on ballots, women aspiring to office and denying the existence of discriminatory barriers will be left with attributing defeat to personal failure, inexperience, incompetence, or a variety of manifest reasons which may be less relevant than the fact of gender. In single file, women will continue to squeeze through the narrow passageway, moving in at a slow-paced rate, one by one, to have a turn inside the club as a minority member. Acknowledging one's outsider status and its disadvantages does not lock a candidate into making gender the subject of her race. It simply creates the awareness and the opportunity to build a campaign which takes into account the real obstacles it may encounter and which explores the means for taking maximum advantage of the outsider's position.

THE ANTIWOMAN BIAS

Certain forms of discrimination women face as political candidates are not so subtle as being excluded from clubs by an insider protection clause, or encountering a quota mentality masked in progressive rhetoric. Some people simply do not believe that women can or should be public leaders. They discriminate blatantly, feeling justified by tradition in their judgment that women ought to know their place and stay there. In 1979, after Anne Martindell was appointed by President Carter as ambassador to New Zealand, she was introduced to Robert D. Muldoon, New Zealand's Prime Minister. He looked at her and announced, "I don't like lady politicians."[3] In New York, a taxi driver muttered, "I can see women running the kitchen, but not the country." He was responding to a radio newscast quoting a female public leader. "What does she want to fool around with that stuff for? Leave it to the guys," he added in a tone of protective concern for the woman.

Female candidates can expect some voters to bypass them on the ballot simply because of their sex. While most women who go out to meet the electorate report that positive support from voters offsets the antiwoman comments of other citizens, it always comes as a shock when the candidate is greeted with these kinds of remarks made during door-to-door canvassing in recent election seasons: "I don't believe in women in political office"; "I ain't voting for no woman or no nigger"; "I wouldn't vote for a woman for dogcatcher"; "Women should stay home where they belong"; "Go home and take care of your family."

A Texas state legislator who does not approve of sex discrimination has said that he does find it uncomfortable running against a woman: "I have all kinds of respect for a lady, and it hurts me that one would want my job," he said. "Some say men want to dominate women, but in this district that is what the ladies want and expect. They don't want any part of women's liberation."

No matter how women and men respond to pollsters, reporters, and candidates' canvassers about women's right to govern, centuries of conditioning sway attitudes and choices about appropriate roles for the two sexes. Cultural habit is still the most important factor influencing the recruitment of candidates, the availability of campaign endorsements and support, and even the hands that pull levers in polling booths on election day. As long as women are considered oddities or interlopers in competitive politics, the numbers of women attracted to candidacies and their electability will be affected by their status as political outsiders.

Certainly a significant minority of citizens is willing to admit favoring men over women for decision-making positions in the public sector. When Nancy Judy organized her 1976 congressional race in a district that includes the urban area of Dallas, Texas, her campaign hired professional pollsters to survey the electorate. Results indicated that 26 percent of voters interviewed preferred a male candidate. In some precincts dominated by low-income white households, the margin of respondents preferring a man increased to 29 percent. No hard data are available to demonstrate the extent to which these kinds of preferences are converted into antiwoman votes, or the extent to which antiwoman votes make a decisive difference in election results. Yet the fact that gender per se is sometimes a relevant characteristic in assessing political candidates means that in seeking nomination and election, women face people's biases about their sex—both pro- and antiwoman. Biases affect the odds for success.

In general elections, when the alternative to voting for a woman running in one's own party may be to vote for a male on the opposite ticket, party affiliation might be a stronger determinant of voting behavior than gender preference, at least among voters who are strongly partisan. But the problem for female candidates may be particularly acute in primary elections when voters face no conflict between antiwoman attitudes and party loyalties. Something of this sort seems to have happened in Oregon's Republican primary for secretary of state in 1976.

Sipping Seven-Ups on the rocks, John Paul Kelting relaxed in a Portland bar and recalled his bid to become secretary of state in Oregon so he could abolish the office. "Jefferson said the masses are asses," Kelting said. "If it could ever be proven, I did it."

Kelting, a political nobody, came out from under his middle-class blues nearly to upset Republican Norma Paulus in Oregon's state-wide primary election. Arrested the night before the election while walking barefoot and wearing cut-off suit trousers on a freeway ramp near Sausalito, California, Kelting fielded an amazing 44 percent of the Republican vote.

A self-employed building contractor from a Portland suburb, Kelting was unknown to Oregon's Republican Party until he filed for the race the day before the deadline. Paulus, a three-term state representative, had been gearing up to run for months. She was one of the party's few shining stars destined for higher office.

Kelting's campaign was a one-man show employing no paid staff, no television or radio ads, and fewer than a hundred bumper stickers. "I was closer to being comedian of the week than I was to being a competent candidate," he said. Paulus, the consummate candidate, had all the trappings of a full-blown campaign—a handsomely paid staff, hundreds of volunteers, thousands of pieces of campaign literature, and media advertising.

For his efforts, Kelting spent less than $600. For her efforts, Paulus, tapping into well-heeled Republican sources, spent more than $32,000 on the race.

The disparities left political pundits scratching their heads. How did Kelting do so well?

Although he had worked on conservative Republican campaigns outside of Oregon, Kelting, 32 years old, had never run for office. At age 17, he campaigned for a candidate for sheriff in Palm Beach County, Florida. In 1962, he helped organize Fresno County, California, for Richard Nixon's gubernatorial bid. "I'm the dumb shit from Coalinga who's been asking for your autograph," Kelting once told Nixon. But in 1976, Kelting had become disillusioned with politicians, even those who had been his heroes. "Nixon finally gave in to the fascists," he said. "He accepted their terms."

It was Kelting's disillusionment with politicians and government in general that sent him to Salem, the state capital, to file for secretary of state. "To be very candid," Kelting said, "it was a farce. To be further candid, they pissed me off."

"They" were the state bureaucrats who had thrown up red tape when Kelting sought his building contractor's license. "They" were the state Land Conservation and Development Commission, whose actions had profited the big land developers at the expense of the little guys, Kelting believed. "They" were the judges in traffic court who had "made a mockery of justice."

Crisscrossing the state in his Chevy pickup, Kelting sought a forum for his views wherever he could find one. His campaign slogan was

"Government by us, not for us." If elected, he promised to abolish the secretary of state's office as well as many state agencies.

The message fell on open ears at the other end of Kelting's CB radio. "Big John," as Kelting tagged his handle, took his campaign to truckers and others up and down the highways. "It was something new," Kelting said. "I was identifying with people in the same bind I was. They were tired of being pushed around. Their theme was the same as mine: 'Throw the bastards out.'"

When the votes were tallied, Kelting had racked up 44 percent of the vote, not only statewide but also in urban Multnomah and Lane counties where Paulus was expected to swamp her opponent. He also carried thirteen of thirty-six counties, most of them rural, where presidential candidate Ronald Reagan also ran well.

While Kelting may have been aided by a conservative backlash around the state and by organizational disarray in the Paulus camp, he also tapped into a hard core of sexist opposition to women candidates, particularly among GOP women. A Republican poll conducted after the election showed that 33 percent of 626 respondents said they preferred Kelting simply because he was a man. Among men, the figure was 31 percent and among women it jumped to 35 percent.

"Let's face it," said Kelting's wife, "he did so well mostly because he was a man."

For some years to come, women who step forward into public life must expect to contend with varying degrees of blatant discrimination—attitudes and behaviors on the part of people to whom any male candidate appears preferable to any female outsider. During the 1978 election season, *Time* magazine reviewed the campaigns of a number of women running for high-level offices around the country. In identifying the issues arising repeatedly for female candidates today, the article stressed, "Perhaps the most basic barrier to women's political success is outright sexism—a feeling, among women as well as men, that a woman's place is in the home, not the House."[4] While there is no doubt that a major source of moral and material support for women's candidacies these days is coming from women everywhere cheering each other on to new challenges, other women disapprove strongly of changes in traditional patterns of behavior. Some have no confidence in their own abilities to govern and find it impossible to imagine other women as able public leaders. Some shun politics as unsavory, feeling that women should remain aloof from the back rooms and bars where political deals are made. Many believe firmly that women's most important responsibilities to society lie in their roles as homemakers, wives, and mothers and that there is no way to fulfill these critical obligations properly while doing anything else as demanding as campaigning or officeholding. Some men concur with these attitudes. Others do not want to deal with a new group of competitors and with an unfamiliar breed of colleagues. Together, these women and men constitute a small but intractable obstacle to women's advancement in public life. They vote for women to stay put inside their homes and to remain locked out of the political world.

ONE WOMAN'S PROBLEMS ARE
ALL WOMEN'S SINS

For the time being, political woman exists as "the other"—as Simone de Beauvoir termed, in *The Second Sex,* the sex whose existence is defined not for its own autonomous qualities but as it appears relative to men and is differentiated with reference to men. His presence defines the activity called politics, and thus is essential; her presence is inessential, noted in relation to an activity defined by his existence. It is in this sense that women are outsiders at a more profound level. Their presence is noteworthy primarily because it is not inevitable in the context as constructed. Thus, political women are viewed first as women, not as individual political people. Seen as women, often they are lumped together as a class, pinned with the same identity (every political woman is a potential Bella Abzug until she proves otherwise), not differentiated at the outset with regard to their diversity as individuals. The manifestations and consequences of this situation range from the silly to the serious.

Individual members of outsider groups are mistaken for one another frequently, and they are assumed to think and behave alike. While no one in a rational moment would suggest that women are hard to tell apart, many political women have been mistaken for one another. After all, it is asked, how many outspoken, politically active women could there be in one district? In a legislative session in Minnesota, a male legislator repeatedly confused two female colleagues and called them by each other's names. Finally, in a moment of frustration, he made the classic remark: "But, you know, you women all look alike."

The public opinion polls in Oregon had reassured the Paulus and Lansing campaigns that most voters would not disapprove of two females serving in statewide office. Nonetheless, with both women on the ballot other problems arose. Faced with two women seeking major statewide offices, some voters could not keep them straight despite the fact that the candidates belonged to different political parties and were seeking different offices. In the course of her campaign, Paulus was greeted frequently with the comment, "Oh, you're the CPA," a title emphasized by Lansing as one of her prime professional qualifications to be state treasurer. While parading at a bean festival in the mid-Willamette Valley, Lansing was mistaken for Paulus by bystanders. Even after the election, when both Paulus and Lansing appeared at a fund raiser sponsored by labor groups, Lansing, who had lost her state treasurer race, was congratulated several times for winning her secretary of state race, a tribute that should have gone to Paulus.

During the primary season in Oregon the situation had been even more confusing for those who could not tell one woman from another. Three women were running for nominations to statewide office. Campaigning during a shift change at a lumber mill on the Oregon coast, Democrat Caroline Wilkins, running to become a nominee for secretary of state, reported the following conversation with a male worker:

Worker: "You were here just a few weeks ago, weren't you?"

Wilkins: "No, not me."

Worker: "I'm sure it was some woman running for secretary of state."

Wilkins: "Was she blond?" [A reference to Republican Norma Paulus.]

Worker: "No."

Wilkins: "Was it Jewel Lansing?" [Democratic candidate for state treasurer.]

Worker: "Yeah, that was the one."

It is understandable that during primary election season voters cannot sort out all the candidates from the same party running for the same office. Male candidates are also mistaken for one another.

It is difficult to tell politicians apart when one has no contact with them except through political advertisements in campaign season. However, confusion about the identities of female candidates has been articulated repeatedly from a position in which women are categorized as a special, separate group of candidates—as women, above and beyond other relevant classifications. Some voters place the category "women" alongside a stereotype meaning "incorruptible" or "trustworthy." For them it almost becomes unnecessary to distinguish one woman from another. As one male voter assured a female legislative candidate, "Well, little lady, I've voted for every woman on the ballot because I knew they weren't politicians."

A further twist in the knot is illustrated by a familiar attitude expressed in Connecticut during Gloria Schaffer's U.S. Senate campaign. Schaffer faced negative reactions from voters and political activists who were unhappy with Governor Ella Grasso's policies and administration. Despite the fact that Governor Grasso did not stand for office on a platform to test womankind's abilities to govern in a popular or successful manner, she has been held accountable for the ways in which other women might perform as public officials, and other women are held accountable for her perceived failings. While there has been a great deal of grumbling about the performance of male elected officials at all levels, few people conclude that their failings are sex-linked or that it would be wise to avoid electing another male officeholder in the years to come. Gloria Schaffer's campaign did hear such grumblings and conclusions about women.

> In her first year in office, Ella Grasso appeared to lack the political acumen of her mentor, John Bailey, and committed one political faux pas after another. By the beginning of 1976, she had alienated many members of her own party, angered labor, and made it clear to liberals who once supported her that she was not one of them.
>
> Concern that the public's growing dislike of Grasso might spill over onto Gloria Schaffer—at that time one of the most popular state officials and the Democratic Party's biggest votegetter—was reflected in a January campaign poll conducted by Peter Hart and Associates of over six hundred respondents. When asked how important Ella Grasso's performance was in judging the ability of women to handle major government positions, a 52 percent majority of voters said it was very or fairly important. Less than a third felt it was not at all important.[5]

The poll asked another question which made it clear that there was a small but significant number of people who would be reluctant to support Schaffer because Connecticut already had one woman in high office. When asked if Schaffer's election to the U.S. Senate would give Connecticut an overrepresentation of women in high positions, 9 percent said yes, and another 27 percent were not sure.

In the next six months, Grasso's popularity fell drastically. In the meantime, Schaffer's campaign was gathering momentum, and she was highly visible in the news after being nominated officially by the state Democratic Party at its convention in July. That same month Schaffer's campaign staff conducted a poll which showed the percentage who felt her election to the Senate would mean an overrepresentation of women increased to 15 percent, and the undecided group decreased to 15 percent.

In the next few months columnists in Connecticut newspapers speculated on what one called "the governor's political disease" and recommended that Grasso and Schaffer not appear to be too close to each other. On several occasions in the fall, when Schaffer campaigned in Connecticut towns, she was heckled by passers-by about Grasso's policies, or was told, "I've voted for my last woman!"

The most concrete opposition which linked Schaffer to Grasso was voiced by the two state employees' unions in October. The state employees were among Grasso's strongest critics. They had expected wage increases with her election after several barren years under an austerity governor, and were angered and alienated when she not only demanded a wage freeze but laid off several hundred employees and tried to lengthen the work week from thirty-five to forty hours.

At a meeting of the Connecticut State Employees Association a straw poll gave incumbent Senator Lowell Weicker 72 percent to Schaffer's 23 percent. In announcing the results, the union president said it was really an anti-Grasso vote and that Schaffer was being turned down because of the governor.

Asked to reply, Schaffer said it was unfair of the association to blame her for Grasso's policies, as she had nothing to do with them. Several days later, Grasso supported this position, saying that "other people" are "not to be blamed" for the fiscal decisions she made. Although other labor leaders said the president had given his personal interpretation, not that of the association, and was trying to make political hay out of the straw vote, Schaffer's campaign staffers still thought the union poll said more about their opinion of Grasso than of Schaffer.

A similar situation arose the following week. During the question period after Schaffer spoke to the Connecticut Independent Em-

ployees Union, one rank-and-file member stated from the audience
that because he had been burned by Grasso, he would not vote for
another woman.

Once again, Schaffer said this was unfair. "Use my record and not
the difficulties you are experiencing with the present state administration, in which I have no policymaking role, to decide whether or not
to support me," she said.

Despite overt expressions of distrust for one woman because
of the behavior of another woman, it is not clear how typical such
thinking is of the general voting population. Schaffer and Grasso
were both high-ranking Democrats holding statewide office. Many
people asserted that if both were men, the fact that they were
members of the same administration would cause the policies of
one to affect the electoral chances of the other. Other Connecticut
voters said that those expressing antiwoman or anti-Grasso sentiments as reasons to vote against Schaffer would have voted against
her anyway, and that these were simply convenient excuses.

Whether such sentiments are symptoms or merely excuses,
however, the fact that they can be uttered so openly indicates that
female candidates are still viewed as women before they are seen
as individuals. As women, they are held responsible for the actions
of other women.

The governor of Connecticut is by no means the only prominent woman for whom all political women are held responsible.
There are those who, not admiring Bella Abzug's outspoken style
and liberalism, or Dixie Lee Ray's conservatism, or the style, substance, and political persuasion of any number of lesser-known
public women, generalize their negative judgments from one
woman to all females.

Disapproval of visible women for their shortcomings is as
likely to come from other women as from men, though often as a
result of different psychological mechanisms. Some women who
articulate a desire to support the advance of other women into
positions of public leadership do apply higher and more stringent
standards for background qualification and for behavior to females
than to males. Sensing that whoever among women achieves public
attention will be viewed as a model of all women, and feeling
uncertain enough about their own ability and stamina for becoming

superwomen, women have been extremely cautious about supporting female candidates who do not meet acid tests for perfection.
Unless the defensiveness recedes and the expectations for performance by political women are similar to those for political men, only
a handful of women each decade will pass muster.

By the same token, the judgment that one woman's problems
are all women's sins is likely to result in depressing the numbers of
women in politics. Only a very small and highly self-selected group
of women will vie for positions in which they are apt to become
victims of special harsh judgment, targets for disapprobation or
derision. Among those few who enter as unwitting standard bearers
for female political leadership, even fewer will survive the application of double standards, the psychological burdens, and the expectations of superhuman performance which await the visible advance
guard. Furthermore, the vicious circle continues to perpetuate itself
so long as there are few enough women in public view that they
inevitably receive special scrutiny by those expecting women to fail,
and so long as their accomplishments come as a surprise to those
who do not expect as much from a woman. At least in one regard
women and men are quite equal—they are imperfect as judged
against the impossible standard of an ideal. Until women are held
no more accountable than men for failing to transcend their human-
ity and manifest celestial qualities, the profile of public leaders will
remain overwhelmingly male.

The way in is strewn with obstacles, some more prohibitive,
others quite manageable. Defining the right image, orchestrating
private and public lives, and establishing a compelling presence as
a respected outsider—to varying degrees, these challenges confront
today's political woman. While their combined effects could result
in containing or strangling political ambitions, events suggest otherwise. By taking cognizance of obstacles in her way, today's astute
female candidate sets out to locate the points of entry most mallea-
ble and receptive to her and to use time-honored political techniques to maximize her advantages, reduce her liabilities, and stay
in the running.

Campaigning

And from the podium at a rally, Queens Borough President Donald Manes says, "She'll make a good Congressman . . . woman . . . person . . . whatever." Replies Geraldine Ferraro: "I'll take it."
                    —Quoted in *Time,* November 6, 1978

Chapter 5
Laying the
Groundwork

*It hasn't been easy. I've worked hard and learned that you don't go out
on stage and play the piano without knowing the whole score.*
     —Bess Myerson, quoted in *The Washington Star,*
     February 9, 1980

The political woman of the seventies was a pioneer in establishing her credibility as a political candidate before the public and the
political parties. Although her ultimate success in winning nominations and elective offices depended on many variables—some unanticipated, or capricious, or related to the passing moment's political
climate, others peculiar to circumstances in a particular district, or
lodged in powerful patterns of traditional political behavior—the
woman candidate was more likely to gain entrance where others
had preceded her. The first woman to announce her candidacy in
an election district is far more likely than the tenth to encounter
automatic incredulity or skepticism about her ambition to hold
office, her familial arrangements, or her tone of voice and style of
dress.

While the long process of building credibility for women's
public leadership has begun, much of the burden still falls upon the
individual woman to crack the barriers to her political advancement. After realizing that she can be a viable candidate and successful officeholder, she must sway many other people to support that
conviction. Men, too, must establish their credibility as political

candidates, but they do so within a social context that already accepts the concept of male leadership. Female candidates meanwhile confront the larger task of quelling doubt about women's very capacity for political leadership. In short, strong male candidates are given the benefit of the doubt, while strong female candidates must earn it.

To minimize the credibility gap and establish solid credentials for political office, a woman must enhance her visibility, convey authority, and, when aiming for higher levels of office, attract recognition from the party and other networks of political power. For this, careful and thorough groundwork is essential.

The groundwork might begin years before she actually runs for elective office. Sometimes it starts with the decision to pursue a particular course of study or attend a certain college or professional school within one's own state in order to make contact with people who can later be useful. Sometimes it involves selection of domicile in a district where specific political opportunities are likely to arise. Often it includes joining local political clubs, business associations, and community organizations as well as contributing time and/or money to other people's campaigns. Some potential candidates establish credentials and contacts by serving as paid staff in the offices of elected officials.[1] New York's Mary Anne Krupsak, Senator Nancy Kassebaum of Kansas, and Chicago's Jane Byrne all worked for other elected officials before running for office themselves.

Sometimes the groundwork is laid when a woman wins an appointment to a local planning board or human-rights commission and consciously begins to promote her visibility and build a base of support for a town council race she anticipates entering two years later. In the case of running for higher office, a state assemblywoman, for example, may set a goal of running for the state senate four years down the road and devise a plan to use her assembly position in building credentials and making contacts for a bid to move to the legislature's upper house. In some cases, a candidate may prepare by running in a campaign that is virtually destined for defeat but which promotes her visibility in the district and serves to mobilize a team of supporters who will be available when the opportunity arises for another, more viable race.

Five basic components can be isolated that helped women establish credibility in elective politics during the seventies. First, candidates utilized the connections and experience they had gained in previous volunteer work, in affiliations with a wide range of community activities, and in working behind the scenes in other people's campaigns. Second, timing was usually a very important element in deliberate efforts to build a candidate's credibility—the earlier the start, the more effective the outcome. Third, establishing a strong base of grass-roots support produced positive results for female candidates. Fourth, a campaign plan grounded in an accurate, detailed, and comprehensive assessment of the candidate and her district worked in the candidate's favor. Finally, every woman determined to establish her credibility as a candidate set out to form constructive relationships with public leaders, win the support of her party, and tap into existing political networks or create new ones.

The women who ran for elective office during the seventies knew how to make good use of some of these essential building blocks, and took strides in employing those which were less familiar. They did so in a variety of ways, to different degrees, and with varying outcomes. Virtually everyone learned something useful from the experience.

Ann Richards is a textbook example of how to build a political candidacy, capitalizing on all five ingredients to achieve success. In 1976, at age 42, Ann Richards of Texas, a woman who had worked for years in other people's campaigns, took on a two-term incumbent in the race for Travis County commissioners court, the legislative body for the Austin area of Texas.

When Henry B. Gonzalez, now a San Antonio congressman, made a gallant attempt at the Texas governorship in 1958, one of his unsung campaign workers drove the more than five hundred dusty miles from Dallas to Brownsville, posting campaign signs on every telephone pole.

In those days Ann Richards was the indefatigable boiler-room girl. She was the energetic young mother who pushed a baby stroller door-to-door to pump up a campaign for a North Dallas precinct chairman. She worked the Dallas precinct desk for the Kennedy–Johnson presidential campaign, sold poll taxes in black grocery stores on Saturday nights, and served as unpaid bottlewasher for many a Dallas Democrat who paid his filing fee for a go at public office.

By 1968, when she and her family moved to Austin, she was

something of a burned-out case. All those hours in campaign storefronts had been less than fulfilling. She was tired of licking stamps.

No political firehorse stays long in pasture in a government town like Austin, Texas' capital city. When Richards reentered the fray it was as a tactician instead of a street soldier. She was advisor to an aspiring young lawyer, Sarah Weddington, who has since served two terms in the Texas legislature, moved on to be appointed counsel to the U.S. Department of Agriculture, and then to the White House as President Carter's special assistant.

By 1975, Richards was ready for stage front center. Translating all those years of political apprenticeship into a carefully planned and superbly executed primary campaign, she unseated popular two-term incumbent Johnny Voudouris.

Richards started giving serious thought to the commissioners' contest in August 1975, nine months before the primary election. In October she called together a group of close friends and politically knowledgeable acquaintances to assess her chances. On November 1, she resigned from her legislative job to devote all her time to her campaign.

The next three months were devoted to rounds of meetings with officeholders, political leaders, community activists, Kiwanis club presidents, and anyone else who might be able to influence votes. She told them that she had decided to run, the reasons why she could win, and she sought their advice. Some tried to discourage her. Others gave her contributions.

Richards also talked to the incumbent, Johnny Voudouris, about her decision. "I told him his record was inadequate. It was nothing personal." She made a list of all those people who would not like Voudouris—his opponents of other years; presidents of senior-citizens groups who objected to his votes against projects for the aged; civic-group presidents who objected to his dealings with water or road projects. Her objective was twofold—to build support, and to freeze out any potential opposition.

"Make an unbiased assessment of yourself. Don't ask your friends if you should run for office," says Richards. Not surprisingly, the unbiased assessment of Richards came out on the positive side. She had her degree in speech and political science from Baylor University and a recent year of experience as legislative aide to State Representative Weddington. Her service in the state capital as well as her close ties to Austin's liberal community gave her a ready network of politically shrewd supporters. Her family situation was ideal. Her husband, a politically active attorney with a statewide reputation for his civil rights work, was totally committed to her endeavor. Her four children were of high-school and college age and willing to sacrifice receiving their mother's attention for the sake of good government in Travis County. The Richardses were moderately affluent and could provide that vital early money necessary to any serious political effort.

Richards carried her decision-making process beyond the realm of seat-of-the-pants conjecture into an analysis of hard data. She decided to let election returns tell her whether a liberal-leaning, urban woman had a chance against a moderate to conservative rural man. "That first calculation—the one that tells you whether you can win in that district—is the most important you can make," Richards said later.

Precinct 3 had been represented for eight years by Johnny Voudouris, who lived outside the city limits and generated more rapport among the families who go steer-roping on Wednesday nights than among the University of Texas students who make up a sizable segment of the precinct's voters. Richards quickly ascertained that 82 percent of the voters lived within the city and that another 7 percent inhabited her home base of West Lake Hills and its sister suburb, Rollingwood, on Austin's western edge. "I knew it didn't make a damn what I could do in the rural boxes," Richards concluded.

She then looked at returns from Frances "Sissy" Farenthold's 1972 and 1974 gubernatorial races, searching for clues about voter reaction to women candidates. In fact, Farenthold had fared better in Richards' precinct in 1974, when she was taking a statewide trouncing, than she had in 1972, when she came within striking distance of the Governor's Mansion. Returns from recent city council elections in which three women won seats convinced Richards that South Austin voters were open-minded to female contenders. A look at George McGovern's votes in the 1972 presidential race gave Richards more insight into her prospective voters' habits.

The statistical groundwork not only clinched her decision to run for commissioners court, but it also provided the numerical underpinnings for her campaign game plan. Targeting votes, based on tedious hours pouring over precinct returns, may be the single most important aspect of any campaign.

Richards' study of past elections convinced her she had six boxes of solid support, eight boxes where voters were ripe for persuasion, and another fourteen—some sparsely populated—which were filled with Voudouris' soulmates. Midway through her campaign, however, when a telephone poll showed that the swing voters were rapidly converting to her cause, she shifted her effort into the most likely of the opposition precincts, with satisfactory results.

Ann Richards was well aware that her campaign needed careful planning, not just to raise her own visibility but to convince many of the voters who supported the incumbent to switch their allegiance. She had to find Voudouris' soft spots and exploit them, meanwhile giving the voters positive reasons why she could better represent them.

Voudouris was vulnerable on several fronts. He had been less than accessible to the homeowners who wanted a chuckhole repaired or a broken culvert replaced. He had voted for an unpopular pay raise for commissioners court; and a money-losing landfill project cast doubts on his managerial abilities.

Since accessibility was to be an issue, Richards decided to be accessible—on the voters' doorsteps. Voudouris was open to charges that he spent county time on his five private businesses. Richards would work hard and long hours for her constituents.

A great deal of her time was spent door-knocking, which any candidate knows is a tiring, tedious way to win a political race. But Richards knew that it was an effective method for women like herself to create an image of credibility with voters. "Even growing up in Waco, I encountered a basic feeling that government is something that costs a lot and doesn't do much good. I think it makes a difference if a voter can see someone on the doorstep and decide, 'Well, that looks like a sensible person.' "

The Richards door-knocking effort was highly organized and meticulously followed through. "I walked those streets. It was my plan and I stuck to it. I thought if they saw me working that hard they'd figure that I would work that hard in office." No door-knocker can afford to waste time on nonvoters, and Richards isolated from precinct returns those hardy souls who had voted in a recent city bond election and in a low-turnout referendum on a new state constitution. Those hard-core voters were listed on 3 × 5 cards by residence so that the stack would lead the candidate up one side of a block and down the other side.

About a week before her planned visit to a particular street, postcards preprinted with her photograph were mailed, informing residents that she would soon be in the neighborhood.

Richards carried with her brochures for the at-home people, doorhangers on which she had written, "Sorry I missed you," and her stack of 3 × 5 cards. If the voter was home, Richards made a simple pitch—"I'm running for county commissioner, and I hope you will read my brochure." She followed with a chatty comment—"What lovely geraniums you have." As she left the home, she made a quick note on the 3 × 5 card—"lovely geraniums"—for later use.

During remaining weeks, whenever she had time, Richards made notations on postcards sent to voters reminding them to go to the polls. Her note mentioned the geraniums, or whatever comment she had made during the door-to-door visit.

Such a personalized campaign can have its drawbacks. A few weeks after the election, Richards answered the telephone to hear an unfamiliar voice say, "Mrs. Richards, I've got your cat." Mystified, Richards replied, "Well, yes, I do have cats."

"No, no," the caller explained. "I mean your calico cat. You said I had a lovely calico cat and if she ever had kittens to let you know. Well, the kittens are ready to go now."

The door-knocking campaign was coordinated with another personal vote-gathering technique—neighborhood coffees. More than 110 coffees were held for Ann Richards. They began six months before the election.

Nothing was left to chance. Each prospective hostess for a coffee received a mimeographed sheet of instructions from the coordinator of coffees. The instructions set a time schedule and discouraged elaborate refreshments, which might intimidate other people from hostessing coffees. Standard procedure had a campaign aide making a brief pitch for support before Richards herself delivered a ten-minute talk about her positions. If a coffee only attracted two or three guests, and some did, it was still an asset, Richards said, because her name had been spread through the neighborhood by the invitation process. "The value is the seed planted in a voter's mind," she said. "Media can sock it all together later."

Political pros refer to voter contact as a "hit." The more hits the better. In addition to door-knocking and coffees, Richards used a phone canvass. Her volunteers called voters with a simple message: "Ann Richards is running for county commissioner in Precinct 3. I hope we can count on your support." If the voter said no, she or he was scratched from the list. If the response was yes, the name was marked for a "Don't forget to vote" postcard. Undecided voters got special treatment—a personal letter from the volunteer who had called telling why that volunteer supported Richards' candidacy.

Richards' mail efforts were supplemented with one mailout directed to Spanish surname voters and another to the few black voters in her district.

When postmortems were conducted on campaigns in the seventies, many female candidates believed it was this type of grass-roots

work—voter contact through door-knocking, canvassing, and mail—
that built their credibility as serious candidates and made the difference between winning and losing. In the Richards campaign, direct
contact with voters was supplemented with the use of media to reach
large numbers of voters.

Mary Beth Rogers, Richards' media advisor, sought to make television spots—run the last week before election—the frosting on the
cake of an already well-executed effort. Richards' door-to-door en-
counters had convinced her that high utility bills (Austin has the
highest in the nation) were uppermost among voter concerns. "Now
a county commissioner can't do anything about utility rates, and Ann
didn't want to purport to, but she did want to key to that concern,"
Rogers said.

Film was shot in Richards' home, a warm and unpretentious but
nevertheless substantial piece of real estate in affluent West Lake
Hills. Richards pointed out that she paid utility bills and she paid
taxes and because of this, she was concerned about keeping government costs as low as possible.

Television was a finishing touch in the Richards campaign. Less
expensive ways of generating the all-important name identification
had been used through signboards, selective newspaper advertising,
and radio.

Richards' radio spots started five weeks before the primary. The
first message was a variety of voices saying, "I'm voting for Ann
Richards because." The next week Richards had scheduled a public
fund raiser with celebrity sponsors, humorist John Henry Faulk and
former White House Press Secretary Liz Carpenter. All that week,
Faulk and Carpenter were heard on radio inviting people to the party
and plugging Richards' candidacy.

During the last weeks of the campaign, radio messages delivered
a skillful attack on Johnny Voudouris, focusing on Voudouris' less
than full-time attention to his commissioner's office. For "get positive" time just before election day, a radio spot reinforced the image
Ann Richards had created for herself through months of building her
credibility with the voters. A whimsical guitar was heard playing in
the background. Over it a number of voices talked about Ann Richards' visits to their neighborhoods, her concern with utility bills, her
commitment to hard work. At appropriate intervals the candidate's
own voice expressed her views on pertinent and serious issues.

Richards attributes her primary victory 85 percent to plan and
15 percent to luck. A victory in a Democratic primary in Texas is

tantamount to winning the general election, which is what Richards moved on to do with little trouble. On a global scale, Richards' "empire" is a modest one, encompassing seventy thousand voters and three hundred square miles of Austin and the surrounding limestone and live-oak hill country. But she scored a rare success: not many first-time candidates for competitive positions offering high status and a good salary manage to win either a primary or a general election in which they unseat a well-known incumbent.

UTILIZING EXPERIENCE

In the 1970s most of the women who handled the task successfully and won election to public office knew campaign politics and had accumulated political equity in their communities. Moreover, they knew where to promote themselves and how to utilize their years of experience in public activities. Most were sought out neither by their political parties nor by business or labor interests; nor were they protégées of established political figures or influential and wealthy community leaders. Encouraged to run for office by their families and friends, many were self-starters who decided the time was right to convince others that their résumés spoke compellingly of qualifications for candidacy.

In an address to the 1979 national convention of the National Women's Political Caucus, Congresswoman Barbara Mikulski of Maryland reminded her audience that while recent attention to women's lives might suggest that women were new to the labor force or political affairs, that was not the case. "Now we are about to be discovered as party activists," she said. "Isn't that nice? After all these years of staffing the headquarters and making the phone calls, of raising the money and walking door-to-door for candidates —we're going to be an overnight success. And somebody's going to say, 'Look at all these women! Where did they come from?' Well, we know where we came from—we know it has been a long road, and uphill most of the way."

When Republican Diane McCarthy was first elected to the Arizona house of representatives in 1972, she could credit herself with a near-lifetime history of building political contacts. McCarthy had followed all the unwritten rules (especially for women) about putting volunteer time into party work. She had also worked at low-paying jobs for party leaders: "I graduated from college with a degree in political science that was worth nothing in terms of a job," she said. "I went to work for the Republican State Committee as a receptionist—as a go-fer, actually." The pay was low, but she found politics exciting, especially as the Republicans were beginning to build strength. She moved from receptionist work to an assignment as administrative assistant to the attorney general.

McCarthy also learned a few unpleasant lessons about politics. After working very hard for a successful candidate, "I was told he didn't need me. This happens to everyone in politics sooner or later. But I was crushed—in tears—I really turned off politics." Nonetheless McCarthy continued to work in the party on the precinct level and in fund-raising activities. When a state legislative seat opened and "no one was anointed for it," she saw it as a perfect opportunity. "I went down to the county GOP people. I knew them." The announcement that she was planning to run received encouraging responses. In 1972 McCarthy waged a successful campaign for the state legislative seat to which she was reelected in 1974, 1976, and 1978. In 1980 McCarthy ran and won a statewide race for a seat on Arizona's three-member Corporation Commission.

The ranks of successful women candidates in the 1970s include many who, like Diane McCarthy, had campaigned for other politicians, using what they learned to personal advantage. Some women even won difficult first races in districts dominated by the opposite party. Such was the case in Barbara McConnell's 1977 campaign for the New Jersey assembly. A Democrat, McConnell announced early and planned carefully for her successful primary and general election races. With years of party work to her credit and with a history of managing two successful campaigns for Congresswoman Helen Meyner, McConnell converted political experience into election victory in a traditionally Republican district, winning a seat to which she was reelected in 1979.

Other women move patiently and slowly through the echelons of local politics. "You know, I started in politics baking cakes for the Democratic club. That's the way a lot of women started," said Sue Mills after winning election in 1978 to the Prince George's county council in Maryland. She believes that "men just decide they want to run for office and do it. Women have to work their way up."[2] That attitude finds voice even among women who have achieved high levels of office. Ohio's State Treasurer Gertrude Donahey believes that "starting at the bottom and working up—stuffing envelopes, licking stamps, going door to door"—is the way women should become involved in politics. She sought the lowest statewide position because "I didn't think the men would mind starting a woman there."[3] While many women would disagree about choosing that route for pursuing candidacies in the future or even today, it is generally the way women have entered political life in the past.

In sum, whether they started at the bottom in vying for public offices or moved directly into races for more powerful positions, most women who launched candidacies during the seventies managed to convert years of political activity and voluntary participation in civic affairs and nongovernmental organizations into practical tools for building their own credibility as candidates. Very frequently, and all over the country, one hears political women echoing the remark "I got my training in the League of Women Voters."

TIMING

Filing and running for office during the campaign season are behaviors which implement and extend a plan of action set in motion much earlier. Among those female candidates who lost races (especially in primaries) during the 1976 elections for state legislative, statewide, and congressional offices that were not considered hopeless to win, a striking number blamed their defeats on timing.

In 1976 when Baltimore City Councilwoman Barbara Mikulski joined Gladys Spellman and Marjorie Holt in Maryland's congressional delegation, six other women in the state had lost primary races for congressional seats. Four of the losers had never held elective office. All were challenging incumbents or front-runners who were considered shoo-ins. Several who were challenging conservative incumbents declared for office late after trying to find other candidates. Only two of these women were at all known in their communities. None was associated with a cause popular enough to mobilize volunteers despite last-minute entries, and none had widespread support from a political organization. Only two of the unsuccessful candidates in the congressional primaries had strong local political ties, and those were limited to her own area in the congressional district. Without lining up sufficient political support before announcing their intentions to run, they had little credibility for a high-level race—no matter how civic-minded their motivations, how respectable their qualifications, or how great their skills at political analysis.

"I had a lot more enthusiasm than expertise," recalls one women who ran unsuccessfully in another state's legislative primary. She decided to run at the last minute and admits, "I didn't even know the district when I filed." While long-range timing alone does not guarantee success, without it a campaign is severely handicapped. With it, a potential candidate can assess her personal history and take good advantage of her knowledge of local politics and community affairs, her work history and professional experiences, and her relationships with friends and associates in neighborhoods at the grass roots. She can study the district and organize her resources. All the raw material is there, in the community and in the experience of her daily life, for launching a public career.

GRASS-ROOTS SUPPORT

Both women and men must build local support for their campaigns and maintain good relations with the people who stand to put them in office. But women's strength more than men's still lies in forging and reinforcing bonds at the grass roots, particularly among campaign supporters and voters who have not previously been reached. Because the established networks of power and sources of campaign support are less familiar, less accessible, and less forthcoming for women than for men, women are challenged to mobilize and then maintain a somewhat different base of support from that on which men have relied traditionally.

This challenge is recognized by forceful political women such as Mildred Barry Garvin, elected in 1977 for a first term in the New Jersey legislature. Garvin knew that local party leaders would not extend themselves to support her candidacy for first-term office. She also realized she had resources among people in her district whom the party leaders did not reach. Those were the people she contacted for support—all the parent-teachers' organizations she had worked with during years on the school board; all the women in local church groups; all the mothers of Girl Scouts and Boy Scouts she had met through years of raising a family. From the day she won her legislative race, even before she was sworn in to serve her first term as a New Jersey assemblywoman, Garvin's calendar for the following year was filling up rapidly. She was going back to the people who put her in office—to the PTA meetings and church club groups—to tell them what she was doing, how she was doing it, and why their dollars and votes were well spent in supporting her to continue representing them in the state's lawmaking body. They did again in 1979.

County Councilwoman Sue Mills of Maryland believes that today's women in office are likely to devote more care to constituent services than are many men. "That kind of thing makes you popular," she says.[4] State Senator Jean Ford of Nevada notes, "I have always found that the best way to campaign for reelection is simply to do my job year-round—to respond to the questions and the requests for help." Ford's approach to campaigning while doing her job includes mailing a periodic newsletter to constituents and campaign workers to keep them informed of what she is doing as an officeholder, and scheduling well-publicized living-room chats throughout the district. In June 1979, when Ford returned from her first session in the senate, she sent a three-page "Dear Friends" letter to over a thousand supporters. "It's good to be home from Carson City," she began. The letter continued, "It's also been great to have some quiet time to unpack and unwind, but I couldn't let too many weeks go by without making a personal report to those many friends who supported my election campaign, as well as new acquaintances made during the legislative session." Ford described her activities in the capital, the issues which aroused most interest, and her plans for the period following the legislative session. She concluded, "You know I'm available—to talk with you personally, to speak at your club meetings, to sit down with you and your neighbors to discuss continuing and new problems as they arise. Thanks once again for all your interest and support and giving me the opportunity to represent you in the Nevada State Senate. It has been a real privilege, and I look forward to continuing to serve you in the months ahead. Let's do keep in touch!"

Ford, Mills, Garvin, and political women everywhere who

have made a realistic assessment of their electoral strengths and liabilities share the recognition that maintaining contact with the grass roots is critical to their success.

CAMPAIGN PLAN

The basic goal of a campaign plan is to make the candidate's credentials and political strengths apparent in the district, both before and during the actual campaign. A person intending to announce should be well educated about her district and the diverse citizenry she expects to serve, and should develop a campaign theme which is in harmony with the needs and interests of relevant voters. She must also plan how and where to identify and mobilize the resources necessary for conducting a viable campaign. And she must plan the strategy for making herself known and acceptable to political party leaders, influential citizens, and community activists as well as to the district's general population of voters.

By the mid-1970s increasing numbers of women around the country were absorbing these lessons in the process of facing defeat and in chalking up well-planned victories. Harriet Woods of Missouri stood on the latter side of the scoreboard. In seeking a nomination, she planned—and gained—a win.

By the time Harriet Woods filed for the Missouri state senate race in 1976 she had won the most crucial part of her election. She filed in January and worked hard through the August primary, but the real work was done during the eighteen months previous to filing. During those eighteen months Woods had publicized her intentions and established her credentials. In effect she had headed off any tough Democratic opposition in her heavily Democratic district. By saying early and loudly that she would pursue the senate seat, and by working hard to make herself a visible and credible candidate, she may also have headed off Republican opposition in the general election.

The Nineteenth Senate District in Missouri belonged to a veteran legislator, Senator Maurice Schechter. As an outspoken opponent of the Equal Rights Amendment who had been responsible for keeping it in committee and preventing a senate floor vote in previous years, Schechter irked many of his constituents, especially those in a part of his district called University City. His remarks about women belonging at home and staying out of the work force had prompted angry women to organize a statewide festival of women in the arts.

Sponsored by the American Association of University Women, the festival specifically called attention in the press to the fact that its organizers planned "to show Schechter that women were not limited to the home." Thus when Senator Schechter talked about retiring, many women and some men thought it only poetic justice that a woman should take his seat. Harriet Woods stood prepared to be that woman. She had served from 1967 to 1974 on the University City council. With a population of almost fifty thousand, University City was the largest city in its suburban St. Louis legislative district. Woods also benefited from the good public image she had gained as an intelligent news producer and interviewer for documentaries on a St. Louis television station.

Making herself available to speak to any group free of charge, Woods had spent nearly a year before primary election season accepting invitations to speak about a variety of subjects. She discussed the recent news documentaries she had produced which addressed social issues such as child abuse and jail reform. She also discussed politics, using a comparison between football and politics for one of her most popular talks. After hearing Woods talk, the wife of a high school coach said, "You know, that woman must understand politics because she really understands football."

Woods covered Democratic ward meetings in her district as well as state party meetings, picnics, and social occasions. She and her supporters kept reminding Missouri Democrats that she was running for office. Steadily and persistently, Woods lined up support, particularly from area Democrats who had considered Senator Schechter a liability to liberals in the party. Concerned about passing the Equal Rights Amendment in Missouri, the Women's Political Caucus encouraged Woods' candidacy and worked for her success.

Candidate Woods had no intention of running a one-issue campaign and risking the election by being identified as concerned solely with feminist issues. Her campaign manager stressed, "Her interests are wide." These wide interests had prepared her to represent a district which included a diverse population of blue-collar workers, many elderly citizens, a large middle-class black constituency, and communities of affluent whites.

As the deadline for filing approached, Woods heard rumors that other strong Democrats would enter the primary. As it turned out —and perhaps because Woods' dedicated supporters had touched all the important bases in their discussions about her candidacy—only one Democrat filed to oppose Harriet Woods in the primary. He was Frank Munsch, alderman from Overland, Missouri.

Munsch's community was half the size of Woods' University City, and it was far less politically visible in the county. Woods was much better known than Munsch. Feeling that Munsch was not a formidable opponent and was pursuing a candidacy because he simply liked to run for office, some party politicians expressed complacency about Woods' success in the primary.

Harriet Woods, however, refused to underestimate a challenge posed by any competitor for the senate nomination. Instead she and her campaign manager developed long lists of tasks, planned a highly organized campaign, and arranged for the candidate to address every Democratic township and precinct meeting it was possible to attend.

The two major township Democratic clubs in Woods' state senate district endorsed her a month and a half before the primary. The Young Democrats of St. Louis County voted endorsement in June. The Missouri affiliate of the National Education Association followed. The Missouri Women's Political Caucus announced endorsement two weeks after she filed. She sought and won labor endorsements, including the Brotherhood of Railway and Airline Clerks, the Greater St. Louis Community Action Program of the United Auto Workers, and the political arm of the Teamsters Union.

Woods did not forget to meet the people who would go to the polls on election day. Three months before the primary election, she began canvassing for three hours every evening near dinnertime. She covered block after block in the district, knocking on doors of those who had voted in previous primary elections. If no one answered a doorbell at the home of a regular primary voter, Woods left a note saying she regretted missing the opportunity to talk. She always left a phone number so that she could be reached to answer questions about her position on public issues.

With temperatures reaching almost one hundred degrees in a humid climate, Woods and her volunteers wore sun hats on their rounds and carried supplies of water. In Overland—opponent Frank Munsch's aldermanic district—several residents offered to vote for Woods just because she had made the effort to visit them despite the awful heat. One woman commented that Munsch, her alderman, had never visited even on balmy spring days during his term in the town's government.

During the campaign, Woods' dining room was converted into an office. Removing most of the furniture, campaign volunteers installed a working table, desk, and file cabinets. One area of the room was set aside for workers to mail out cards acknowledging Woods' front-door visits and stating her pleasure in meeting each voter.

Charts, maps, and clippings from local newspapers replaced pictures on the walls. Some of the wall charts explained telephone campaign techniques, including directions for answering basic questions. Posted warnings discouraged volunteers from offering personal opinions about subjects not included on the issue lists. Guidelines suggested that volunteers take names and phone numbers of callers so that Woods could telephone herself to discuss unanswered questions.

Woods' campaign manager kept strict lists of volunteers' schedules and assigned duties. Volunteers were expected to work in the dining-room campaign office—not in other parts of the Woods house, and not in their own homes. "We want to be sure it is done," said Woods' campaign manager. "If people take some work home, it may not really get done. They forget, become distracted."

The organized and efficient campaign operation supervised by Woods' manager allowed the candidate to concentrate totally on meetings with groups of voters and on person-to-person contacts. She did not have to worry about who would scratch voter lists, address envelopes, and make the basic phone calls. Her job as candidate was with the people.

By devoting months to establishing her candidacy and promoting her visibility through speeches, meetings, and door-to-door contact with individual voters, Woods built a solid campaign for the state senate nomination. Woods had refused to be complacent about the weakness of her opposition. Her political instinct told her to campaign hard.

Primary opponent Frank Munsch found an issue—abortion. It was an issue that hit an emotional nerve for many voters, and the Woods-Munsch race heated up in the month before primary election day.

For the first time, in 1976, the Roman Catholic Archdiocese of St. Louis' Pro-Life Committee made a massive effort to let Right-to-Life advocates know where most political candidates in eastern Missouri stood on the issue of abortion. Candidates were surveyed concerning their opinions on an antiabortion amendment to the Constitution, and candidates' speeches and voting records were studied to assess whether they would be likely to vote for such an amendment.

A massive effort was made to distribute the voting records of most primary candidates in each parish of the Archdiocese of St. Louis. All of Harriet Woods' district was in the Archdiocese.

Parish voters were asked to leave their names in a box at the back of churches after services. The Pro-Life Committee then mailed letters and enclosed the voting records of parish candidates. Letters ended with, "We hope this information is helpful to you, and we urge you to see your vote as a moral act, giving support to those candidates who will take a stand in favor of morality."

Frank Munsch strongly supported the antiabortion Human Life Amendment. Pro-Life Committee members in his parish began to tell voters about what they saw as a dark spot on Harriet Woods' record. Woods was accused by a few emotional antiabortion spokespersons of being the "founder and maybe even owner of an abortion clinic."

Years before, while Woods was serving as a University City councilwoman, an antiabortion group had requested the council to rezone a building where The Ladies Clinic, an abortion clinic, was preparing to open for business. Woods had spoken out against such a zoning change. During the legislative primary race Frank Munsch's supporters dug out the old story and began passing it around.

It was a difficult issue for Woods to handle. Voters confronted her with questions about abortion. She chose to remain vague, calling the issue a "matter of personal conscience" and attempting to separate the role of government from the matter of individual morality. She was asked about the issue in Overland, Munsch's town, as well as in Catholic areas of University City.

During the last days of the campaign, extra volunteers arrived to work for Woods. They had assumed she was a safe winner. Now they worried about the potential impact of the abortion issue. Women from other areas volunteered time and energy in Woods' district.

Three months before primary day most Democrats expected an easy victory for Harriet Woods. People knew her. She carried a record of experience as an officeholder. She was highly respected and well liked.

On primary day 1976 Harriet Woods did indeed win her race for the Democratic nomination in Missouri's Thirteenth State Senate District—with Woods tallying 12,751 votes and her opponent, Munsch, scoring 8,989 votes. The margin of victory was much narrower than Democratic pundits had predicted three months earlier. Had she not organized to win, the election count might easily have gone against her.

Political candidates usually devote the late summer and early fall to intense campaigning for votes in November general elections. But Harriet Woods was able to relax her campaign schedule after the August primaries. With a Democratic nomination in a Democratic district, and with no Republican opposition, Woods was guaranteed a seat in the Missouri state senate on the day she won the primary election. Her victory, however, resulted from two years of massive effort.

PARTY SUPPORT

The importance of the role played by political party leaders in individual campaigns varies across the country depending on differences in state election laws, party rules, endorsement procedures, and local political traditions. In many areas, a candidate's credibility is extremely fragile without the support of party leaders and influential citizens. A candidate must plan how to acquire it as early as possible, as Harriet Woods did. Once that support has been obtained, and she has become the designated candidate of a major political party, it becomes relatively easier to gain visibility and attract financial support, campaign workers, and endorsements. Moreover, she can count on acceptance by a significant body of voters. Despite widespread and serious disillusionment with politicians and government, most voters continue to exercise their franchise within the two party system, relying on traditional political circles to screen and select an array of qualified, acceptable candidates.

Political party leaders and other decision makers are still far more likely to seek out, encourage, groom, and actively support the nomination of men for open seats in upcoming elections. Indeed, the political parties have even been charged with discouraging women's candidacies. When Wisconsin's Susan Shannon Engeleiter mounted a credible and effective congressional primary campaign in 1978, she believed and said that the party does not contribute money to primaries. Her understanding was that even when the local party endorses a candidate, the national party does not send in money. However, two or three weeks before the primary, her opponent received $10,000 from Republican Party organizations at the state and national levels—money which enabled him to advertise on television, and which was very likely responsible for her defeat in a close race which she lost by approximately five hundred votes out of seventy-one thousand cast.

Women often discover that they have to score a victory outside their political party before they can gain acceptance within it. Only after building massive grass-roots support leading to a primary election upset was Jane Byrne accepted as a candidate in the 1979 Chicago mayoralty race by a skeptical and unwelcoming party. Similarly, other women running for office have had to create an independent political base with enough strength to win against primary opponents before the local clubs and influential individuals in the party acknowledged their credibility and supported them in general election campaigns and thereafter.

It was early January, time for the 1977–1978 Minnesota legislative session to take up its business. First-year lawmaker Arlene Lehto settled down to work in the St. Paul capitol building.

Senate Majority Leader Nicholas Coleman spied her, came over, and put his arm around her. "You don't know what your election means to us," he said in an affectionate welcome.

His warmth contrasted sharply with the cold shoulder Lehto's candidacy had earned from a number of Democratic-Farmer-Labor (DFL) Party regulars. Since the beginning of her campaign for a seat in the Minnesota legislature, influential members of her party had looked with suspicion and disfavor on her public-minded concern about the environment. Lehto, a spokesperson for environmentalists, was called the person "who can save Lake Superior . . . if anyone can."

Strong and vested interests in the DFL Party considered her campaign a threat. Labor unions and mining companies did not trust her. They worried what added leadership for vigorous environmental policies might do to their jobs, their pocketbooks, even to the future of their communities.

Arlene Lehto was not the one anointed by the party leaders of her district to carry the torch of representation from Duluth to St. Paul. She had done her share of party work, beginning with a job as chairwoman for Hubert Humphrey in Lake County in 1969. But she was not inside the party power elite. She was not part of the "machine," as some called it. Those who had been calling the political shots for years were not keen about some upstart, especially some upstart woman, moving in and challenging their leadership.

Lehto took the long road. She had been learning how to build power and use it for years. As a young woman barely out of beauty school, she challenged unfair, restrictive cosmetology-licensing regulations in Texas. Back in school at the University of Minnesota in Duluth in 1969, she became co-founder and president of the Save Lake Superior Association. Between classes and political-party activity, Lehto traveled from Duluth to communities in several states to organize chapters of her environmental organization.

Lake Superior had been the focus of Lehto's major political effort in Duluth and surrounding areas. She loved the lake virtually from birth, growing up on the small family resort her parents operated on the lake's famed North Shore. But when she began to campaign for the state house of representatives in 1974 and continued that campaign through to her victory in 1976, she worked hard to inform voters that she stood for office as a candidate concerned about many issues.

The legislative campaign took two years—through defeat in 1974 to victory in 1976. Lehto campaigned tirelessly, admitting that she never really stopped after she lost the 1974 election. She kept on pounding the pavement, knocking on doors, talking with voters day after day, month after month.

Ignoring advice from her campaign staff that she say only a few words and move on, she preferred to sit in the kitchens or stand on porches in her district, sometimes for nearly an hour, discussing issues and getting to know her potential constituents. Candidate Lehto began to develop a reputation as a woman who knew what was going on. People began calling her for information. Sometimes they would ask a political question, sometimes pose an environmental problem.

Lehto's public image was helped when she and her husband entered partnership in a printing and rubber stamp business. The business spread her name around the district. People who might have hesitated to intrude on her at home readily began calling her at the print shop, which turned into an "action line," or information-and-referral service, for Duluth residents. As a partner in a small business and as a member of the Duluth Chamber of Commerce, Lehto also developed support from some sectors of the business community. Even a few small union locals went on record for her candidacy.

At the district's 1976 endorsing convention, Lehto managed to block endorsement of Gary Doty, who was expected to win his party's official support handily. Shortly after the convention, Doty surprised the district—and Lehto—by withdrawing his candidacy.

In an eleventh-hour move to provide opposition to the strong environmentalist, DFL leaders turned to Brian Halverson, a Duluth junior high school teacher, to oppose Lehto in the September primary election. Labor and mining interests backed him. Labor newspapers even targeted his race as critical.

Well after the election was all over, Governor Rudy Perpich told

Lehto that before the election, he would not have bet "two cents for her to win," although he quietly favored her candidacy.

Arlene Lehto's intense campaigning and her bold, open approach to her district's voters was aided somewhat by allegations about Halverson's personal life and discontent with his candidacy among black residents of the area. Her perseverance paid off, yielding her a margin of victory on primary day far beyond what she had anticipated. Two and four years later she won reelection to her house seat with no opposition from her party.

A significant number of women running for office in recent years propelled campaigns with the encouragement, endorsement, and support of other women, either on an individual basis or through organized women's political groups. Arlene Lehto discovered that while the DFL Party did not work for her nomination, its Feminist Caucus and the Minnesota Women's Political Caucus came forward as the only organizations to give her strong public support until she beat all odds and won the primary election.

With prodding from women, the two major national parties have taken some steps toward inviting women's fuller participation in political activities—among them, an ongoing series of regional political workshops for women sponsored by the Republicans in the last years of the decade under the leadership of Mary Crisp, former national co-chairperson of the party; on the Democratic side, a resolution approved at the 1978 mid-term convention to require fifty-fifty representation between women and men at the 1980 presidential nominating convention. Yet there is still a vast distance to travel before national, state, and local party leaders place high priority on seeking out their female delegates and recruiting active rank-and-file women for places on the ballot.

At a press conference in 1978 Senator Donald Riegle of Michigan, calling attention to the underrepresentation of women in national politics as a serious problem, stated that "both political parties need to do a great deal more to encourage women to run on their tickets."[5] Few women would disagree with Riegle. Many would add that at the very least party leaders should refrain from discouraging candidates like Susan Shannon Engeleiter and Arlene Lehto—women who are not waiting to be discovered, but who are recruiting themselves and stating their interest in candidacies.

Of course, some office seekers do benefit from strong party support. More often than not, a female candidate who is solidly backed by her party in a district where the party has an even or better chance of winning is someone who has been a hardworking party loyalist for years. She is well known to party leaders. Almost invariably, she has taken pains to build her candidacy in all the requisite ways. By the time she decides to pursue a first elective position or reach up for higher office, her credibility is solid gold.

Such was the situation for Gladys Spellman, a hard worker who had been active in her district for over a decade before Maryland sent her to the U.S. House of Representatives in 1974. While her success in the general election was not guaranteed, she had earned the support of party leaders, which proved vital to insuring her designation as the Democratic candidate.

Mounting a challenge for better education in 1960, Spellman and her local allies had been told they had to prove people were willing to pay the costs of raising teachers' salaries and ending classroom shifts. In one week they collected fifty-seven thousand signatures on petitions and motorcaded to the state capitol at Annapolis. "We brought about a complete reversal on the state's role in education in our county," Spellman said.

In the early 1960s no woman had ever served on the county governing body in Prince Georges, Maryland. Using her visibility as "the PTA lady," Spellman ran and won in 1962. She served until 1974. Learning to work with the old-line politicians, she became part of a faction that took control of the local Democratic Party away from the Southern Maryland courthouse politicians. "The Old Guard ended up coming with us," she says. "I was willing to work with them as a member of the team—when I liked what they were doing."

Spellman's steady accretion of influence developed over years of working as a team member within the party, almost never missing a public function no matter how small or insignificant, and constantly building grass-roots support through personal contact with constituents. She began to think about running for Congress eight years before she found the right opening at the right moment. In 1974 she launched a congressional race when no other Democrat wanted to face Larry Hogan, an apparently unbeatable Republican incumbent. Later, Hogan decided to run for governor. When other Democrats indicated an interest in bidding for the newly opened congressional seat, party leaders stood by Spellman. They knew and respected her from years of working together, and they acknowledged her willingness to risk entering the race before the incumbent withdrew. With a record of public service and a party reputation as a loyal, hard worker, Spellman succeeded in retaining organizational support and moving up to the seat in Congress that she held for the rest of the decade.

OTHER NETWORKS

Important as it is, the party is not the only political network that confers credibility on candidates and from which they seek support. In the 1970s fewer Americans affiliated themselves strongly with a party, and increasing numbers of voters identified themselves as independents. During the same period the implementation of direct primaries across the country, which eroded party control of the candidate-selection process, also contributed to the growing strength of politically influential networks outside the parties. Every aspiring officeholder recognizes the potential benefits of belonging to networks in which many people are linked by common interests. Powerful formal and informal networks which political candidates have courted traditionally are labor unions, circles of professional people, individuals who share business and commercial interests, citizens associations, special-interest groups, ethnic and religious communities, veterans' organizations, and so on. If any of their members can be enlisted to carry the good word about a candidate into a network's leadership circles and from there to spread the word through its channels of communication, the candidate can count on expanded visibility, on public endorsements and campaign resources where legally permissible, and on votes at election time.

Women, however, are vastly underrepresented at leadership levels of organized labor, business, industry, and many of the professions. Associations of doctors, lawyers, undertakers, or contractors show virtually all-male leadership; chambers of commerce, church hierarchies, rifle associations, and veterans' groups are like fraternities in their membership.

The result is that traditional networks of political influence have not been readily available to aspiring political women. And although female candidates did make efforts to tap these resources, collectively they did not make major gains in penetrating male preserves during the 1970s. As one 1978 state legislative candidate said after appearing for an interview with an AFL/CIO group: "I had done more to further their [the union's] interests than my opponent, but I didn't get the endorsement because they aren't used to supporting women."

In the future, as more women across the country enter public life, it is probable they will receive increasing support through the traditional political networks. For the present, however, female candidates are seeking support through other channels as well. In addition to covering familiar ground in the neighborhoods they know well and building their credibility through grass-roots politics, they are uncovering and even creating new networks among women to work for their candidacies. Unfortunately, these groups are far less numerous and, on the whole, less powerful than the established ones and, as female candidates have discovered, they do not always give formal endorsements and support as organizations. After her successful race for a seat in Maryland's state legislature in 1978, Paula Hollinger recalled, "Individuals will come out for you, but not organized groups of women." She observed that women are found in the PTA, the League of Women Voters, and other groups which cannot endorse or support candidates. Saying that this was the "most frustrating thing I found running as a woman," Hollinger regrets that "women haven't learned to be political." "We're not part of the men's networks, and we don't have women's networks. We've got to go out and work on our own"—a troubling observation at the end of a decade marked by a striking increase in women's interest in politics.

Yet many women running for office during recent years did successfully reach out to the formal and informal women's associations that had developed under the impact of the feminist movement. In some instances (for example, Arlene Lehto's support from Minnesota's political feminists), these groups were politically sophisticated. Well-connected feminists also provided access to pockets of support outside the organized women's community.

Some women discovered informal networks in strange places. In one primary campaign a candidate tapped "the social community of unmarried people" in her city through the bars where they gathered, and especially through the bartenders. "There's nothing like having bartenders on your side," she said. "I used systems I was already involved in. Women really have incredible networks, untapped resources. Look, the political network gets tired. It gets split. So you should get some experienced people, yes. But bring others into it, too. They get so excited and so devoted to you." New Jersey's Barbara Sigmund recalls that when she first ran for local office, she called on a "nursery school network." Local politicians joked that she had sent her three sons to different nursery schools deliberately, in order to build a base of support among a variety of nursery school parents.

Women also developed support from other women in female-dominated occupational networks. For example, in her legislative race, Maryland's Paula Hollinger was unable to gain useful support as a serious candidate from her political party. She won her race by turning for help to hundreds of individuals, among them an informal network of nurses. Herself a nurse by occupation, Hollinger activated her colleagues to contribute time to a grass-roots campaign which focused on health issues, mental health, senior citizens, and children's welfare.

When Arizona's Sue Dye decided to run for state senate in 1974, she was a political unknown. But she was a realist who understood how to assess her connections. She had taught high school journalism in Tucson for ten years. Other teachers might support her, she concluded. They did. She had taught more than fifteen hundred local students. She had worked for several summers on the *Arizona Star,* with bylines on her stories. She held membership in a local press club and in a state press organization. When her son was young, she had been player-agent for the Little League, meaning that she put three hundred boys on teams and had met numerous coaches and parents. Dye had also been active in the Tucson Education Association, the American Association of University Women, and the League of Women Voters. Having identified her connections, Dye knew where to seek support in building an image of credibility for her first race.

A political aspirant at the *local* level must have contacts with networks of whatever origin, for without them she has no community of shared interests to convert to the cause of her candidacy. But when an ambitious political woman raises her eyes to the top of the elective ladder, popular support in the neighborhoods and her good relations with community groups are not enough for political advancement. The tools and tactics are similar for planning, organizing, establishing contacts, and building support; but the campaign game is played on much tougher territory—territory in which women candidates have been strangers and where their numbers remain very low. Greater demands for credibility loom in the climb to higher office. The competition is intense. A great deal of money is required to retain professional services, buy media time, and pay for a campaign organization. Powerful vested interests and traditional political networks exert great influence on the fate of top-level candidacies.

The 1970s view reveals only a few women even reaching the starting line for high-level city, state, and national primary races—and they lost many more than they won. In 1976 every woman who entered a race for the U.S. Senate lost, including several who were highly experienced politicians, who planned their races far in advance, organized serious campaigns, and could point to long records of achievement in public life. All but one were knocked off the ladder in the competition for nomination at the primary election stage.

Two years later, in 1978, a handful of thirteen women across the country sought major party nominations for U.S. Senate seats. Eleven were defeated in primaries or nominating convention. Of the two whose primary races were successful, one woman—Jane Eskind of Tennessee—faced an unbeatable incumbent. But in Kansas, Nancy Landon Kassebaum ran for an open seat, and she surprised the oddsmakers by winning a race in which she was considered the underdog despite some inherited credibility as the daughter of one-time Republican presidential candidate Alf Landon.

It takes enormous self-confidence to put oneself forward in competition for the highest elective offices. More women than ever before have been expressing new confidence in their potential for major leadership positions. Yet few women have won any level of office unless they have yoked that confidence to an image of credibility—a credibility which has been built by taking deliberate and painstaking steps to lay the groundwork for a viable candidacy. Even then, a viable candidacy simply insures a solid race. It does not guarantee enough votes to win. This was apparent in 1980 when Democratic Congresswoman Liz Holtzman was narrowly defeated in New York's Senate race. A highly credible candidate who campaigned long and hard, and who followed all the rules, Holtzman could neither overcome the problems she faced in an unexpected three-way race nor emerge a winner in a landmark Republican senatorial and presidential year. Through hard-earned victories as well as disappointing defeats, a growing population of ambitious political women in recent years experienced these types of realities in the elective process.

All the career and issue credibility in the world does little good if a candidate gets into a race late, challenges an opponent who has been working the territory for months, faces an unmovable incumbent, runs in a district with a stable population traditionally rooted to the opposition party, or simply has fewer political debts to collect than does her opponent. And all the confidence in the world does little good unless the office seeker manages to use her carefully developed credibility as a means of attracting ample resources to organize and wage an effective campaign. A candidate's credibility can grow light and flimsy unless it is bolstered by a healthy supply of basic campaign resources and the skilled use of time-honored campaign techniques.

Chapter 6
Getting and
Spending Resources

The object of a campaign is to win. To win, the candidate conveys a message to a sufficient number of voters a sufficient number of times to convince enough of those voters to go to the polls and vote for her. . . . And ultimately, of course, a campaign is also much more than an emotional connection with voters. A campaign must also be seen as the strategic management of resources.
—National Women's Education Fund, *Campaign Workbook*

Some political scientists and observers claim that voters' decisions are less determined by campaigns than they are by party loyalties, political ideologies, socioeconomic status, and racial or ethnic affiliations. No one, however, has proposed seriously to do away with political campaigns. In fact they seem to be growing more elaborate and more professional with each election season. And there is general agreement that campaigns certainly influence election results insofar as they promote candidate visibility, kindle political activists' competitive spirits, and mobilize voter turnout. To execute winning campaign strategies, candidates of both sexes seek and use resources that will influence election-day results in their favor. Time, people, and money—these are the three resources most important to political campaigns.[1]

How much of each resource is required depends on many factors and varies from race to race. Sometimes it is possible to begin with little more in one's resource kit than a few dedicated friends and a modest amount of time, plus ingenuity and energetic determination. New York's Carol Bellamy has said that after a few friends prodded her to vie for a seat in the state senate in 1972, she was acutely aware of her invisibility as an unknown candidate and felt awkward about approaching voters for support without so much as a campaign flyer to leave behind as a reminder of her existence. Thus it developed that her first race was launched with four formidable resources—a camera, several rolls of film, a friend who played shutterbug, and a handful of unsuspecting pedestrians. Out on the busy streets of Brooklyn, Bellamy left her friend behind at an appropriate distance and approached a number of voting-aged citizens to ask, "Pardon me, could you tell me the time?" During the moment it took to pose the question, Bellamy's friend snapped a photograph. With plenty of shots to choose from, the Bellamy campaign developed its literature—a set of brochures depicting the candidate talking with the people. She found it much easier after that to greet the voters by handing them a piece of campaign literature while saying, "Hi, I'm Carol Bellamy, and I'm running for the state senate."

At the other extreme, it is possible to win an election by simply announcing one's candidacy. When an office seeker's name and political credentials alone are enough to keep the field clear of opponents, additional campaign resources are less important. This was the situation in 1978 when Polly Baca Barragan decided to relinquish her position as a state representative and make a bid for the Colorado senate. Having won her first office in 1974 and in 1976 moved into the third highest leadership position among Democrats in the lower house of the legislature, she was highly visible and well respected in the district. When the senate seat opened, several men who were considering the race contacted her first to ask if she planned to run. A contingent of Democrats visited her home to urge candidacy. Close supporters and campaign workers from previous races were unanimous in encouraging her to bid for the senate seat. Polly Baca Barragan telephoned each of the other Democratic hopefuls to inform them that she would enter the race—two had already dropped out, and the other two men withdrew their candidacies upon hearing her decision. Without a primary contest, she was free to focus attention on planning the general election campaign. Even that became unnecessary, however, because the Republicans decided not to enter a candidate against her in November. In January 1979, Polly Baca Barragan was sworn into the Colorado senate as the first woman and first Hispanic from Adams County to serve in the upper chamber of the legislature. Credibility was a sufficient resource in this case to guarantee her the victory.

The overwhelming majority of political candidates face the issue of campaign resources from a position somewhere between where Carol Bellamy stood in 1972 and where Polly Baca Barragan found herself in 1978. Whether a race is for the local borough council in a district with a population of five thousand or whether the prize sought is a statewide or national office, most candidates cannot conduct strong campaigns without some initial resources and without gaining access to additional resources as their campaigns move forward. Indeed a potential candidate who is serious about winning bases her or his decision to run in the first place on a careful assessment of whether enough time, people, and money will be available to compete reasonably well for a particular office. The total amount of each resource adequate for a campaign varies according to the level of office sought, the nature and political climate of the district, the strength of the opposition, the aspiring officeholder's name recognition, and her or his status as challenger, incumbent, or a candidate for an open seat.

The need for resources depends heavily upon the credibility a candidate brings to the campaign, as does the availability of those resources. A highly credible, well-known candidate may be required to spend less time, recruit fewer people, and use less money to wage a successful campaign than an unknown who has to build an image of credibility within political circles and among voters. Likewise, the more familiar candidate usually will have an easier time recruiting people and raising money to support her or his race, at least at the outset. Insofar as credibility is linked to attracting campaign resources, the advantage of incumbency is obvious; and so is the disadvantage most women face as challengers and newcomers to candidacy.

Women develop campaign strategies to minimize these disadvantages wherever possible. They also seek to enhance the benefits of those resources that are particularly available to them as women. Certain patterns of getting and spending resources can be identified as more common to women's campaigns than to races conducted by their male counterparts. Some of the differences which do exist in this regard probably will fade as greater numbers of women run as incumbents and move into the nation's centers of power. At the moment, the most important issue is money. Here women face the biggest handicap in acquiring resources because they are less likely than men to attract large sums of money for expensive races. As a result, the other campaign resources of time and people may assume greater value for women than for men these days—at least for those elections in which money is not virtually the sole determinant of victory. The more time a woman can find for campaigning and the more committed people she can recruit to work for her, the better her chances of compensating for a campaign treasury which may be harder to fill and smaller than her male opponent's.

I.   Time

Campaigns eat up prodigious amounts of time for both women and men seeking elective office. They also consume the time of a candidate's close supporters. A 1978 state legislative contender reports a familiar timetable for a contested primary race: "My two unpaid campaign managers worked fourteen hours a day for seven months." She worked the same hours for fifteen months. After serving as campaign manager for a male candidate's successful U.S. Senate race in 1978, a female campaign expert observed, "It's exhausting and difficult to be a candidate. Women may be showing good sense by not running!"

Those women who are running may acknowledge that it is exhausting and difficult—but they know who they are and usually enjoy the experience. Shy, retiring people do not become candidates. Political people generally thrive in public, mingling in large groups and making person-to-person contacts. Recalling her congressional race with obvious pleasure, Geraldine Ferraro tallies her time on the campaign trail in handshakes: "Every night I shook a thousand hands!" She says that she was "everywhere" during the 1978 election season, and everywhere she went she gave out campaign buttons—thirty-five thousand buttons distributed by the candidate herself. A month after winning her first election to the Congress, and even before she had been sworn into office, Ferraro remarked, "I'm already running for reelection in 1980."

Losers who make serious bids for office usually spend no less time meeting the voters than their successful opponents. Congresswoman Marjorie Holt of Maryland describes Sue Ward, her Democratic opponent in the 1978 general election, as an "articulate, good candidate" who ran a "good campaign."

Sue Ward is a social worker who had been active in parent-teachers associations, the League of Women Voters, and the Women's Political Caucus; but she had never held office before entering the congressional race against Holt. An unknown candidate with little political credibility, her biggest resources were energy and time. As reported in *The Washington Star,* on a typical campaign day she followed a schedule of "getting up at dawn, climbing into her 1964 Buick Special, and heading off for a day of campaign appearances that would last past midnight and take her all over Anne Arundel County. 'When you've got no name recognition and no money, that's about the only way to do it,' she said. 'You just have to get out there in person and meet the voters.' " Meeting the voters included attending such annual occasions as the Anne Arundel County Liquor Association's bullroast, where almost three thousand people enjoyed a picnic meal as Ward moved through the crowd shaking hands and distributing campaign literature. Although Marjorie Holt, a popular incumbent, won the November election, she considered Ward a formidable adversary because of the well-organized, energetic way in which she conducted her campaign. Ten months after beginning campaigning, Ward said, "Last January . . . no one knew me. Today there are a lot of people who know my name, want to meet me, ask questions."[2] The time had been well spent earning political visibility.

In New Jersey, another congressional candidate in 1978 entered the race being described as "an unknown woman" and emerged after her November defeat as a credible candidate for the future. Marge Roukema challenged Congressman Andrew Maguire, a two-term incumbent, in a first-exposure campaign in which she made a respectable showing by earning 47 percent of the votes in the general election. Working with less name recognition and fewer dollars than her opponent, Roukema says, "I went door-to-door selling myself and the concept that we had a plan and knew what we were doing, and that we had a reasonable hope for success. We documented how we were going to do it."

During the summer and fall of 1978 Roukema spent seven days a week on the campaign. She devoted many hours to research —studying her opponent's record and educating herself in the issues. Her typical day started at 7:00 A.M. with desk work at home, followed by a breakfast meeting with a local organization, a walking tour ringing doorbells in neighborhoods, visits to shopping centers, a stop at campaign headquarters to meet with staff and place telephone calls, and personal appearances at luncheons, dinners, and scheduled meetings of civic groups and other organizations.

Roukema's schedule also included seven evenings a week out on the campaign trail—at Republican Party events, social functions, coffees, or wherever people gathered. "We'd find out where there was going to be a crowd, and I'd appear," Roukema recalls. On Friday evenings the campaign plan called for finding crowds waiting in line at popular movies or converging on local bowling alleys. She remembers, "Originally it was determined I should have an afternoon and an evening off each week, but that soon fell by the wayside." Not only does Roukema believe that her 1978 campaign time was well spent in winning a substantial number of votes, but she used that time as an investment for her successful congressional race in 1980.

HIGH-INTENSITY VOTER CONTACT

In the months and weeks preceding election day, women and men bent on victory believe they cannot overlook canvassing that last street of front doors, shaking hands with the last group of shoppers at the supermarket, stopping by to chat at each table during dinner hour at the local restaurant, or speaking at that evening's club meeting. To neglect any of these opportunities might mean the loss of a crucial vote on election day. During campaign season every moment not absolutely essential for earning money to buy food and pay the rent or mortgage, or being at home to tend children, must be spent directly on campaigning. A tough campaign manager does not care if the candidate has a bad cold, a fever, or even a broken leg. If there is a speech to give, a crowd to meet, some hands to shake, the candidate is expected to take aspirins, bring the sickness along, and carry on.

Even personal crises do not stop most candidates from plunging ahead on their appointed campaign rounds. During one Texas legislative race in 1976, candidate Leon Richardson's house burned to the ground a week before the election. Richardson handled the situation as a challenge to be confronted rather than a disaster to collapse under. Speaking with a reporter on the phone when news of the fire reached her, Richardson brushed it off until staff members convinced her that it really was an emergency. "I remember her standing in the ruins of her patio," said her press aide. "The television cameras were gone, and it was suddenly very real." Richardson turned to her press aide and said, "I'm still in the race. It's not going to lick me."

Neighbors offered to house her five children, but Richardson moved them into a motel in order to keep the family together. She made only one concession to disaster by bowing out of a Kiwanis luncheon speech. Staff members bought her some new clothes, and she went to a League of Women Voters debate that night as scheduled.

While Richardson's particular experience was unusual, personal crises are not uncommon during campaign season. With only so many days to campaign and a great many voters to reach, candidates know they must keep running—despite crisis, or fatigue and illness, and regardless of the morning's weather forecast. Moreover, candidates must keep running even when the odds for success are stacked against them. Running hard and long means making useful contacts and building name recognition. It means gaining experience which textbooks and manuals describe, but which only immersion teaches. For today's political women— usually challengers, and frequently novices as candidates—there is no alternative to the day-in-day-out, door-to-door, person-to-person campaign grind.

Is it worth it? One candidate whose block walking touched twenty thousand households felt it was "good for the image and I like doing it, plus I get a lot of feedback. There is nothing more humbling than knocking on doors. It also gets you back to the real problems of the district. To run a good campaign you've got to know what's out there." Many women believe it was high-intensity voter contact—through door knocking, direct mail, and telephone canvassing—which made the difference between their recent victories and defeats.

The characteristics of the urban electorate have foreclosed some options traditionally used by candidates to attract attention. Citizens jaded by television are unlikely to turn out for a political rally unless the candidate can draw them there with a superstar. Few people these days can be wooed away from home for evening coffees and meetings. Large urban newspapers tend to ignore campaigns below the congressional level except for announcement statements and voter's-guide wrap-ups. For most women and men running in local or legislative races, television advertising is not an economic use of campaign resources. Few candidates feel justified in paying enormous television-time prices to reach large numbers of people who cannot vote in their districts. The options that remain are the tried and true telephone canvass, direct mail, and especially the block walks.

"If you like talking and meeting people, door knocking isn't so hard. There's just so much of it," says Irma Rangel, state legislator from Kingsville, Texas. Candidates must go where the voters live and congregate. It is a type of campaign which costs relatively little in dollars, but a fair amount of shoe leather—and a great deal of time.

WOMEN'S TIME AND MEN'S TIME

In general, current differences between the two sexes in finding time to pursue public office are based largely on individual economic situations and the culturally influenced personal choices about how one's time should be allocated. The level of office sought, the size and nature of the election district, and local political traditions also affect the way office seekers use time. Before running for election, all potential candidates must assess time as a highly valuable campaign commodity. They must make a clear determination of the amount of time available for campaigning and the number of votes needed to win—and then they must come up with an effective plan for using the one to gain the other in a particular race.

Given great individual variations, a number of patterns do emerge as more common to one sex or the other in how time is spent campaigning. In some cases they work to the advantage of women, in others to their disadvantage.

INDEPENDENCE FROM WORK AND
FULL-TIME FAMILY OBLIGATIONS

Among campaign resources, time is the one available to some female candidates more often than to their male counterparts. For those unemployed political women whose husbands' incomes adequately finance the household and whose children no longer require hourly supervision, there is time to expend on meeting the voters. Marge Roukema is not employed outside her home; therefore, she was able to devote seven months to full-time campaigning in the primary and general election races during 1978. Sue Hone, vice-mayor of Berkeley, California, won her first race in 1973, after being appointed to the city council in 1971 to fill a seat vacated two years before the term expired. In 1977 she won reelection as part of a slate of four candidates running in a nonpartisan, citywide campaign. Observing that the seven-day-a-week campaign schedule is "heavy and full during the last month" before mid-April elections, Hone says that in her races, because she carried the "ongoing responsibilities of an incumbent," she was required to attend council meetings and handle council business while campaigning. But she acknowledges that she still had more time than candidates who had other jobs as well. She feels that women who do not have to earn a living have an advantage in politics. "Men who are more career-oriented are unwilling to turn over responsibilities to partners or colleagues," Hone believes.

The fact that a sizable proportion of women running for office does not hold down full-time jobs outside the home has two related advantages. It enables these women to organize a type of campaign well suited to their preference for people-to-people politics as well as strategically most appropriate for cultivating grass-roots support and public credibility outside established political networks. An unemployed female candidate is one who may have adquate time to run a strong door-to-door campaign in which she personally canvasses an entire district.

Democrat Mae Yih of Oregon waged a successful campaign using time as her most valuable resource. Yih is the wife of an affluent industrialist who supported her candidacy and whose financial resources adequately support the household. Active in community affairs, Yih was an elected member of two local school boards in Oregon's mid-Willamette Valley, but she was otherwise unemployed. As a first-time legislative candidate in 1976, Yih spent four days a week going door-to-door in her largely conservative district, which was unaccustomed to that type of campaign. Her efforts paid off in the general election, where she upset Republican incumbent William Gwinn, a fourteen-year veteran of the legislature and vice-chairman of the House Ways and Means Committee. Gwinn, a developer, grumbled after the election, "I had to work for a living. I couldn't afford to run that kind of campaign."

Men and women candidates who have to work for a living usually cannot match an unemployed candidate hour for hour on the campaign trail. Neither can they easily take time from the heavy demands of business or professional life to serve in time-consuming but unremunerative public offices. At those levels of political life where elected officials—both men and women—earn little or no salary for serving in office, women whose husbands are the bread-winners have a time advantage over candidates whose income depends on their own full-time employment. In Decatur, Georgia, for example, former Mayor Ann Crichton earned $250 per month in the mid- and late 1970s—$200 for serving in office, and $25 per session for attending each of the twice monthly city-commission meetings. The other four elected officials who served with her on Decatur's city commission earned $50 per month plus an additional $30 attendance fee. Crichton, the first woman to serve as mayor of Decatur, was married to a man who provided the family income, leaving her full time to spend on her elected position. "The job is viewed as public service, and not as a profession," she says. But it is very time-consuming, and she recalls that the last mayor, a man, "really couldn't do it and keep up his law practice."

In addition to campaigning and serving in office, Crichton has been very active in national and regional associations of public officials as well as in political party affairs. Pursuing a deep interest in issues of economic development, housing, and community development, she traveled frequently to Washington to attend meetings and to testify at congressional hearings.

There are still many women who can manage the time to campaign for election, serve in an office with little or no salary, be active in local, state, and national affairs, and even respond to the needs of a broad public beyond their constituencies. Those who are not burdened with heavy demands for earning the family income and who have energy and talent to offer in public life are becoming more and more aware of their opportunities as political candidates. They have an advantage over both men and women who must fit campaigning around their jobs, and must run for only those offices which do pay a professional salary—or stay off the campaign trail altogether.

FULL-TIME CHILD-CARE AND HOUSEHOLD WORK

For the many women and tiny minority of men whose full-time presence is required by the needs of young children and the requirements of household management, time for campaigning is difficult to find and even more problematic to organize. Free hours may be available, but usually they are scattered in bits and pieces throughout a schedule responsive primarily to the varying routines of different family members. With few exceptions, a woman responsible for the care of young children, a husband, and a household is on duty twenty-four hours a day, constantly available for call. She can hardly base a viable political campaign on stolen moments—slipping out to make a speech or canvass the block while a neighbor watches the baby; going on a round of fund-raising appointments while one child is in morning nursery school and her toddler visits a friend; attending political events between trips to the supermarket and the family mealtimes.

Women in this situation may be able to run for some offices, but only for relatively undemanding positions close to home. Similar problems exist for a handful of men who find themselves assuming the woman's traditional role in the household. Such was the case, for example, in Madison, Wisconsin, when Eric Schulenburg entered the local school-board race in 1979 after determining that he had some "extra time on his hands and could handle the twenty-hour-a-week responsibility." The "extra time" was available because he had given up a law practice the year before in order to stay home to tend the house and two children while his wife worked. Concluding that he could not "be a househusband" while practicing law, he commented, "You can't call a court date off. A sick child is not a valid excuse."[3]

EMPLOYED CANDIDATES,
MEN AND WOMEN

When male or female candidates are employed full time in addition to seeking office, flexibility in work schedules is very important to the campaign's success. Here men often have the greater advantage of flexible time both at work and at home. Men are more likely to be self-employed or found in occupations where they can take time off to campaign, particularly the large number of political men who are lawyers. Furthermore, men's candidacies often receive support from colleagues and employers who perceive their own interests served by the candidate's potential victory. A law firm stands to benefit, at least in enhancing its prestige, when one of its partners wins elective office. So does the public relations agency, the insurance and real estate office, the construction firm, the investment company, and the restaurant or hotel business.

In contrast, employed women are not likely to own their own businesses or hold partnerships in law firms. Most come from positions of relatively low status as employees in companies or institutions which are less interested in the women's political aspirations than in the time they spend on the job. Women who hold jobs with short-day or flexible schedules—for example, teachers or nurses—and women who hold part-time jobs are in a better position to find time for campaigning than those with full-time office responsibilities. The latter group of women is likely to dismiss the idea of running for office; and some who do decide to run do so at heavy personal cost.

In Oregon's 1976 races not all the women seeking office were in as fortunate a position as Mae Yih. Republican Virginia Vogel, who narrowly lost her bid for a first term in the state legislature, had only two weeks off from her job as personal services representative of the U.S. National Bank of Oregon in Medford. In addition, she was serving on the Medford city council. Her opponent in the general election had resigned from his post as an aide to Oregon's Congressman James Weaver in order to devote his full time to campaigning.

In another legislative race, Gretchen Kafoury emerged as one of the few candidates to squeeze a successful campaign into a schedule dominated by a full-time job. The effort required a prodigious performance. Employed as a technical assistance coordinator in the state Civil Rights Division, Kafoury arrived home from work at 5:30 every afternoon. Between 5:30 and 8:30 each day, she canvassed her district door-to-door. Later in the evening there were phone calls to be returned and strategy meetings to attend.

In the Oregon state treasurer's race during the same campaign season, Democrat Jewel Lansing initially decided that she would campaign only on weekends and in the evenings after putting in a full day at her elective job as Multnomah County auditor. Shortly after she announced as a candidate for state treasurer, Lansing told a member of the press corps that the public need not fear that she would neglect her job during the campaign. When it became apparent that she could not conduct a statewide campaign without devoting more time to it, Lansing reversed her position and decided to campaign during working hours. The decision did not come easily. It resulted from consultation with numerous advisors as well as with male candidates who held down full-time jobs while also campaigning. She wrangled with her own conscience. "I finally decided that I could be virtuous and no one would ever know it," Lansing said. "On the other hand, I could lose handsomely and it would benefit no one."

FULL-TIME WORK PLUS
PRIMARY FAMILY OBLIGATIONS

Women and men who must hold down demanding full-time jobs in order to support themselves face real difficulties in finding enough time to seek or serve in most public offices above the local school board or municipal council levels in small districts. And when domestic duties call for running a household and caring for dependents on top of the burdens of employment, time is very scarce for serious political activity—whether before, during, or after campaign season. Since women still bear primary responsibility for domestic management and child care, the employed woman with family obligations has the least time of anyone to pursue elective office. While some women do hold jobs, manage families, and campaign for office with lesser or greater personal conflict, a much larger population of women interested in politics either never considers running for office or dismisses the idea as an impossible dream. They conclude that the same woman cannot be present in two or three places at the same time—that a twenty-four-hour day cannot accommodate a job, a family, and a political campaign. What comes first, what comes second, and what comes third in a list of priorities affecting the way an individual's time is expended has been different for women and men. This is especially true between the ages of 25 and 45 for people who marry and produce offspring. Most women have decided that time to spend on candidacy and officeholding is still lower on the list and comes later in life than time to spend on child rearing.

Time is an extremely valuable campaign commodity for all political candidates. The more time an office seeker can allocate to campaigning, the better her or his opportunity for making direct contact with large numbers of voters. Regardless of how much money a candidate raises and how many volunteers join the campaign, the candidate must be available to project a personal presence in the district. Nothing substitutes for it.

Finding and managing time are similar challenges for office seekers of both sexes. They are benefited or hindered by individual economic circumstances, professional status, family roles, and the politics of a particular campaign in a given district. Individual variations notwithstanding, some broad differences do emerge between women and men who need time in order to run for office. The large population of women with primary household and family responsibilities as well as full-time jobs is in the worst position to seek political office, followed by those men and women with inflexible employment whose income-earning responsibilities leave no room for campaigning, and those women who may be unemployed but whose daily presence is required by the needs of young children. Self-employed candidates and those with part-time or flexible employment and no pressing obligations at home are in a relatively good position to devote time to campaigning. More men than women fall into this category. Time is the most available resource for economically independent candidates with minimal family demands. A small group of wealthy individuals of both sexes and a larger group of unemployed women whose husbands earn a comfortable living benefit from these advantages. They are in the best position to find the time it takes to wage a viable political campaign.

II. People

No candidate would refuse the services of a magician to work for her victory on election day. In 1973, when Barbara Curran first ran for the New Jersey legislature, that is exactly what she had. A businessman who was a personal friend of Curran's had practiced magic in his younger days—and he volunteered to perform his repertoire of tricks for the Curran campaign. On Saturdays, the campaign van stopped in parking lots at local shopping centers. While Curran and a group of supporters entered supermarkets to talk with voters and distribute campaign literature, the shoppers' children were kept entertained out in the magic van. At the end of the show, the magician asked, "What's the magic word?" He also provided the answer: "Barbara Curran for Assembly." Curran believes that her magician was a critical campaign resource, a major asset in a race which she managed to win by 130 votes.

Professional staff alone do not a political campaign make. Most modest campaigns like Barbara Curran's, especially at local levels, have little or no budget for paid staff. Yet all candidates for elective office need many people to work on their races. Among a candidate's fundamental campaign resources, people power is critical. Volunteer campaign workers have been a cornerstone of the American electoral system. Even in the present era of high-finance campaigns, well-paid political consultants and carpetbagger campaign experts have not replaced the need for a corps of volunteers to send out the word and bring in the vote.[4]

VOLUNTEERS

"The people working in my campaign are my friends," Ernestine Glossbrenner noted. "We trust each other. It's a joint effort because we are working for what we all believe in." What they believed in was good government in an area of South Texas notable for its absence. With the help of her friends and colleagues, Glossbrenner pulled off a nearly impossible victory in George Parr country, the heartland of Texas' most formidable political machine. Glossbrenner won that race by 136 votes.

Campaign teams are peopled with volunteers—family members, friends, colleagues, concerned citizens, students, and campaign addicts who take responsibility for the numerous tasks and details no candidate can handle alone. Their numbers vary depending on the size and population of the district to be won, the candidate's ability to recruit committed supporters, and the importance of people power in campaigns short on funds or in districts where electronic and print media may be largely irrelevant. While the size of a campaign staff depends on these various circumstances, every candidate should have a campaign manager and someone to coordinate campaign finances—preferably as paid staff members, but as volunteers if necessary.

In her 1978 race as a three-term incumbent for the U.S. House of Representatives, Elizabeth Holtzman of New York hired a campaign manager, an assistant campaign manager, and a part-time fund raiser. Beyond these three paid staff members, the campaign operated entirely with volunteer workers—approximately 450 area residents, including large numbers of senior citizens and students. Holtzman, a strong incumbent in a heavily Democratic district, won the race with approximately 82 percent of the votes. In Ohio, Mary Rose Oakar won her first congressional reelection race in 1978 with the help of between three hundred and four hundred volunteers. New Jersey's Marge Roukema utilized about one hundred volunteers in her 1978 congressional primary race and several hundred more in the general election race.

It is not uncommon to find several hundred volunteers in races below the congressional level, even in the campaigns of candidates who do not have the power of incumbency to help in attracting willing unpaid recruits. In Jean Ford's 1978 state senate race in Nevada, over three hundred volunteers helped to put her in office. And in Maryland during the same election season approximately six hundred volunteers ultimately joined Paula Hollinger's successful race for the legislature. Between fifty and a hundred volunteers are commonly found in races for local municipal and county offices in small districts.

In addition to family, friends, and politically active area residents, volunteer campaign workers can also be recruited from among individuals, professional groups, and voluntary organizations with which the candidate has some formal affiliation or informal contact. To whatever extent women and men are segregated by sex in the labor force, private clubs, and in civic activities and voluntary organizations, they are likely to draw campaign workers from different pools of volunteers. Where there is overlap in affiliations and constituencies, the differences diminish or disappear.

In the spirit of "getting one of us into office," numbers of volunteers from among members of women's organizations have been attracted to female candidates in recent years. One candidate, who had been an active member and officer in her state's League of Women Voters, ran for the state legislature with the help of seven hundred volunteers, many of them league members who had known her over the years. They conducted telephone canvasses, mailed out literature, and delivered campaign materials to neighborhoods all over the district. She won the election in an area which had a long history of voting for candidates of the opposite party. While the League of Women Voters and other nonpartisan or nonpolitical women's organizations operate under policies which preclude them from endorsing candidates, individual members of these groups are entirely free to work on political campaigns. Not surprisingly, they are likely to sign onto campaigns with a candidate who belongs to the same organizations in which they hold membership. Quite common in men's political networks, this pattern of support is developing among publicly minded women.

Candidates often find campaign volunteers among the people they know professionally. Women's professional networks exist on a formal and informal basis where there are large numbers of women employed in a given occupation. Thus when Ernestine Glossbrenner organized her 1976 campaign for the state legislature in Texas, she fueled her low-budget race with teacher friends. A teacher herself for twenty years and past president of two local teachers' organizations, Glossbrenner sought help from people with whom she had worked. "Teachers are our ace in the hole because they have the respect and trust of the population," Glossbrenner said. "They used to be encouraged not to get involved in politics, but they've become a lot more active, with cause. Back in the 1950s we had forty kids to a classroom, and we thought nothing could be done. Now we have a teacher surplus, and we still have forty kids to a classroom."

Not all candidates can count on volunteers as dedicated as Glossbrenner's—whether professional associates or fellow club members. Despite the popular perception that female candidates

attract armies of committed housewives, some women would have
traded in these volunteers for a battalion of organized labor stal-
warts to handle the phone banks and knock on the doors. "A lot
of women are bridge players and den mothers, and it's difficult to
get them out for night phone banks," said one woman who
managed a campaign in an affluent state legislative district. "They
didn't like getting doors slammed in their faces, and they didn't like
having phones hung up on them. I am just convinced that a lot of
the work didn't get done."[5]

A well-heeled candidate can overcome volunteer shortcomings with money. Phone banks can be handled by paid workers.
Direct mailouts can be contracted to commercial mailing services.
Paid campaign workers who do a poor job can be sent packing
more easily than a volunteer who is dedicating time and energy out
of commitment to the candidate or a personal need to participate
in political campaigns. But most candidates draw on limited campaign treasuries and cannot afford to pay large staffs. The volunteer
remains a critical campaign resource, one which is available to
female candidates in at least as ample supply as to their male counterparts. The challenge to women running for office today is to
develop a pool of supporters—perhaps from untraditional sources
in the women's community—as dedicated and disciplined as the old
party regulars.

In the give and take of campaigns and public life, a candidate
is served by groups of volunteers whose interests she will promote
and guard once she is in public office—whether they are teachers
concerned with classroom size, nurses concerned with their status
in the health profession, senior citizens worried about the problems
of fixed incomes, environmentalists pressing for strict enforcement
of pollution-control standards, or citizens advocating passage of the
Equal Rights Amendment. People join campaigns as volunteers for
many reasons, all of them self-rewarding or self-gratifying at some
level. The candidate must know how to discipline and use their
services for her own benefit. In her turn, she will owe them, at the
very least, an attentive ear and mind. Business and political affairs,
after all, operate on the most fundamental level as two-way, invest-
ment-benefit arrangements.

Often candidates reward particularly valuable campaign volunteers with paid jobs on their staffs once they are elected to office,

or with contacts for seeking appointments to governmental boards and commissions. The campaign organization is a good laboratory for testing energy, loyalty, judgment, commitment, and talent.

Also, in order to perform for her constituents, an elected official will seek support from political party members and colleagues in public life. In return for their support of her programs or legislative goals, she is likely to be receptive to particular issues which they advocate in the interests of their constituents. As a candidate and an officeholder, she accrues debts, and she pays them.

THE CAMPAIGN ORGANIZATION

Campaign organizations come in all shapes and sizes—from elaborate productions with paid professionals and hundreds of supporters to small operations working from family basements and dining-room tables. But political operatives agree that there must be an organization, and it must work. If the organization breaks down—a common occurrence in the heated atmosphere of election season—it must be replaced, restructured, or abandoned before it sinks the campaign. Modifications are made throughout the campaign season as conditions require. For example, during the summer of 1978, Jean Ford's race to gain a seat in Nevada's state senate benefited from the services of teachers who were free to volunteer when school was closed. When fall arrived and teachers went back to their classrooms, the campaign organization adjusted to a new shift of volunteers—summer vacationers who returned to the city after Labor Day.

Successful campaign organizations keep growing, but not in a haphazard fashion and never at the expense of structure and control at the core. Paula Hollinger built and sustained her large, winning organization with care, control—and index cards. A small team of committed supporters who worked with Hollinger for more than a year of campaigning never left home without a stack of index cards to fill with names of people whose services could strengthen the organization. One of Hollinger's two campaign managers was an avid tennis player. By always setting out to find new games and meet new players, she made sure that each day a few more people left the courts with a new commitment to fulfill—that of doing volunteer work for the Hollinger campaign. Other campaign workers recruited volunteers in shopping centers. In addition to attracting many of her nursing colleagues, Hollinger found friends from the League of Women Voters willing to help. But most of all, the organization filled its ranks with volunteers who signed up at one of Hollinger's fifty coffees held over twelve months. The candidate attended each coffee accompanied by a campaign worker whose assignment it was to mingle with the guests, distribute index cards, and enlist recruits to fill spots where help was needed most. Steadily building momentum, the campaign organization grew from a core of thirty to sixty people at the beginning to an operation of six hundred by election day.

Whatever the size of the campaign organization and whether it is composed exclusively of volunteers or a mixture of paid professionals and volunteers, it must operate according to an explicit plan, with responsibilities, roles, and relationships clearly defined and understood by all participants. A plan explicitly sets forth goals, strategies, maps, timetables, and budgets for all phases of the campaign operation—including research and polling, fund raising and accounting, targeting and voter contact, media and advertising, scheduling, headquarters and materials, staffing, and candidate activity. To make the plan work, each phase of the campaign operation must be organized, administered, and staffed by people who can be trusted to meet all obligations they have agreed to undertake. Unless the candidate can rely on responsible workers to keep the organization functioning smoothly, she is not free to do the jobs most critical for her to perform—making major policy decisions and especially being available to meet the greatest possible number of undecided voters. The candidate's success in playing her part well depends, first, on her ability to acquire the services of a sufficient number of talented paid or volunteer staff and consultants, and second, on her willingness to place confidence in their capacities to handle assigned tasks.

DELEGATING RESPONSIBILITY

Some candidates decide to manage their own campaigns, but all campaign experts agree that this is a serious, potentially costly error in virtually all competitive races. Many candidates, both male and female, also choose to work as nuts-and-bolts artisans—writing their own press releases, editing their own television and radio spots, and trying to keep their fingers on the pulse of every precinct. Such attention to detail may pay off if the candidate has the necessary expertise, the energy of several persons, and a district no larger than congressional size. The prevailing advice, however, is that the candidate delegate the details, pay attention to the big strategy decisions, and listen to advice from appropriate members of the campaign team. Whenever possible these members should be experts in their particular areas. It is important for the candidate to trust and follow their advice, even down to such small details as what color blouse to wear for a television appearance.

There is some feeling among political observers that more women than men are reluctant to relinquish their authority over dotting the i's and crossing the t's. One of the complaints emerging from campaign personnel is that female contenders preoccupy themselves with stationery design and photograph selection and balk at advice from the campaign operatives they enlist to counsel them. Some candidates hazard the opinion that women have less experience with delegating responsibility. Many women have labored for years in relative isolation managing households and caring for children or working in low-status occupations with few opportunities to delegate chores and supervise staffs. One candidate explains that career women have inched their way upward in the working world by assuming individual responsibility and by ensuring that no one under their supervision performs in a way which would reflect unfavorably on them. Whatever the reason, a failure to delegate authority in campaigns can mean decisions not made, projects not carried out, and low morale among the workers who watch their advice go unheeded.

"I tried to raise my own money and make all the decisions," said one candidate. "I had a horror of anything going out under my name that I had not seen. I wouldn't let it go without reading it myself." She lost her congressional race, and says of her attention to details that if she ran again, "I would do that differently." Her opponent had not been very good at delegating duties either, but he had the advantages of incumbency, which included high name recognition and a substantial campaign treasury. She had more to do to raise support and become known among voters. Problems that she thought were partially due to her insistence on carrying the ball herself included a weak fund-raising effort resulting from her unwillingness to turn over that duty to a finance committee early in the campaign.

Carrying the burden for handling a multitude of campaign details is sometimes not so much a consequence of inexperience in delegating authority as of women's status as challengers in uphill races for which very little financial support can be found. This is especially true in primary election races when, with limited access to traditional political and financial networks, female candidates often take on campaign tasks they would rather recruit and pay experts to perform.

"Nothing went out in writing unless I saw it," said one woman who lost her primary race for a congressional nomination. "Nobody ever talked to the press, except about my schedule, except me. Nobody ever gave my views on issues. I insisted on signing checks. That's a very inefficient way to run a campaign, but I felt I didn't have a choice. I couldn't pay people; and if you can't pay, you haven't much choice."

THE CAMPAIGN MANAGER

According to campaign experts, candidates for most offices above local levels in small districts should find funds to hire at least a few critical staff members and part-time consultants—among them a campaign manager, an office manager, and legal counsel. Those candidates who can afford to do so should recruit the best political experts available, and then trust their judgment, especially the judgment of campaign managers. "There is nothing worse than a candidate who is her own manager," said one candidate who learned the hard way. After deciding that she trusted no one's judgment as well as her own and sticking to the determination to manage her own campaign, she recalls, "I would come home at night exhausted and weep and weep and say I can't do it anymore."

Whether paid or volunteer, the ideal manager is a twenty-four-hour-a-day support system, able to provide both emotional support and hard-nosed advice to a candidate who may need a kind word or, conversely, a tough critique. It is not easy to find such a person. Out of loyalty and gratitude for past support, some women vying to move up to high-level offices have asked old friends to manage their campaigns. But kind friends who offer sympathy and warmth may feel reluctant to take a strong stand with the candidate or may lack experience for running high-pressure campaigns, especially in statewide competitions.

Familiar difficulties in handling the recruitment and proper employment of managers and other high-level campaign team members plagued the races of some women in the seventies, among them Oregon's two statewide female candidates in 1976. Their situation was not exclusive to one sex, but it did highlight some conflicts that increasing numbers of women in political and professional life have begun recently to anticipate and resolve.

Jean Skillman sat in the living room of her ranch-style home in affluent South Salem, Oregon. "My daughter tells me maybe I should take assertiveness training," she said.

Sixty miles north in Portland, Marge Floren talked over lunch in a downtown tavern. "For me, it was an ego blow to know I was not capable of doing it," she recalled.

Both women had experienced being deposed as campaign coordinators for two female candidates on the 1976 statewide ballot. Republican Norma Paulus, candidate for secretary of state, hired Skillman to run her primary campaign because Skillman had effectively organized Paulus' earlier races for the state legislature. Once she won her primary, however, Paulus picked a more experienced and politically savvy woman to head up her general election campaign. Faced with a pay cut and an envelope-stuffing job, Skillman quit the campaign entirely.

After going through two other campaign managers in her primary election, Jewel Lansing, Democratic candidate for state treasurer, had promoted Floren from finance coordinator to campaign coordinator. One month into the general election, however, Lansing hired a man with more experience for the top campaign post, moving Floren to the job of Portland-area coordinator.

To a large extent, both women were the casualties of political naïveté on the part of the candidates, a circumstance that was not uncommon among women running for office in the mid-1970s. As women sought higher office, they assumed their campaigns could be run by personal friends whose willingness to work made up for their lack of management expertise or political experience.

Paulus had placed all her state legislative campaigns in the hands of Skillman, a personal friend and neighbor for over fifteen years.

But Paulus' statewide race for secretary of state wasn't the same homey affair. It required coordination of speaking engagements around the state, sophisticated media advertising, and lots of bucks. Skillman, by her own admission, was not qualified to handle the job. "I recognized the fact that I was out of my depth and I needed help," she said. "But I asked for help and I never got it."

When two other campaign managers had left Jewel Lansing in her Democratic primary race for state treasurer, she turned to the one woman on her campaign staff whom she had known the longest and trusted the most, Marge Floren. Her ties to Floren, with whom she had been active in a local Unitarian fellowship, went back fifteen years. While she was eager to work, Floren's previous campaign experience was almost nil. She had walked a few precincts for several state legislative candidates and had run a garage sale for Lansing's earlier race for county auditor. But she had never held a major staff position in any campaign organization.

"I didn't map out a campaign plan for the general election," Floren said. "I just didn't know how to do it. There were also managerial skills that I had never developed. Like kicking asses."

Besides feeling out of their element, both women found their personal friendships with the candidates got in the way of campaigning. "It's hard to be a campaign coordinator for someone you know," Skillman said. "It was very difficult to say to Norma, 'Look, you need to be spending your time here instead of there.' " On personal matters, such as what Paulus wore while campaigning, Skillman found herself giving advice to one of Paulus' key male advisers to pass on to Paulus, rather than confronting Paulus herself.

The candidates themselves found the situation just as uncomfortable. Here were two long-time intimates, loyal and willing workers, who had devoted night and day to their friends' political aspirations. What's more, they were serving only because they had been sought out and asked. Although painfully aware of their managers' inadequacies, both Paulus and Lansing put off decisions to dismiss them. And when the decisions were finally made, they were not communicated with the utmost directness.

Skillman was simply informed that the campaign would be coordinated from Portland and that she could continue to run the Salem office in Paulus' legislative district if she wished. Floren was informed she would be replaced. She heard the news on the same day Lansing told her steering committee. Although they knew the changes were necessary for the best interests of the campaigns, both women felt hurt about the way they were informed of their replacements.

Other members of both campaign teams had other complaints about their candidates. Paulus was charged with rejecting staff advice; accepting any and all invitations to speak, thereby expending valuable travel time in visits to sparsely populated parts of the state; devoting steering-committee meetings to minor matters, and spending more time selecting photographs for campaign brochures than making key strategy decisions. Complaints about Lansing riveted on her unwillingness to give up control over trivia; her resistance to campaign schedules that ran her ragged; her objections to campaign plans that marketed her like a commodity.

Paulus won and Lansing lost in the general elections. Probably none of these issues was the critical factor in deciding the outcomes. Certainly none of these campaign troubles is the private property of women's campaigns. Complaints about priorities, leadership styles, managerial skills, and methods of coping with ineffective paid or voluntary personnel emanate from all political campaigns no less than from all enterprises in which groups of people work together for common goals. With regard to women's growing political aspirations, what is important about these problems is that they exist to be recognized and solved.

FINDING THE RIGHT PEOPLE

The female candidate of the seventies, like all office seekers, appreciated the value of services provided by both women and men who expressed confidence in her potential for leadership by joining her campaign team. Even at the stage when women were deciding whether to enter political races, people were a critical factor. "When I knew I had the commitment of several key people to work for me, I decided to run in 1978," said Nevada's State Senator Jean Ford. She had served in the lower house of the legislature for two terms, and then been defeated in a 1976 bid for the senate. In 1977 Ford switched from the Republican to the Democratic Party and contemplated her chances for a return engagement on the campaign platform. People told her she had "deserved to win in '76" and that they were ready to support her wholeheartedly for another race. Ford concluded that if she could recruit five key people on whom she could rely for running the campaign so that she could "let go of the details," she would announce her candidacy for 1978. In the last election campaign, she recalled, "I hadn't let go, and it worked against me. I had more confidence I could do that in 1978. And it worked."

A key supporter told Ford, "My next five months are yours." Becoming the chairperson of the campaign's finance committee, this supporter was joined by four other women filling major roles in the organization—a campaign coordinator, an office manager, a treasurer, and a precinct coordinator. Their support gave Ford the confidence she could win, the services her campaign required, and the freedom to do her part in making contact with the electorate in a district where over ninety thousand citizens were registered to vote.

The rest of the campaign organization's people power consisted of over three hundred former supporters, senior citizens, ethnic groups, public employees, university students and faculty, individuals from the League of Women Voters and Common Cause, and women who had worked with Ford a year earlier, when she had coordinated Nevada's statewide women's meeting and then led the Nevada delegation to the National Women's Conference in Houston. On primary election day in a race in which five contenders competed for three nominations, Jean Ford came out first, leading the ticket of a party she had joined only a year earlier. In 1978 Ford knew where to find the right people and how to utilize them properly for building a victory.

People power fuels the campaigns of female and male office seekers alike. While there seem to be no major sex differences between candidates in the manner of recruiting and utilizing people as a campaign resource, there is sometimes a distinctive spirit on the campaign teams of women running for office nowadays. The women working for a female candidate are likely to identify with her personally. The candidate becomes a mentor symbol—someone whose example teaches women on her campaign team that their own life choices can include becoming candidates as well as campaign workers. The route leading upward in the campaign hierarchy is not blocked implicitly by the presence of men holding a monopoly on the candidate's slot. While most women who participate in politics on campaign staffs may never aspire to seek election themselves, under these new circumstances the choice can be more individual and freely made. Furthermore, in addition to elective office, there are many influential positions in the political system to which female campaign workers may aspire once they sense that pathways are open.

There is also a spirit among workers in women's campaigns similar to that found in campaigns of ethnic candidates, minority candidates, and candidates affiliated with special (often underrepresented) constituencies. Since many women run as underdogs, and all run in a political climate that has bred very few women as officeholders, their campaigns produce intense feelings of personal victory or defeat among supporters who feel strongly about electing to public office a new type of candidate, someone from their group. In an atmosphere where workers identify with the candidate and make a personal investment in chalking up a victory for one of their own, women's campaign teams today are peopled with supporters who feel that "if she wins, we win." It is a feeling that contributes a distinct flavor to women's campaigns.

III. Money

"If you can't ask for help and money, don't run," says one politically sophisticated woman after defeating an incumbent in her bid for first-time office.

Women must usually surmount inner obstacles before asking for other people's support to further their own personal ambitions. But that challenge pales when compared with conflicts experienced by women in soliciting money on their own behalf. It is all right for a woman as Lady Bountiful to raise money for "those less fortunate" and for all manner of worthy causes. Women have developed valuable expertise in organizing fund-raising events and donation drives for community projects, hospitals, ballet societies, museums, parks, and certainly many a political candidate. But when it comes to raising money for herself, a woman recoils.

"Money raising is a nightmare time after time," said Congresswoman Pat Schroeder after her fourth successful congressional race in 1978.

"Asking for money is the hardest job a candidate has, and I'm convinced it keeps a lot of good people away from seeking office," says Connecticut State Senator Audrey Beck, who chaired the senate's Finance Committee. Having served in the legislature for over ten years, Beck has not found fund raising growing any more appealing during six campaigns.

One 1976 legislative candidate in Texas failed to organize a full-fledged finance committee or major fund-raising event early in the campaign and did not even send out her first mailing for money until September for a November election. A formidable fund raiser, she had brought in a great deal of money for Republican Party events, and her long experience in Republican campaigns told her where the money was. That was one matter, but it was quite another to ask people to donate to her own campaign. "I am just more comfortable asking for money for another person," she said.

Despite their know-how, most women judge themselves as poor fund raisers when wearing the candidate's hat. Even women with long experience in electoral politics hate this part of political life. In their U.S. Senate races, both Bella Abzug and Gloria Schaffer disliked doing personal solicitation. Abzug acknowledged, "It's difficult to ask for money," but she added, "I overcame it because I was so determined to win this race." Schaffer not only "hated to ask for money," but admitted that her campaign was affected because "fund raising was the area where we were the least professional."

Republican Diane McCarthy of Arizona, a decided extrovert, learned during her first campaign for the state legislature in 1972 that promoting her own candidacy did not bother her: "Men don't like to knock on doors; it's beneath them. I love it," she says. "You are no different from a salesman selling a product. The product is yourself. I'm outgoing and really didn't have a problem with that —some women do." McCarthy continued, "But the hardest thing, and the thing I really hated, was to ask for money."

"I would gear myself up until I could eat ground glass," recalls Ann Richards of Texas. No more eager to make a personal appeal for money than the next candidate, Richards would push forward to see how many checkbooks she could pry out of custom-tailored suits.

Hers was no starry-eyed spiel about how her election would

benefit Travis County. Contributors were more interested, Richards decided, in hearing whether she could win. She marshaled her analysis of voting habits, the impressive turnout at her announcement party, and her skilled cadre of supporters as proof that she was a strong contender. She also learned to ask for a specific amount. If a potential contributor seemed likely to give $50, Richards asked for $75. If someone seemed in the $100 category, she pitched for $150. Later she invited potential donors in to hear radio spots which needed financing in order to be aired properly.

Ann Richards, who unseated a two-term county commissioner, operated with a total budget of $22,000—enough to run a quality campaign. But it took serious, continuous effort to make her candidacy an appealing investment to contributors, and even then Richards had to supply $6,000 from her own bank account.

In the context of big-time politics $22,000 is barely a beginning. It can be raised from small contributions. But as a political unknown facing a popular incumbent, Richards had to labor nearly as hard for her $22,000 as Bella Abzug, a three-term congresswoman with a national reputation, had to work for her $600,000 Senate race.

A great many women approach the money end of politics as the root of all its evils. They hate to ask for it and fear they cannot get it. Often they do *not* get it. It is little consolation that many men have much the same problem, especially those who share with women the status of challenger and newcomer to office seeking. Whether pursuing a small campaign contribution or a large check, candidates of both sexes almost invariably find fund raising the worst of campaign tasks. "I have never overcome the feeling of asking for charity, of personally asking for something for myself," says Connecticut's Audrey Beck. Yet there is no way around it— ask for money they must. And men usually get more of it than women.

CAMPAIGN MONEY:
WOMEN VERSUS MEN

All political races cost money, and the variations in costs of campaigning are enormous among states, districts, levels of office, and depending on the status of a candidate. But several generalizations can be made safely about the costs of running for office. First, the prestigious high-level, high-salaried offices in any state are few in number, competitively sought after, and very expensive to win. Few women have sought or won them. Second, while incumbents may need less money to win reelection races because of the enormous advantage of name recognition, their established political credibility allows them to raise more money with less effort than is required of challengers and newcomers. In general, the financial rewards of incumbency are enjoyed by both female and male candidates, with one great and obvious difference—by the end of the 1970s there were nine times as many male as female incumbents in elective office. And third, while races have been won by both challengers and incumbents who spend less than their opponents (women among them), those candidates who raise more money for any election campaign are considered more likely to win. In general, women candidates find it difficult to raise campaign chests which equal or outweigh those of their male opponents.

A campaign chest is raised to buy goods and services for establishing a campaign organization which promotes a candidate's visibility. Depending on the size of the campaign, funds may be used simply for printing brochures and flyers and paying for postcards and stamps, or in more expensive campaigns they may be used for salaries and consultants' fees, headquarters costs, polling and research services, travel costs, and political advertising on billboards as well as in the print and electronic media. The money to pay campaign bills is raised through mail and telephone solicitation, personal visits to individuals and organizations likely to make political contributions, and fund-raising events.[6] Campaigns also operate with money borrowed from lending institutions and other sources, including the candidate's personal or family money. Debts are repaid with contributions raised both during the campaign and after election day in those cases where outstanding obligations remain on the books.

While female and male candidates aim to raise funds from similar sources to pay for the same kinds of campaign goods and services, observable differences existed in the 1970s in two closely related areas of campaign money. First, there were differences in attitudes and emphases between the sexes in methods of fund raising. Second, there was some variation in the sources of financial support for women's versus men's campaigns. Unsurprisingly, these differences arose in races where women were challengers, but more significantly they also arose in races where women entered primaries and general elections as candidates vying for open seats. While women felt that it was harder for them to ask for money and to succeed in attracting amounts equal to those raised by comparable male candidates, many of them did raise the sums required to mount competitive races.[7] If they had not, the decade could hardly have produced the phenomenon of an emerging political woman running competitively and winning increasing numbers of public offices. Looking back on a decade of successful campaigning, Audrey Beck observes, "Money is easier *to get* now that I'm an incumbent and chair an important legislative committee. But it remains as hard *to ask* for it."

Psychological Differences

Given a universal distaste for the fund-raising task and the high cost of campaigning, broad differences between the sexes should be viewed psychologically as well as under the light of hard political reality. Psychologically, women's self-image and self-esteem have traditionally rested on a concept of the female as provider of services. Whereas men have been encouraged to put a price on their services and to judge their worth in financial terms, women are accustomed to judging their worth on the basis of their ability to perform unpaid services in the domestic sphere and in the community. A woman has been raised to expect payment in the form of praise and gratitude (sometimes flowers or chocolates) if she succeeds in keeping a nice home, raising fine children, and serving as helpmate to her husband. It is no surprise that many women seeking elective office place top priority on their intentions to serve constituents, seeming to underplay their own interest in holding positions of power within the institutions of government. Power and money traditionally have not been associated with women or controlled by women. As strangers to their combined charms, and suspicious of their corrupting influence, women tend to feel uncomfortable in their presence.

Feeling better when they can offer something in return for money received, many female candidates look favorably on fund-raising events for filling campaign chests. An event—whether a picnic, a fashion show, a theater party, or a Halloween dance—offers contributors a pleasant social occasion in return for dollars spent. Frequently the candidate herself assists with arrangements. Unaccustomed to relying on other people to shop and prepare food for her parties, much less for an event planned in order to raise money for her personal advancement, a woman running for office is often found pitching in at the bean-salad-and-casserole level of preparation. Leaving the preparation to campaign workers might seem inappropriate to many women, might even produce guilt in the candidate and resentment among the women assigned to washing the vegetables and setting the tables. Without doubt, women can get accustomed to being served by others and to attending fund-raising events as guests of honor, but many women still feel more comfortable in joining their supporters in the kitchen than in being waited on at the dais.

Differences Imposed by Political Reality

Added to the force of psychology is the weight of hard political reality. Female candidates find it more difficult to raise money than their male counterparts because women are not influential in established formal and informal financial and political circles. Elizabeth Holtzman's administrative assistant, Rod Smith, observed: "Women are just not part of the money-raising network. There's no overt discrimination, but they're not in the network because their friends are not the presidents of corporations. They're left out of money, information, and influence by being overlooked unconsciously." He calls it a "sin of omission."

Maryland's state legislator Paula Hollinger feels that "women just don't raise the kind of money men do. The special interests give the money, and women don't get it." In her 1978 first race for the legislature, Hollinger says that some of her opponents had campaign treasuries ten times as large as hers because they were running "with special-interest support." And another state legislator who put together two successful campaigns with people power and small budgets: "Women don't have access to money, to the Kiwanis and the Rotary Clubs and all the men's networks."

Big-money political contributors are usually men active in informal male networks, and they are usually shrewd judges of electoral tides. Likewise, the lobbying interests, which still fuel the majority of campaigns, tend to look as closely at the odds as they do at the ideology. A businessman who occasionally must deal with government officials to protect economic interests, or a lobbyist who earns a living asking for legislative votes, usually will not contribute money to the unlikely quest of a challenger and thereby risk an incumbent's disfavor.

"Women are less involved in business activities," says Connecticut's State Senator Audrey Beck. She continues, "Men deal more frequently with lobbies than women. Women know they can offer nothing back—they're 'cleaner' on the whole. But if more women get into office and go on banking, insurance, real estate, and finance committees, things might get different." Although Beck finds fund raising extremely distasteful, she acknowledges that it gets easier to attract the money "particularly if you hold a key position." As a result of her role as chairperson of the senate's Finance Committee, she got reelection money both from industry and labor, and in 1978 lawyers and bankers also contributed to her campaign.

Upset because her race was ignored by the political arm of her state's medical association, one candidate called it "a very selfish organization," which "never paid me the courtesy of interviewing me." She described the organization as operating under "a friendly-incumbent clause."

"That's not a clause; it's a cardinal principle of politics," countered the lobbyist for the medical association. "If someone in office does a good job for you, it's just human nature to support him. It's nothing more than common sense." In this case the incumbent, a tried and true friend of local physicians who had championed their malpractice bill in the state legislature, was rewarded with a campaign contribution exceeding $6,000.

THE COSTS OF CAMPAIGNING

By 1978 races for the U.S. Senate cost an average of more than $900,000 per candidate, with winners spending an average of almost $1.2 million each.[8] In the larger states the costs were even higher, and they are going up drastically all the time. In 1979, when administrative assistant Rod Smith talked about whether or not

New York's Elizabeth Holtzman would make a bid for moving up to the Senate in 1980, he indicated that a major part of the decision would rest on the feasibility of raising required funds—an anticipated $2 to $3 million to cover the New York primary and general election races. Holtzman did make the Senate bid in 1980, raising and spending almost $2 million for a race she lost.

In her reelection race for the U.S. House of Representatives in 1978, Holtzman had spent approximately $40,000—almost twice what it cost in 1974 and 1976. The tab increased despite Holtzman's status as a strong, entrenched incumbent in a district that returned her to office with 82 percent of the vote in 1978, 83 percent in 1976, and 79 percent in 1974. Congressional races in 1978 among incumbents ranged in cost from as little as $14,000, spent by House Speaker Thomas P. O'Neill, Jr., of Massachusetts, to almost a quarter million dollars each spent by several House leaders in both parties.[9]

In 1978, expenditures for women seeking congressional office for the first time as major party candidates in the general election rose above $100,000. Marge Roukema's race against an incumbent in New Jersey cost $18,000 for a successful primary campaign and approximately $125,000 for the general election defeat. Two years later, Roukema's winning congressional race cost over a quarter million dollars. New York Congresswoman Geraldine Ferraro's successful bid for office cost over $130,000. In 1980 her winning reelection race cost about $75,000.

In statewide and large city races few candidates for top offices can get by without attracting long lists of thousand-dollar contributions. In states without funding limits, the amounts of single contributions can go considerably higher than a thousand dollars. Gubernatorial campaigns in states like Texas, New Jersey, or New York are undertakings of well over a million dollars these days. Primary races bring the figures up much higher. In New York State Hugh Carey spent over $5 million for his first gubernatorial race in 1974. In 1977, in New York City's mayoralty race, the cost of the Democratic primary alone hovered around $1 million per candidate.[10]

Below the top offices in populous states and urban areas, costs for campaigning decrease dramatically. In a small state like Vermont, for example, Madeleine Kunin won the lieutenant governorship in 1978 in a race which cost her $36,500 for the primary and general election campaigns. Nonetheless, no serious-minded political hopeful sets sights on statewide office without first assessing financial resources. If early money is not there, the good tacticians back off and wait for a more opportune moment. No amount of diligent door knocking and no army of dedicated volunteers can offset the impact of a media blitz, for example, in any of the populous states.

When running for elective offices below congressional and statewide levels, candidates raise between a few hundred dollars and a hundred thousand dollars depending on the office and the district. In urban districts, where voters must be wooed with media or mail or both, money often makes the difference between winning and losing. In California's big city districts, a $100,000 campaign chest is considered essential for a state assembly race. A similar situation exists in Texas. But it is also possible to win a state legislative race in Texas with a campaign costing less than $10,000 if the race is in a rural district where courthouse contacts, yard signs, and newspaper advertisements are still mainstays in the campaign manual. In Nevada, Jean Ford spent $72,000 in her 1978 state senate race in a district which included the metropolitan area of Las Vegas. In the same year Polly Baca Barragan, running without opposition for a seat in Colorado's senate, spent a mere $1,500. According to Baca Barragan, in a typical race with opposition, a campaign for Colorado's state senate would cost between $15,000 and $20,000. In Connecticut during the 1978 election season, State Senator Audrey Beck spent $6,000 for her reelection race. Several years earlier when she campaigned successfully for a seat in Connecticut's lower house, Beck spent $1,000 on the race, and in Vermont Madeleine Kunin's first race for the legislature in 1972 cost a total of $350 for the primary and general election campaigns. Her reelection race, when she faced no opposition, cost $100. In Maryland, Paula Hollinger spent $7,000 for her successful 1978 legislative race, but some of her opponents in the primary campaign spent as much as $70,000 to $80,000, according to Hollinger.

At the county level, a commissioner's race may cost $20,000 to $40,000 in some states. But in Iowa, for example, Black Hawk County Supervisor Lynn Cutler spent only $5,000 in her first campaign in 1974 to run at large in a county with a population of 136,000. Four years later she spent $7,000 for reelection and considered that an expensive race. The additional cost was necessary because she was opposed by someone with the same last name. In other states a county-level race may cost only a few hundred dollars.

Campaign costs for municipal council and mayoralty races vary as greatly as for other levels of office. They range from $100 or less for council seats in small municipalities to the $1 million already cited for New York's mayoralty primary.

Lack of access to large-scale political money is indeed one of the formidable barriers looming to block almost any newcomer's political aspirations for first-time office or for climbing to higher office. Whatever the level of office, wherever the race, money is essential for building a campaign machine and making it work. Convinced that they did not have access to large amounts of political money, over the last decade many women attracted to politics decided not to run for office, especially not to bid for higher offices than the ones they held on local councils or in legislatures. In 1974, when Audrey Beck considered moving up to higher office from her seat in Connecticut's lower house of the legislature, she felt qualified and ready to vie in a congressional race. Instead, she chose to run for the state senate because it would have taken $100,000 to mount a viable congressional race. "I thought I couldn't get it," she recalled, "because I didn't have access to major business interests or to a wealthy constituency in the district."

While women with ambitions for congressional and statewide offices have remained at local levels or foregone candidacies primarily because they could not attract levels of financial support required to launch viable campaigns, men often make the same decision for the same reason. But it is important to notice that in the panorama of U.S. campaigns and elections men run in virtually 100 percent of contests which require large campaign treasuries. Almost no women show up in those races, even in the decade of the seventies, when more women than ever before became candidates. While money is hardly the only reason for that difference, it is by no means an insignificant one. This situation is unlikely to change markedly until political contributors consider a woman's election to office both appropriate and worthy of financial support.

SUPPORT FROM SPECIAL-INTEREST GROUPS— CRITICAL AND ELUSIVE

Incumbency is no guarantee of support from established interests if a candidate is not perceived as a trusted insider, which is often the case when the men controlling political purses do not feel comfortable with a female officeholder. Incumbent Congresswoman Pat Schroeder has said men and women are not friends with each other. Noting that she is a member of the House Armed-Services Committee, Schroeder says she does not "go out drinking with the lobbyists" and is not involved in the networks that spend money on politics. "My friends give $15, not $1,000," observes Schroeder. This situation is not exclusive to incumbents in high-level, well-paid elective offices. In a small Southwestern town, a woman who had held office for four years on the local council was defeated in 1978 because "the business community bought my seat." Believing that "at the local level the business community really doesn't want equality of treatment," she recalls that during the week before the election her opponent spent more money on newspaper and radio advertisements than she had collected in her entire campaign budget. "I had almost a hundred little contributors, and he had ten biggies," she says. The local media acknowledged that she had done a good job on the council, but they endorsed her opponent because, she says, "he spent money in the media."

Even when women vie for open seats, they are likely to face opponents in primaries and general elections who have more name recognition and credibility in established financial and political networks. In such a situation the woman is still seen as a high risk for someone betting money on an election outcome. Nevada's Jean Ford recalls that in her losing race for the state senate in 1976, she got less money from the same sources as her opponent. "I was not considered as serious a candidate because I was a woman," she says. But two years later "things were different because of our tenacity and the positive way we went about it." In the 1978 race Ford raised $74,000, which turned out to be $2,000 more than she spent. The money came from 990 contributors, some individuals and some corporations. Contributions ranged from $5 to $2,500, with about 20 percent of the contributions coming in amounts of $500 or over and 65 percent coming in amounts of $50 or less.

Special-interest groups—particularly political action committees representing corporate interests, professional organizations,
and labor unions—contribute heavily and steadily to political campaigns at all levels of the elective system. In 1979 *The New York
Times* reported that in the previous fall's congressional elections
these special interests alone contributed almost $1 million to the
campaigns of eight congressional leaders.[11] In a 1977 statement
delivered at a meeting of the Senate Rules Committee's deliberations about laws governing campaign finances, the National
Women's Political Caucus and the Women's Campaign Fund in
Washington, D.C., discussed the difficulties facing women candidates in this area. Arguing that a strong relationship exists between
campaign expenditures and election-day outcomes, especially in
primary races, the two organizations noted that a review of finance
reports in recent years reveals that in primary campaigns for congressional office non-incumbent women regularly are outspent by
male opponents. The two reasons given for the patterns of differen-
tial funding between female and male candidates were, first, that
"so few women have a personal network of sizable contributors,"
and second, that there was an "unwillingness of major funding
sources to acknowledge the credibility of women candidates." In
the view of the National Women's Political Caucus and the
Women's Campaign Fund, in instances when funding sources such
as labor union or corporate political action committees do "consider a primary [campaign] contribution, the risk is regularly taken
in support of the male candidates."[12]

Whether in primaries or in general elections, the candidate
who receives support is one political contributors know personally
or through someone else, and with whom they feel comfortable
identifying themselves. That person is almost bound to be a man.
Based on frustrating experiences in 1976, a fund raiser for Jewel
Lansing's statewide campaign states a basic fact of political life:
"Large contributors seem to be very practical about playing the
odds on who's going to win. If you're running against somebody
who has . . . name familiarity, it's real hard for these people to take
you seriously. They give you a token contribution. They say, 'She's
great. She's qualified,' but like one guy said, 'I can't be taken off
the fence for this.'"

Lansing's biggest problem was that her opponent, Oregon

State Senator Clay Myers, the ultimate victor, had high name iden-tification and a long-standing acquaintance with the largely Repub-lican financial community. One businessman backed Myers with $5,000 and Lansing with $150. Small groups of businessmen who were invited to Lansing fund-raising luncheons backed out. "It gets frustrating when you talk to somebody on the phone and they tell you, 'Sorry, Clay is a personal friend.' They won't even argue qualifications with you," said a member of Lansing's campaign staff.

"From every guy who would ordinarily give $500 to $1,000, I would get $25," said one exasperated candidate who lost her congressional race against an entrenched incumbent. Where poli-tics and money intersect, few people contribute willingly to lost causes. And according to the pure logic of vicious circles, those candidates who cannot attract financial backing begin to look more and more like losers.

Here is how one man—both husband and fund raiser to a candidate—views the situation. Ron Warner handled fund raising for his wife's 1976 primary campaign for a U.S. Senate seat in Arizona. The Carolyn Warner campaign raised about $300,000— a great deal of money. It was $200,000 less than the resources reported by Dennis DeConcini, the candidate who defeated Caro-lyn Warner on election day. Ron Warner believes he could have raised more money if his wife's entry into the race had been better timed. She announced in June for a September primary. A year is considered minimum effort in most Senate races.

Despite his conviction that with more time he could have raised more money, Warner also concludes that women lack access to networks of influence, to well-heeled contributors, and to the businessman's confidence. Ron Warner, a businessman himself, used his leverage to raise money for his wife's campaign. "I'm not at the highest level of the establishment," he noted, "but I might be at the second level. I call most people in town—we're talking about money people—by their first names, which helps. The money is still controlled by the men. Women may inherit it. But it's a buddy system. The guys you play golf with, the guys you have lunch with—they're willing to give to each other."

Warner also suspects that businessmen think women are not tough enough and perhaps just a shade too principled. "I think that men suspect that when faced with a tough decision—one that might even compromise a little on ethics—women would say, 'That's morally wrong. That's not right.' Now what this brings up is the double standard of what boys are allowed to do and what girls are not supposed to do. A woman would say something is morally wrong. A man would say, 'But it's practical. I don't give a damn if it's moral or not.' Take the question of kickbacks to foreign countries by large American corporations. I'm not saying it's right or wrong. I'm just saying that the businessman's posture is, 'This is just the kind of world we live in.' "

BYPASSING THE CENTERS OF POWER

Many women in the 1970s sought elective office via routes laid to bypass traditional centers of political power, whether in the political party system, labor union groups, business circles, or among other powerful special-interest groups. And the most common bypass taken by political women in the seventies went directly to the electorate. By building credibility in neighborhood networks and finding campaign resources and ballot strength in grass-roots politics, women forged bonds with the people they sought to represent. Nickel by nickel, dime by dime, handshake by handshake—it is the long and arduous route to elective office.

While bypass routes do not usually lead to victory in races for highly competitive, powerful offices, it should be remembered that the overwhelming majority of female candidates in the 1970s were running in state legislative, county, and municipal elections. At those levels in most districts, local fund-raising events which ask for relatively small donations in return for an enjoyable afternoon's or evening's social occasion can be a highly successful means for attracting both financial and human resources to a campaign. In Paula Hollinger's successful 1978 legislative race in Maryland, for example, campaign money came from two sources: small contributions sent by individuals in response to a mailing; and $3,000 to $4,000 raised by selling $15 tickets to a wine and cheese reception followed by a theater party. In Hollinger's case, where a $7,000 campaign resulted in victory against opponents who spent as much as $70,000, the candidate assessed money as third in the list of resources accounting for her success. "It was people—the corps of volunteers—and the time we all put in; then money," she concluded.

On the other hand, money played a critical role in purchasing billboard, radio, television, and newspaper advertising in Jean Ford's 1978 race for the state senate in Nevada. Her $72,000 campaign, supported by almost a thousand contributors from within the state and around the country, also depended heavily on mail solicitation and fund-raising events. During election season, the Ford campaign held raffles, sold items, and sponsored a luncheon style show in which campaign workers modeled. Entitled "The Politics of Dress," the fashion show was held in a discotheque and drew 250 guests, each paying $20. "It got a lot of attention," says Ford.

Jean Ford observes that "women have the advantage of knowing how to put on fund-raising events because they've always done it." But she has also learned the importance of seeking help from men, both as large contributors and as active supporters at the nickel-and-dime level. In 1978 the Ford campaign included a men's auxiliary that was organized and run by a male professor from the local university. Among its contributions to the campaign, the men's auxiliary sponsored and conducted a fund-raising event, albeit the type of event which usually has been left to women to run —"the men put on a very successful bake sale," the candidate recalled with satisfaction.

NICKEL AND DIME-ING IT

In January 1977, with the next gubernatorial election almost two years away, Governor Dolph Briscoe of Texas—a rancher whose net worth is estimated at $40 million—invited the state's leading political contributors and lobby representatives to a friend's ranch. The purpose of the barbeque was to help Briscoe pay off some debts accumulated in his 1974 campaign, in order that he could be off and running again in 1978. People who attended reported that the afternoon resulted in approximately $1 million in pledges.

In May 1976, with the primary election close upon her, Barbara Boxer of California—a woman in her early thirties, the mother of three young children, and a district aide to a congressman—met with the four women who served as top strategists for her campaign to become a county supervisor in Marin County. The purpose of the session was to plan last-minute details for their major fund-raising event—a home-cooked dinner of barbequed fresh salmon for one hundred people to be held outdoors at a friend's house two days later. Discussion of final details included where to get chairs and tablecloths, whether to expend money on renting outdoor heaters, and whose responsibility it would be to provide fresh vegetables for the curry dip. The event turned into a success—an enjoyable evening with guests donating $10 each to raise nearly $1,000 toward the $15,000 needed to finance the primary campaign.

Boxer won her race to become a county supervisor in California. Briscoe lost his 1978 bid for an unprecedented third term as governor of Texas despite available money. The most telling differences between Briscoe's million-dollar barbeque and Boxer's thousand-dollar dinner are not revealed by noting the amounts of money raised for each politician, since there are enormous differences in costs between statewide executive and county legislative races. The important differences between candidates like these are in expectations regarding money, in approaches to fund raising and level of involvement by the candidates, and in sources of money available to each candidate. Briscoe and Boxer hold credibility in different political universes. These differences will affect their outlooks, their aspirations, their planning, and the nature of their participation in the money side of political life.

If more women begin political careers, as men often do, under the tutelage of influential mentors who introduce them into monied circles and promote them actively in the places of power, or if more women gain access to more of the traditional sources of large-scale political money through concerted and sustained efforts to enter the political mainstream, there may be less need in the future for female candidates to rely as heavily as they do today on the nickel-and-dime route to filling campaign coffers. Nickel-and-dime fund-raising events usually require great investments of time and energy, often for minimal gains in the campaign treasury. Yet, it must be noted, there are compensating benefits which many women recognize and acclaim in that approach to fund raising. It can attract popular support, magnetizing people where they are really needed for grass-roots political participation in ways perhaps worth more than money for certain types of races.

Unsurprisingly, attitudes differ sharply among female political practitioners about the reasons for and the benefits to be derived from low-yield fund raising. An active member of the Women's Task Force of the California Democratic State Central Committee who has assisted in planning fund raisers for a number of women's organizations concluded that women have difficulty asking high prices as admission to these events. In her view, "there's a dichotomy" between whether to stage "an expensive fund raiser and eliminate a lot of people or have a less expensive one and accept the fact you're not going to raise as much money." Acknowledging that both types of events are the same amount of work, she notes "there is a concern we'll be elitist if we charge over $15." Go higher than that magic number, she says, and someone asks, "Over $15? Grrrrr. All right, $16.50. But that's all."

Women are wary about accepting money that has strings attached, suspicious that almost all money is attached to someone's demands for repayment of some kind, dubious that expectations of return favors can be considered as savory or aboveboard. Women feel reluctant giving or taking money on a large scale. There is suspicion that the more the money, the greater the likelihood of corruption. There is also a "just plain folks," working-class ethic among women when it comes to money and politics, an attitude that says a hard-earned dollar may be more worthwhile than an easy windfall. Rationally if not realistically, honest hard work is associated with material rewards and personal satisfaction. Strangers to reaching goals via high-risk wheeling and dealing, most women are more accustomed to tasks they accomplish themselves in a step-by-step process of individual effort.

Even for races at the congressional level women spend a great deal of time and effort raising small money. For example, while Bella Abzug's campaign for the U.S. Senate carried a formidable fund-raising burden, it staged very few exclusive affairs. Abzug's supporters held nearly sixty money-raising functions during the primary campaign. More than half these events asked contributions of $15 or less. Only seven events sought more than $50 a ticket. Abzug's staff complained that a low-yield event takes as much time and effort to stage as an expensive one. However, the chief fund raiser for the campaign reported that she was criticized by indignant Abzug supporters whenever she tried to set the price of tickets high. She was told often and in no uncertain terms that that was not

Bella's image. It is not generally a woman's image. High-priced women have been models and movie stars, not professionals or politicians. Abzug's image as a "people's candidate" suggested that there be many affairs that the "people" could attend.

In raising her treasury of $600,000, Abzug necessarily had to depend on large contributions as well as small. Nearly fifty of her contributors reached the $1,000 limit. Pamela Harriman, wife of former Governor Averell Harriman, staged a lavish Manhattan party that provided an entrée to major money. Abzug made from five to ten phone calls each week to selected prospects, informing them of campaign progress and asking their assistance. In addition to the direct mailing to a "women's list," a commercial mailing house donated its services and its lists of members of liberal organizations to the Abzug campaign. One mailing to two hundred thousand names on these lists raised about $75,000. However, mailings tended to produce smaller contributions than fund-raising events. Only 10 percent of mailed donations were larger than $25.

In Arizona, Pat Fullinwider's 1976 congressional campaign raised money from sales of T-shirts, direct mail solicitations, and one three-day telephone campaign which asked for one-dollar contributions on the spot. It raised about $1,000 and consumed dozens of hours of volunteer time. Meanwhile Fullinwider's opponent, Congressman John Rhodes, stoked his campaign with $1,000 checks sent in response to minimal urging.

Resorting to the nickel-and-dime path to political office frequently leaves candidates wondering from day to day whether there will be money to pay the bills. In the 1976 Texas legislative races, for example, Ernestine Glossbrenner recalled that "the week before the election I needed very badly to get on the radio. There just wasn't any money. We were stone broke. I was on my way to the station, but I didn't know what I would do when I got there. I stopped by my mailbox on the way, and there was a check for $300 from the teachers' organization." It was a large check for the Glossbrenner campaign, and it saved the day.

WOMEN CONTRIBUTORS

More women must be willing to place money on women's races. Efforts to educate women in the fine art of political check writing have not proven highly successful to date. "Many women who think nothing of spending $50 for a dress or pair of shoes think you're crazy if you ask them for $50 for a political campaign," says Melinda Bass, a political activist in New York. Bass observed that "a woman prominent in New York financial circles, who earns a large salary, contributed only $15" to Carol Bellamy's 1977 campaign for city council president.[13] In Oregon, when Secretary of State Norma Paulus sought support from well-heeled women in her own Republican Party and from business and professional women on both sides of the party line in 1976, she encountered considerable reluctance and political naïveté. In 1978, when Sharon Sharp ran as the Republican nominee for secretary of state in Illinois, she was approached after a speech by an expensively dressed woman who enthusiastically handed her a check—for $5. "Men are more comfortable contributing large amounts," and "they also have access to it," says Jane Eskind, Tennessee's 1978 Democratic candidate for the U.S. Senate.[14]

Some female candidates do seek and acquire important financial contributions to their campaigns from individual feminists and from groups of women organized to support other women running for office. Candidates like Bella Abzug in New York, Gloria Schaffer in Connecticut, and Barbara Mikulski in Maryland all used mailing lists of women in their fund-raising drives. They met with varying degrees of success, discovering that some of the key early money for their campaigns came from women around the country who supported them, as well as from women within their states. However, the consensus among female candidates is that women do not yet give money proportionate to their financial ability to make political contributions. It will take some time before women are of the mind and in the position to see their own best interests served by contributing their own money to the electoral system.

INVESTING ONE'S OWN MONEY

In addition to seeking money from men and from women, a candidate often must invest his or her own money in the campaign. This is particularly important in the early stages of a campaign when start-up money is critical but difficult to raise. Personal money or family money is likely to be contributed on a loan basis, then paid back after sufficient funds have been raised to cover campaign costs. Nevada's Jean Ford believes that it does get easier to raise money the more one does it. "It grows on you as you grow in confidence and knowledge of the political process," she says. But the first time she ran for a seat in the legislature in 1972, she simply could not bring herself to make appointments to ask potential contributors for money. She and her husband decided that it was important for her to run for the legislature, and they agreed to launch her effort with a $4,000 contribution from their family funds.

In recent years many women who have decided to return to school after fifteen or twenty years of homemaking refuse to use the family's money to pay costs of their own education. They consider it selfish to spend the family's money for their personal improvement, and they suffer guilt at the thought of draining off resources. For similar and additional reasons, some female candidates for elective office refuse to fund their own campaigns. Some because of principle: "I don't believe in buying a seat," said one state legislator in Minnesota. Some because of personal considerations: "I promised my husband I wouldn't borrow," said a legislative candidate in Texas.

Candidates who are well heeled have been known to invest considerable fortunes in political careers, and the overwhelming majority of them have been male. A report in *The New York Times* at the end of 1978 indicated that in the U.S. Senate "about one of every four members is worth $1 million or more."[15] When Nancy Kassebaum of Kansas entered the Senate in 1979 as one of its millionaires, she was virtually unique as a very wealthy woman holding high-level political office. In considering a 1980 candidacy for the Senate, New York's Manhattan Borough President Andrew Stein commented, "I think being able to spend my own money— $800,000, $900,000, a million—gives me an advantage."[16]

Recognizing the importance of launching viable candidacies with personal money, some women who are in a more fortunate position financially have begun to conclude that they will have to underwrite their political ambitions until they can attract outside contributions. In the 1978 congressional races, for example, two successful female newcomers—Olympia Snowe of Maine and Geraldine Ferraro of New York—invested personally in their campaigns. So did some losers, among them Georgia's Virginia Shapard and Tennessee's Jane Eskind.

In Geraldine Ferraro's case, she was led to believe that substantial labor union and business money would be contributed to the primary race. Promises did not materialize, and she and her husband had invested an initial $25,000 in the primary on the assumption that the loan could be paid back through later contributions. "Once you're determined and you spend," she says, "you can't just walk away from it." The Ferraro campaign continued to draw on personal resources, borrowing up to $130,000 in family funds, including the children's college accounts and insurance policies. In Ferraro's race, family money amounted to approximately one-third of total primary and general election campaign receipts, with other funds ultimately coming from individual contributors, political action committees, party committees, and loans. Congresswoman Ferraro acknowledges that she was in a fortunate position. She also had the self-confidence and determination to take a major risk.

In a less expensive race, Billie Coopwood of Texas took aim at an open seat in the state's house of representatives in 1976. Heavy spending by her husband and his family probably contributed decisively to her success in winning a place in the runoff election. About $9,500 of her $29,000 in contributions came from family sources. "The campaign wouldn't have gotten off the ground if I hadn't put my own money into it." she said. "I had no political connections."

Coopwood lost the primary in the runoff. While critically important, personal or family money cannot guarantee victory. It is a high-risk investment in a political career made by those who can afford it and who have the confidence to put money into a race during its early phases when the candidate's strength has yet to be tested. It is still an uncommon practice among women because women have not been prepared for or accustomed to making financial investments in their own careers or political advancement.

A candidate able to raise money is a candidate whose race is taken seriously. To whatever extent women are not confident enough to take themselves seriously in political life, and to whatever extent they are not taken seriously by political contributors, they still face greater difficulty than men in finding the dollars to fill campaign treasuries. The situation for women will get better by degrees—as more and more female candidates prove that their races are good investments.

Women's
Political Movement

Time: Election season 1976

Setting: Fund raiser sponsored by the Connecticut Women's Political Caucus

Keynote Speaker: Gloria Steinem

Question from Audience: "Do you support Gloria Schaffer because she is a woman?"

Answer by Steinem: "No, I don't support her because she is a woman. I support her because I am a woman."

Chapter 7
Organized Support

Women Running for Women Running for Office
—Title of a five-mile road race sponsored
by the Massachusetts Women's Political Caucus
and the Amateur Athletic Union, June 10, 1979

Early in the 1970s some feminists recognized the need for women's voices in electoral politics. Increased participation in political parties, campaigns, and public offices was viewed both as an end in itself and as one means for advancing social reforms which reflected women's needs and sought to improve women's lot. Thus, the organized women's political movement (that is, the branch of the contemporary women's-rights movement most active in the electoral arena) established groups and support mechanisms for boosting women in political life.

These groups have been able to channel a modest but growing amount of support into campaign politics. When and where they are able, they contribute money, volunteers, and expertise to aspiring political women who meet certain criteria established by each organization. They have also released position papers on selected women's issues, and have set up special workshops designed to motivate women to run for office and to teach campaign skills.[1] Another valuable type of contribution has come in the form of services donated by consultants with campaign expertise.

205

Political consultants sent into the states from national offices of women's organizations based in Washington, D.C., discuss campaign strategy and offer advice to candidates. For example, in 1978 the Women's Campaign Fund sent consultants to advise Madeleine Kunin and Nancy Stevenson in their campaigns for the lieutenant governorships of Vermont and South Carolina. A year before Montana's 1978 primary election, the Women's Campaign Fund hired a pollster and paid for a poll to aid in assessing the viability of Dorothy Bradley's plans for a congressional bid.

The extent of organization, the availability of resources, and the capacity for providing useful support vary greatly around the country. In a few noteworthy cases, campaign support mobilized by feminists has responded to election-season situations with a type of organized energy and political sophistication that has earned respect and local power for the women's political movement. In the judgment of political feminists in Texas, such were the results of their activities in the mid-1970s.

One of the more fascinating case histories, featuring the Texas Women's Political Caucus, involved two races in the primaries of South Texas, where campaigning is important and poll watching is crucial to guard against corruption in counting votes.

Texas had been one of the first states to ratify the federal Equal Rights Amendment. As anti-ERA activities grew across the country, Texas produced its share of advocates for rescission. While the rescission movement did not succeed in Texas, its existence caused feminists to concentrate on strengthening their voices in the state legislature.

"We were greatly frustrated by the rescission efforts," recalled Martha Smiley, 1975 president of the Texas Women's Political Caucus. "We felt we could not afford to spend all our energy on ERA for several more sessions. And we were acutely aware of our lack of clout. Legislators treated us like nobodies. We had no votes to draw on." The result was a decision to target legislative races, field viable candidates, offer them technical and financial assistance, and generally aim at becoming a force demanding respect in the legislature.

The state caucus did best in two South Texas districts which by November of 1975 had emerged as targets, the 58th and the 49th. In the 58th District, 43-year-old Ernestine Glossbrenner had mounted a creditable race against the George Parr machine. Parr, the legendary Duke of Duval, had held sway over three of the four counties in his statehouse district for over thirty years. His hand-picked candidate in the 58th District had been Terry Canales, whose two terms in office showed a heavy absentee record. By 1975 Parr was dead; his son, County Judge Archer Parr, was in federal prison; and the old party machine was coming unhinged.

Glossbrenner had won the Woman of the Year award from the Texas Women's Political Caucus in 1974. She had formed a chapter of the caucus in her local area. Narrowly defeated in a 1974 legislative race which many people felt had been stolen from her during the vote count, she was also still scarred from a bitter defeat in a 1975 race for the Alice city council.

In November 1975, a quartet from the state Women's Political Caucus went to Alice to set up a telephone poll and assess Glossbrenner's legislative chances. The poll, conducted by Glossbrenner volunteers under caucus guidance, indicated that notwithstanding the 1975 council race, the teacher had not lost significant ground in the Anglo community.

The Texas Women's Political Caucus also was eyeing the adjoining 49th House District, where the incumbent was seeking reelection despite an indictment for misuse of house staff. Mexican-American caucus members were pressuring a Kingsville attorney, Irma Rangel, herself a Chicana, to make the race. The district, whose counties rank near the bottom on every economic scale, contains a population almost 80 percent Mexican-American.

On the November swing south, the four caucus members called on Rangel to talk about issues, her contacts, her potential base, and her natural constituency. An articulate woman, Rangel also demonstrated a deep understanding of the plight of the poor. "We told her there was a hope of money from the caucus and a promise of hard work," said caucus coordinator Mimi Purnell.

The state caucus collected about $5,700 for its various candidates with pledges from members and the usual assortment of receptions, bake sales, and garage sales. Glossbrenner and Rangel each received $1,750 in March 1976, a sum later supplemented with contributions from individual caucus members.

Mimi Purnell, who was responsible for organizing the technical assistance to the two South Texas women, had begun her weekend trips from Austin south to the farmland towns of Alice and Kingsville to organize populist campaigns there—a series of journeys which she later estimated cost her two tires, three fanbelts, three thermostats, and four windshield wipers for her car.

A former Dallas County coordinator for Governor Dolph Briscoe, Mimi Purnell was experienced in campaign techniques. Her Austin location gave her access to the voting and attendance records of the two legislative incumbents Glossbrenner and Rangel were facing in the May primary elections. As spring approached, she concentrated on communication by telephone—estimating that she made more than 125 calls to each campaign, to help with problems and assess progress. "I called to keep the lines of communication open and let volunteers take out their frustrations on me instead of the candidates."

Both Glossbrenner and Rangel survived the primaries to face runoff elections. Winning the runoffs would insure victory since there were no Republican candidates for the general elections. But the Texas Women's Political Caucus members were highly concerned about Glossbrenner's chances because of the way in which votes had been cast and counted in Duval and Starr counties in the past.

"We argued with Ernestine about impounding votes in the primary," said Purnell. "We had a brief drawn, and all she needed to do was ask the district attorney to impound. But it has to be done in advance, and she didn't do it until Sunday after the election. She wanted to trust them. In the runoff, we decided the hell with Ernestine. We would just do it."

In another preventive measure, the Texas Women's Political Caucus invoked the authority of the state's new Voting Rights Act to have six caucus members deputized by the secretary of state as official observers. The caucus also conducted a workshop for League of Women Voters members who volunteered as poll watchers.

"I'm convinced those special deputies saved the election," said Glossbrenner after she won by 147 votes.

Rangel, also a winner, noted later that the caucus was one of the very few organizations that "supported me and endorsed me" in the primary election.

There were other victories and some defeats for the candidates supported by the Texas caucus, which gave Mimi Purnell its outstanding service award that year. "The overall result of the 1976 effort," said Caucus President Martha Smiley, "was to make our point." Political feminists in Texas could point to electing a few women, scaring some incumbents, and gaining credibility as a political organization. Smiley noted the biggest victory: politicians learned that "they have to deal with us."

Success like that in Texas, albeit still rare, illustrates an impor-

tant recent development in campaign politics—the potential for
effective action when women organize to support each other's political interests. As a special-interest group capable of affecting the
nominating process and the conduct and outcome of elections, the
women's political movement is far from matching the clout of
established pressure groups. Yet it did become visible and forceful
enough during the 1970s to be acknowledged as a presence to
reckon with in the electoral process.[2]

MAJOR ORGANIZATIONS

The WOMEN'S CAMPAIGN FUND was established in 1973 and
remains the only national organization to provide financial support
and technical assistance services exclusively to female candidates.[3]
As such, it plays a unique supportive role for aspiring political
women with progressive views about women's rights and opportunities. Its bipartisan board meets frequently to review staff research on emerging campaigns, to interview female candidates who
come to Washington seeking support from national organizations,
and to determine how best to spend relatively slim resources most
effectively. Throughout the year, the Women's Campaign Fund
raises money through direct mail solicitation and a variety of fund-
raising events, with 90 percent of its contributions coming from
women. In addition to dispensing funds and hiring technical consultants for women's races, the Women's Campaign Fund functions
as a headquarters office and as a voice in Washington for female
candidates around the country, convincing other funding sources
(particularly labor unions) to contribute money to individual
women's races and facilitating introductions for female candidates
who plan to visit Washington in search of money and endorsements.

The NATIONAL WOMEN'S POLITICAL CAUCUS (NWPC) has
received the most attention of any organization formed during the
1970s to support women's advancement in politics. The caucus
aims to function in a bipartisan manner as an interest group primarily concerned with women's-rights issues and with candidates of
either major political party who support those issues. For the caucus, issues of major concern are women's access to elective and
appointive offices, and support for ERA.

According to the national office, by 1979 membership in the

caucus exceeded forty thousand members and supporters—an increase from about thirty thousand people in the middle of the decade. Approximately three-quarters of the members are Democrats, 10 percent are Republicans, with the rest not identifying with either major political party. Despite the fact that its membership is heavily Democratic, since NWPC's establishment in 1971 its leadership has come from both major political parties and from various parts of the country. Indeed, bipartisan leadership is guaranteed in caucus bylaws, which require representation among top officers from the political party opposite to the chairperson's.

The organization maintains "a real commitment to women's races," but sometimes faces "the painful issue about whether to support a good man," says a national staff member. The issue has arisen in legislative races in states that have not ratified the ERA. The largest proportion of money raised by NWPC comes through direct mail solicitations, fund-raising events, and door-to-door solicitations. The money comes largely from women, and is contributed to political campaigns through the organization's political action committees: a Campaign Support Committee that supports female candidates in statewide and federal races, and an ERA Fund, which in 1978 endorsed and supported 143 pro-ERA female and male candidates running for state legislative seats in seven states that had not ratified the Equal Rights Amendment.

The national organization will issue endorsements when local affiliates recommend them. Guidelines for endorsements are determined locally, with a favorable position on passage of ERA remaining the single issue required for endorsement, and other concerns such as abortion rights and employment issues receiving varying attention depending on local affiliates.

Local caucuses affiliated with NWPC participate in a range of campaign activities from staffing telephone banks to conducting door-to-door solicitations to sponsoring fund-raising events. Strong caucuses in such states as Iowa, Texas, Minnesota, and California have maintained a high level of activity in women's races for all levels of office throughout the decade. In 1978, for example, California's caucus was involved in fund-raising and voluntary activities in the statewide election to confirm Rose Bird's appointment as Chief Justice of the California Supreme Court, notwithstanding the fact that the candidate herself did not campaign actively because she considered it inappropriate for someone in her office to engage personally in soliciting support from special constituencies and interest groups.

By the mid-1970s the NWPC headquarters office in Washington, D.C., was receiving requests regularly from women around the country seeking assistance for their campaigns. Many asked the caucus to send prominent female politicians and entertainers to their states to make speeches and help in raising funds for their candidacies. These requests indicated not only that female candidates valued and needed support from women's groups but also that the organized women's political movement had developed a reputation for being there to provide assistance.

The caucus recognizes its responsibility, noting, in the 1978 winter issue of its newspaper *(Women's Political Times),* that as "NWPC moves into 1979, plans are already underway to see that the goal of electing more women, of giving them the tools, the money, the volunteers, and the technical advice to win is achieved." In October 1979, the caucus newspaper reported that the NWPC Administrative Committee had proposed a budget of $1.5 million for 1980 in order to "make the regional organization work, to get more women in office and the ERA ratified. . . ."

In the mid-1970s the NWPC established Republican and Democratic women's task forces to deal with partisanship issues. Both task forces promote the concepts of support for female candidates, an increase in the numbers of female delegates to the parties' national nominating conventions, and inclusion of statements supporting women's-rights policy issues in the platforms of the two major political parties. Their individual agendas are flexible and their emphases somewhat different.

The REPUBLICAN WOMEN'S TASK FORCE has focused its attention on reaching out to develop networks among Republican women. Publishing a national newsletter from Washington, D.C., the task force informs women around the country about Republican women running for office, encourages readers to send contributions directly to the campaigns, announces election results, and prints current data on Republican women's status as candidates and officeholders. While the national task force has not established its own political action committee to funnel money directly to candidates, it plays advocacy and broker roles in encouraging other political action committees to support Republican women's races. It also provides candidates with advice and introductions to the business community and other sources of direct campaign support. During Olympia Snowe's 1978 race for Congress, for example, a fund-raising event in Washington, D.C., brought in about $3,000 for the campaign. The invitation to the event was signed by several members of Congress, and the Republican Women's Task Force turned out in large numbers and encouraged other people to attend.

While the national task force has remained active all year round, local groups working cooperatively with the Republican Women's Task Force in various states operate mainly during campaign seasons. In the San Francisco area, the Women's Resource Exchange has provided funds to state legislative and local races launched by Republican women. The Southern California Republican Women's Task Force has supported women's races, including Marilyn Ryan's legislative candidacy, for which it helped her to raise $3,000 in individual contributions. In Minnesota, a GOP feminist group has been active in assisting female candidates, as are other groups in Oregon, Arizona, and elsewhere.

One incredulous candidate asked, "Why are you doing all this?" Pat Goldman, chairperson of the national task force from its inception in 1975 until 1979, believes in doing it all because she is committed to advancing women in political life. In her view, "Women are the future of the moderates and progressives in the Republican Party." Indeed, the Republican Women's Task Force evolved in the environment of a party whose numbers were diminishing and which was increasingly dominated by conservatives. Isolated within a conservative milieu, moderate Republican women have been able to use the Women's Task Force as a vehicle for identifying with the party. By the time Goldman turned over the chair of the task force to Susan McLane, then a state legislator from New Hampshire, she was able to look back over a four-year period in which she had discovered "a tremendous solidarity among women."

On the other side of the aisle, the DEMOCRATIC WOMEN'S TASK FORCE has dealt less directly with candidates for office—leaving that activity to the heavily Democratic National Women's Political Caucus—and has channeled its energies to exerting pres-

sure on the national Democratic Party for responsiveness to feminists' concerns. The Democratic Women's Task Force was established after the 1974 mid-term convention of Democrats in Kansas
City. Headed by Millie Jeffrey, who was later elected national
chairperson of NWPC, the task force served initially as a catalyst
for including women and their concerns in regional forums held for
presidential contenders. At the 1976 convention the task force
strongly advocated women's issues in deliberations with the platform and rules committees and in negotiations with candidate
Jimmy Carter regarding the promotion of women within the party
and the appointment of women to governmental positions.

In 1978 the Democratic Women's Task Force, then chaired by
Joanne Howes, was a key force in the move to require equal numbers of female and male delegates at the 1980 presidential nominating convention. Considering this an important victory for women,
Joanne Howes stresses that "running for delegate is a good beginning step in the political process." She believes that after many
more women "go through the step of getting elected as delegates,
they will move on to races for city councils and other offices because
they'll know they can win."

In addition to the rules change regarding convention delegates, the 1978 Democratic mid-term convention passed several
resolutions reaffirming issues promoted by the Democratic
Women's Task Force. These included continued support for passage of ERA and for appointing more women to high-level governmental positions. The mid-term convention delegates also agreed
on other goals: an early increase in the numbers of women in
Congress and as members of state legislatures, and a tripling of the
numbers of women holding office at all levels of government.[4]

Outside the organized partisan task forces, the issue of support
for women is a delicate one for the politically active woman with
strong partisan affiliations. Public endorsements, party loyalty, and
political self-interest complicate the issue of gender-based support.
While no hard figures have been collected on a county-by-county
and state-by-state basis, it is commonly thought within the organized women's political movement that more of its members are
Democrats than Republicans—a situation hardly surprising, since
the partisan distribution of the general population has been about

two to one Democratic. Certainly larger numbers of Democratic women ran for office in the 1970s. As to the distribution of money, by early 1979 the Women's Campaign Fund had helped candidates from both parties—79 percent of the candidates were Democrats and 21 percent were Republicans.

In general, the women's political movement supports the principle of bipartisanship, yet dilemmas often arise. Republican women frequently encounter the issue of party loyalty when an appealing Democratic woman runs. Democratic women who favor increasing the numbers of Republican women running for office face conflicts about abandoning acceptable male candidates of their own party. Both sometimes endorse a sympathetic candidate in one election season only to be faced the next time around with the dilemma of whether to abandon the incumbent's campaign because their own party demands loyalty and perhaps even offers to nominate a candidate more strongly supportive of women's-rights issues.[5] As with other potentially conflicting components of an individual's identity, one's partisan loyalties and feminist commitments may not always coexist comfortably.

Founded in 1966, the NATIONAL ORGANIZATION FOR WOMEN (NOW) became increasingly active in electoral politics as the seventies unfolded. At national and state levels, NOW developed guidelines for endorsing candidates, for providing campaigns with volunteers and services, and for contributing funds through its political action committees. NOW support has been based on ideological criteria regarding feminist issues and is available to both male and female candidates.

By 1978, NOW had established political action committees at the national level and in a number of states. The organization is interested in supporting candidates of either sex and either major political party who can demonstrate solid support for the issues which concern NOW. Support for passage of ERA and for abortion rights remains fundamental; these are issues for which NOW holds candidates accountable. In addition, it is interested in a wide range of feminist issues in the areas of civil rights, employment, education, and economic equity. The national organization distributes only a small amount of money directly to political candidates, and that goes to politicians whose track records in office with regard to feminist issues deserve acknowledgment. NOW has preferred to distribute its limited political money ($110,000 in 1978) to its own political action committees, particularly in states around the country in which ERA ratification seemed possible. In turn, NOW groups in the states organize their own local efforts to work for the election of individual candidates.

In general, "We are trying to elect people where there is a chance of winning, and we often have to turn down our own people because they don't have a chance," says a national NOW spokesperson. She also emphasizes that NOW will not desert its friends, particularly incumbents who have been loyal. A case in point was former U.S. Senator Edward Brooke of Massachusetts, who had been a "very good friend" on the abortion issue. He received $1,500 from NOW in 1978 even when his chances for victory appeared slim. "We will not oppose a solid male friend even for one of us who may decide to get in," she explains, "and at the first opportunity, we will target and go after the turncoats." A candidate like New York's Elizabeth Holtzman "would get support because she's outstanding and did so well for us on the ERA extension." But "there are lots of women running who are not supportive of women's issues," remarks a NOW officer who stresses that whether woman or man, the candidate who receives NOW support "must be a feminist."[6]

Getting women into office and advancing an agenda of women's-rights issues remain key concerns for the women's political movement. The movement faces challenges in the years ahead precisely because it has been successful in identifying a need for collective action and in creating an appetite for support which its limited resources have only begun to satisfy.

MOVEMENT DOLLARS

On the subject of hard dollars, the organized women's political movement is not well heeled compared to established political-interest groups and considering the extraordinarily high costs of American elections. Since the beginning, there has been the dilemma of how to spread slim resources among many worthwhile candidates; also, whether to target limited resources for races where the odds for winning are great or to invest heavily in highly risky races where appealing female candidates are desperate for campaign support. An enormous disparity exists between the demand and the supply.

Nonetheless, it is important to note that in the course of its first ten years, the movement has steadily increased its ability to raise money for contributions to the campaigns of women and feminist supporters. At the national level, the Women's Campaign Fund began in 1974 with $20,000 to distribute among female candidates. In 1976 the figure more than tripled to $63,000 and in 1978 it increased to $103,609. For the 1980 elections, the fund increased its contributions modestly and distributed approximately $125,000 to female candidates. In 1974, the National Women's Political Caucus gave no funds to candidates, but by 1976 the NWPC had established a political action committee for candidate support, contributing almost $25,000 to women running for office that year. In 1978, this committee gave $45,000 to female candidates seeking statewide and national offices, while at the same time the NWPC/ERA Fund gave about $350,000 to pro-ERA women and men running in unratified states.

In comparison with the amounts of money donated by business, labor, and other organized interests across the country, funds raised specifically for women's races by the feminist political movement may count for relatively little. But women candidates who receive campaign money from women's groups acknowledge emphatically how welcome that support is for their treasuries and for the morale of their campaign organizations, especially when it comes early and helps to build the credibility necessary for attracting other support. Furthermore, in some modestly budgeted campaigns where most of the money comes from small donations by individuals, the contributions from women's organizations have outweighed those received from any other single source. This was the case in Madeleine Kunin's 1978 campaign for Vermont's lieutenant governorship. In primary and general election races which cost a total of $36,500, Kunin depended most heavily on small contributions from over a thousand individual donors. Two donations totaling $2,372 in cash and services from the Women's Campaign Fund were the largest contributions she received. Kunin believes that it is "very important to have campaign organizations for women candidates."

At the state level, women's organizations have also provided money to women's campaigns. In California, for example, among the organizations contributing specifically to women's campaigns in 1976, the three making the largest donations were the local affiliate of the Republican Women's Task Force, the Women's Task Force of the Democratic State Central Committee, and the Women's Coalition, a group of feminist women of diverse ages and occupations. Even so, women's groups were not among the state's top fifty major donors. Business interests and employee groups contributed from $50,000 to $500,000 to their favorite candidates.

Women candidates acknowledge that the women's political movement has helped them with financial as well as other kinds of campaign support. In Oregon, State Representative Gretchen Kafoury said that many of her one hundred campaign volunteers emerged from her affiliations with the National Organization for Women and the Oregon Women's Political Caucus. While pursuing her own campaign in 1976, Kafoury also demonstrated her personal commitment to the women's political movement by helping other women's campaigns, including that of Jewel Lansing, for whom she not only sent a letter of solicitation for funds but also staged a fund raiser which netted about $1,400. Although Kafoury was embroiled in her own legislative race at the time, she said she felt a responsibility to raise money for Lansing because "I really felt strongly about getting her elected."

In Connecticut, the coordinator of volunteers for Gloria Schaffer's Senate race felt that the Women's Political Caucus was an important resource in the campaign. In addition to a $500 contribution from the national caucus, the Connecticut Women's Political Caucus held a fund raiser for several of its endorsees, splitting receipts among them. Schaffer's share was $2,500, and she also received several contributions from the Women's Campaign Fund totaling $5,000.

While organized support (as well as individual support) by women for women's campaigns is hardly uniform across the country, women supporting women politically is a familiar occurrence nowadays. In addition to receiving two contributions totaling $6,000 from the Women's Campaign Fund, Geraldine Ferraro's 1978 congressional race was supported by members of the Queens, New York, chapter of the National Organization for Women. In

her successful 1978 race for the lieutenant governorship of South
Carolina, Nancy Stevenson received contributions from the National Women's Political Caucus and the Women's Campaign Fund.
Locally, the state's Business and Professional Women's Clubs endorsed her race, and supporters came from a number of other
women's groups in the state. In addition, a story about her candidacy in NOW's monthly publication resulted in over $2,000 of
campaign contributions sent by individual women. "It was great to
receive those unsolicited donations," she says. While $2,000 con-
stituted only a drop in the bucket in Stevenson's $280,000 total
expenditure for the primary, runoff, and general election campaigns, the money told her that many women across the country
cared about supporting women's races.

Unquestionably, the women's political movement has begun
to stake a claim in campaign politics—with the bulk of work remaining to be done if the efforts of women's groups are to carry real
political weight nationally. While the women's movement has come
nowhere near exercising the type of influence available to business,
labor, and other interest groups which contributed over $30 mil-
lion to congressional races in 1978 alone, the birth and growth of
efforts to support female candidates has itself been a significant
event of U.S. political history in recent years.

IDEOLOGY, PRIORITIES . . .
AND CANDIDATES

There is widespread consensus about general objectives
among politically active feminists; at the same time, there is inevitable diversity in points of view about specific agendas and about the
best means for reaching particular goals. Electing more women to
public office is one agenda item, but it does not take precedence as
the top issue for all facets of the women's political movement. There
are other pressing and sometimes competing goals. In a struggle for
definition and for increased political sophistication, the women's
political movement has been grappling with its own internal differences as they affect hard decisions about priorities, which candidates to support, where to allocate slim resources, and how to be
most effective in the political arena. Unsurprisingly, there are various points of view about ideology as it relates to strategy within the

movement as well as to individual women dealing with the political realities of the districts where they are seeking office. Diversity is common in any broad social movement, whether labor, civil rights, or women's rights. As it attempts to mesh its collective interests with a wide range of political circumstances and practitioners, the women's movement no less than any other has coped with its own inevitable variety and conflicts.

At its weakest, the organized women's political movement has sometimes floundered in attempting to discover a useful balance between enthusiasm and hard realism, between the demands of ideological purity and political compromise, between talk about women's political progress and solid follow-through in commitments of time, people, and money. Sometimes it has also been in danger of remaining insular—active in its own small networks, but ineffective in forging working relationships with the flesh and blood political woman out on the campaign trail who is in need of support but judges it unwise to be vocal on feminist issues during an election season.

One female officeholder, who has been very supportive of feminist issues and who campaigned to move up to higher office in 1978, reports that early in her campaign she was invited to speak at a local NOW meeting. "Instead of knowing how to handle it," she says, "they asked me to state my position on abortion and gay rights. They should have known better than to put me on the spot in front of reporters and get all of that in the newspapers." As a result of this experience, the candidate was wary of placing herself in that type of situation again. In her view, "Either they were naïve, or they don't care if you lose so long as you agree."

In politics when idealism does not find a counterpoint in solid political realism, the result is likely to be an election-day defeat. By the end of the 1970s, more often than not the women's political movement was basing its decisions to encourage and support women aspiring to elective office on realistic assessments of each candidate's political strengths and on election-day odds. Good women who faced almost certain defeat running against popular, well-financed incumbents could not assume the women's political movement would contribute significant portions of its very limited resources to their campaigns. And while the Women's Campaign Fund and some local women's groups did function as instruments of encouragement to female candidates by investing in difficult races, as the decade wore on more and more emphasis was placed on tough political judgments about channeling support to women who had a real chance of winning. It had taken time and the trials of experience to develop the confidence needed for making these hard political decisions.

Beyond enthusiasm and endorsements, realistic activists in the women's political movement recognize their responsibility to follow through with palpable campaign support. But when that responsibility is not acknowledged or fulfilled, candidates feel resentful. As one prominent political woman complains, "We haven't been taught to close ranks. The local Women's Political Caucus people told me they thought it was great I was running, but they didn't come out and help." Sometimes there was a degree of irresponsibility or naïveté even in telling a woman it was a good idea for her to enter a race. For example, during the 1976 campaign season in Missouri, Republican state legislator Mildred Huffman was actively encouraged to enter a race for secretary of state. The statewide race made little sense to political oddsmakers because Huffman's Democratic opponent in the general election would be James Kirkpatrick, a very popular incumbent who had held the office for twelve years. He had strong support from Democrats all over what is a heavily Democratic state and had polled higher than any other member of his party in several elections. Huffman had been a valuable state legislator for feminists because she strongly supported passage of the Equal Rights Amendment in Missouri, where it was still unratified. Instead of firmly discouraging her from leaving the legislature to enter a hopeless race, a member of the Missouri Women's Political Caucus urged her to run. While the caucus endorsed Huffman's race, verbal endorsement was not followed by active support because the state caucus refused to give working or financial endorsements to any woman not running for the state legislature, where its first priority—the Equal Rights Amendment—desperately needed votes. It was a common situation in which the issue of female representation in elective office came into conflict with another feminist agenda item which had been targeted as top priority.

Huffman worked hard in her primary and general election races, but she was defeated heavily at the polls. Notwithstanding the fact that women had urged Huffman to enter the race, she herself was responsible for the decision to announce as a statewide candidate. Yet if it is important to convince women to run for elective office, it is at least equally important that women's groups be able to follow through and provide the support needed to wage campaigns. Leaving someone perched alone on a limb after having encouraged her to make the climb is unacceptable political behavior, particularly since politics is almost totally dependent on group effort and team support.

Because Bella Abzug had depended on women and worked on behalf of women's interests throughout her career in Congress, it surprised no one when she turned to the women's movement for the initial push in her U.S. Senate race. When Abzug lost the primary election by only 1 percent of the vote cast, an Abzug supporter complained that the National Women's Political Caucus had made ERA its priority when attention also should have focused on getting Abzug elected to the Senate. The candidate expressed similar feelings, obviously disappointed that she had lost the race by such a narrow margin. Seeing herself as "a product of the women's movement," she felt she had a right to expect more feminist support. Greater effort might have included turning out a larger Abzug vote on election day and exerting organized, effective pressure on influential members of the Democratic Party to support her, thereby perhaps persuading other primary candidates to drop out before election day.

When priority issues such as the Equal Rights Amendment and abortion rights do not absorb most of the resources potentially available to female candidates from the feminist women's political movement, decisions regarding which candidates should receive money and technical assistance rest heavily on the odds for winning. The more sophisticated and realistic women's political groups divide their resources among candidates who hold feminist views on women's issues and who also have a reasonable chance for election-day success. Candidates such as Mildred Huffman, whose views are sympathetic but whose electability in a particular race is doubtful, can expect more spiritual than material support. Despite the relatively small numbers of female candidates, demands for help and assumptions that it exists in abundance far outrun available supplies. Some candidates are bound to be disappointed because publicity about the women's movement has resulted in overexpectations about its ability to deliver funds and services.

Electing Women and Ratifying ERA

The women's political movement regularly has to make painful choices about the distribution of its small resources. Efforts to ratify the federal Equal Rights Amendment have had a major impact on those choices. The text of the proposed ERA is a simple statement: "Equality of rights under the law shall not be denied or abridged by the United States or by any state on account of sex." However, the battle to incorporate those words as an amendment to the Constitution of the United States has been anything but simple. It has absorbed enormous amounts of time, energy, and money.

By 1980, the ERA was still a key issue for the organized women's political movement—with thirty-five states having voted ratification, three more states needed for passage, and rescission movements active in various parts of the country. The women's political movement led a successful campaign in 1978 to win congressional approval for extending the original 1979 deadline for ratification to June 1982. But with even the legality of the extension challenged by anti-ERA forces, everywhere ERA proponents turned, they encountered the need for political strategies and resources to wage the fight for ratification.

Women running for office in states which had ratified the ERA were asked to understand that resources from national women's organizations must be funneled to elect supporters and defeat opponents—both female and male—in states where ratification was still an issue or where serious rescission efforts were underway. Within unratified states, candidates for offices which have no direct affect on passage of constitutional amendments learned not to count on the support of organized political feminists during campaign season.

Those people who comprise the organized women's political movement as well as the overwhelming majority of candidates who seek out their support favor passage of the ERA. Yet sympathetic as she may be, the individual candidate trying to win an election campaign sometimes sees the ERA as having grown into a hungry giant with an appetite for swallowing up resources which might otherwise be available to feed her race for office.

Opinions vary as to the impact of the ERA struggle on support for women's entry as candidates for elective offices. Some activists in the women's political movement believe that the ERA has served as an organizing tool which brought many women into active participation in the political system. Some feel that it has diverted money which, once the issue is settled, will be available for electing women to office. Acknowledging that the ratification campaign politicized many women who might later run for office and therefore benefit women in the long run, one hardworking fund raiser wished the issue resolved because she continually encountered people who said, "I'm putting all my women's money into ERA this year."

Acting as something of a political lightening rod, the amendment and the pressure imposed by a deadline for ratification did focus and concentrate people's concern with women's issues. Whatever the ultimate fate of ERA, it appears unlikely that there will be a halt in women's advancement as political candidates and elected officials. The questions are whether and how collective feminist resources will be used to influence and shape that advancement. According to one high-ranking member of the National Organization for Women, her organization "will continue to escalate its fund-raising efforts and educate its membership about the political process so that the mystique vanishes." In her view, NOW will always look for hard-line, strong feminist candidates of either sex who support new feminist issues as they emerge. "We'll continue to push for feminist issues that have a sharp edge," she believes.

Social Issues versus Female Representation

How critical and sharp-edged an issue is gender itself? How high on the list of priorities is the item of representation itself, of pouring resources into increasing the numbers of women winning office simply because that itself is of special importance? During the 1970s the issue of representation often was proclaimed as important in principle, and women's organizations were pleased to see women stepping forward as political candidates. When it came to setting organizational agendas and distributing sparse resources, however, very few argued successfully for representation as a top agenda item. While large organizations like the League of Women Voters, the American Association of University Women, and the Federation of Business and Professional Women's Clubs joined in support of many feminist issues and sponsored workshops to educate their membership about the political process, they stopped short of setting representation as a top priority in their national agendas.

In the women's political movement, the Women's Campaign Fund has been the only national organization to make representation *the* top priority issue. Other organizations also support male candidates who take pro-feminist positions, particularly on ratification of the ERA. In the case of ERA, women's organizations have supported men in part because they realize that they cannot yet elect enough pro-ERA women to insure ratification. Even for the Women's Campaign Fund, representation is considered in ideological terms. While all its resources are distributed to female candidates, the positions those candidates hold on feminist issues are critical in decisions about whether or not the Women's Campaign Fund supports their campaigns.

Women's groups sometimes face the dilemma of being sought after for endorsement by both female and male candidates in the same race, each espousing feminist ideologies. In campaigns against strong female candidates, male opponents sometimes use women on their campaign staffs to persuade feminist groups they are worthy of endorsement. An active feminist on a male congressional candidate's campaign staff wrote letters to feminist friends arguing his worthiness and describing him as a "political feminist who, by accident of birth . . . happens to be male." One male candidate for statewide office who did not receive the endorsement of a state women's political caucus concluded that he was the "victim of reverse discrimination."

Most women's groups deal with the matter of endorsement by establishing criteria assigning higher priority to a candidate's position on issues than to the candidate's sex. This leads to agonizing discussions and decisions regarding who is a better candidate in a man-woman contest. In 1974 the Women's Campaign Fund endorsed female candidates based on a set of general criteria related to the organization's assessment of how progressive they were. The fund's brochure stated: "Candidates receiving financial assistance will be selected from among those women who have: a progressive stand on issues affecting the quality of life and human needs, a demonstrated commitment to establishment of a more just society and a recognition of the particular concerns of women in the process of social change; the ability to conduct a vigorous professional campaign with a realistic chance of winning; a need for financial help."

Betsey Wright, who later became a member of the Women's Campaign Fund board, remembers that in 1974 she noticed that the fund did not support Barbara Mikulski in her U.S. Senate challenge to Charles Mathias, the liberal Republican incumbent. "In those days," Wright recalled, "a woman had to be more progressive than her opponent." To increase women's representation in elective office, "We're going to have to run against some good guys," says Wright, "particularly because the districts that are likely to elect progressive men are also the districts most likely to be receptive to electing women to public office." That was her attitude in 1978, when New Jersey's Marge Roukema challenged the liberal Democratic incumbent Andrew Maguire. In that year, the Women's Campaign Fund donated $500 to Roukema. By then the fund had also expanded its statement of criteria for endorsement to indicate that its board of directors would "look at a broad range of issues in assessing a candidate" and would be "particularly sensitive to her capacity for leadership and originality on issues of importance to women, the most critical of which are support of the ERA and legal abortion which is accessible to all women."

Decisions about support from women's groups often are complicated by situations in which male incumbents with good records on women's issues face female candidates who have not yet had the opportunity to establish public records of accomplishment on women's issues. Endorsement meetings also argue into the night about supporting a male candidate to whom women feel indebted and whose incumbency makes him likely to win versus the desire to endorse a female challenger. In a slightly different version of this dilemma, New York's feminist political women debated and disagreed about whether to support Lieutenant Governor Mary Anne Krupsak's gubernatorial primary challenge to Governor Hugh Carey in 1978. Carey had been a trustworthy supporter of women's issues during his first term, and he needed women's active support during a time in primary season when his popularity with voters was low and his reelection appeared far from assured. Many women chose to lie low, speaking out for neither candidate, but some prominent female politicians such as Bella Abzug and Carol Bellamy who hold solid feminist credentials found themselves on opposite sides of the fence. Among organizations in the women's political movement, the New York City chapter of NOW endorsed Carey while the New York State NOW and the Manhattan Women's Political Caucus endorsed Krupsak.

Feminist Endorsement Criteria

Women running for office have complained about the endorsement criteria used by some feminist groups, claiming that the guidelines shift unexpectedly and decision making seems fuzzy. Sometimes criteria have seemed too rigid. Conservative female candidates and candidates who view themselves as moderate but who, for example, may not support abortion rights have charged that endorsements are too tightly controlled by purist feminist liberals. Which criteria most properly define feminism? How much purism can an endorsement require? These questions have hounded the endorsement process wherever women's groups have met to discuss candidates' merits.

One women's group appointed a committee of three members to interview candidates at weekly endorsement luncheon meetings held during campaign season. An observer at these sessions noted that any suggestion of an impure feminist opinion exposed the candidate to repeated grilling on that item. At one endorsement luncheon, a state senate candidate acknowledged under questioning that her top paid staff member was a man. When asked, she also refused to commit herself regarding how many women she would appoint to her staff if elected. "When women are elected," she merely said, "they tend to appoint other women." Displeased, her questioners became more harsh. When the candidate was asked later whether she felt under attack at the meeting, she replied: "I've found in interviews I've had—labor, environmental groups, employee groups, and doctors' groups—the most difficult are women's groups. They are well informed, and the most skeptical. You would think they'd be sensitive."

Women's groups have not necessarily agreed with one another's assessments of an individual candidate. Sometimes their endorsements differ because of the extent to which a candidate's gender is the important criterion, or because of relative loyalties to political party ties and local powers, or because the definition and distinguishing characteristics of feminism vary among women's groups. At one extreme of the women's-rights movement, radical feminists will endorse no candidate for public office because they feel involvement in the established electoral process itself necessitates a corruption of principles. At the other end of the ideological spectrum, such a conservative candidate as Maryland's Congresswoman Marjorie Holt resents not receiving the endorsement of the state's Women's Political Caucus despite her unsupportive position on basic feminist issues.

Near the midpoint on the spectrum the situation is murkier, as it was in Connecticut when two major feminist organizations disagreed on the endorsement of Gloria Schaffer's U.S. Senate race. In its statement endorsing Schaffer, the Connecticut Women's Political Caucus said that "she has consistently supported feminist goals. For example, she has spoken out forcefully for day care for working mothers, provided invaluable support during the campaigns for ratification of both the Federal and State ERAs, indicated by the introduction of election reform legislation the need to open the political process to women at the highest levels, and publicly stated her support for the Supreme Court opinion on abortion."

These strong feelings of support by the caucus were not echoed by the Connecticut National Organization for Women that year. Early in 1976, Schaffer had requested an endorsement from NOW, which prompted the state organization to hold a lengthy meeting to decide on its endorsement policy. Changes in tax laws governing political endorsements by nonprofit organizations had just recently enabled NOW to make endorsements, which accounted for the situation of its having no general policy or tradition for endorsements.

Connecticut's NOW decided not to endorse Schaffer. Alice Chapman, the organization's state coordinator in 1976, explained, "We are very timid about making endorsements, and decided we would only endorse feminists. Gloria Schaffer is supportive of feminist issues, but she is not a feminist." To illustrate that Schaffer was not a feminist, Chapman cited Schaffer's critical attitude toward feminist events, particularly the controversial event entitled "Alice Doesn't Day" when NOW asked women to strike by not performing their customary duties and services at home and at work. Chapman continued, "How can we be fair to men who give us 100 percent support if we then turn our backs on them and support a woman? This doesn't encourage men to be feminists." The "100 percent" referred to ratings given by national NOW on the voting performance of incumbents in Congress. Senator Lowell Weicker, Schaffer's opponent, was one of only a few officials to receive a 100 percent rating.

In her U.S. Senate race, Gloria Schaffer's own attitude toward the women's movement had been a cautious one. According to the only active feminist on her campaign staff, Schaffer would appear at functions of the Women's Political Caucus when other candidates would not, but "she has been very careful not to say too much about abortion" even though she was frequently asked about it. She replied that Senator Weicker's and her positions on abortion were the same, making it not an issue. Schaffer's staff did not wish to surround her or identify her heavily with feminists. Nonetheless, Schaffer did seek the support of organized women's groups, and she supported the issues which had been identified as "women's issues."

Ideology versus Reality

Sometimes it seems as if there have been more stringent applications of feminist criteria to female candidates than to their male opponents. It is as if women expect other women to know better and to behave according to purer standards simply because they are women. Unsurprising, this type of implied double standard is predictable among any strong partisans who expect more loyalty and discipline from one of their own group than from a sympathetic outsider. Equally understandable is the woman candidate's point of view that simply because she is a woman her candidacy should earn points toward endorsement from women's groups. At the extremes, she asks them to treat a woman's candidacy as a top priority for endorsement, and they ask her to embrace feminism as a dominant ideology shaping her positions on issues. Political and social realities indicate that most women will not be bound to support only other women for office, while conversely, overly stringent requirements for ideological purity will result in few candidates for endorsement.

Bella Abzug is a national feminist leader, a woman genuinely supportive of advancing women's opportunities and status. On behalf of women's rights, she has sponsored legislation to eliminate sex discrimination, contributed time and energy working for feminist goals, and subjected herself to risk and even ridicule in speaking up for women. Serving as an example, her courage and commitment have inspired many women to seek out new challenges. Abzug's public life has made a difference for women across the country. Not many public officials can claim such an impact. It is precisely because Abzug is who she is that the political realities of her experience as a candidate are noteworthy. When Abzug formally declared her candidacy for the U.S. Senate in the spring of 1976, she opened campaign headquarters—and she hired a man to manage her campaign. Abzug supports women and has hired many women on her congressional and campaign staffs. As a candidate for high-level office, she needed support from women, and she received it; but she also needed credibility with the press, access to influential people, and an image that would prove she was not anti-male. In dealing with her feminism as well as the hard facts of political candidacy, she made compromises. Sometimes they dealt awkwardly with women loyal to her, in this case the woman who had done all the campaign work for a year prior to Abzug's formal announcement of candidacy. The will to win recognizes the rules of an old game, while loyalty to feminism recognizes the responsibility to provide opportunities for women. Today's female candidates frequently find themselves caught between these two compelling and often incompatible demands.

Recognizing that rigid adherence to nonnegotiable ideologies sows dissension and reaps defeat, effective political women operate as realists. They know that politics at its best is a matter of compromise; that no one wins nominations and elections, stays in office, and moves on to positions of influence and power on the basis of one set of issues and one group of supporters. They know the value of teams, coalitions, and diversified support.

Apathy and inactivity would be worrisome omens for the organized women's political movement. By contrast, lively and even contentious debate about priorities and strategies often signifies development and growth. Following the enthusiastic—usually clear and simple—opening stage of any movement, the tensions which develop are largely signs of health. They signal the inevitable emergence of complexities—neither surprising nor unwanted in any situation of real social change. The key point is that within a few short years, the women's movement arrived on the political scene and took strides forward in supporting the campaigns of women seeking elective office. The tests for the future are how useful the movement will be to individual women's races, and whether it will continue to develop by using to conscious advantage its own diversity to further women's representation in politics. From the point of view of female candidates, there is no doubt but that greater collective political strength among women is needed. At the same time the very existence of collective resources and the ever-increasing demand for them are evidence that something remarkable has been happening to women's awareness of their own rights and their stake in electoral politics.

Chapter 8
The Larger Context

*The national wish to return to the good old days works against elected
women and women seeking office* because *they represent change.*
—Rosemary Ahmann,
former Olmsted County Commissioner,
Minnesota

It takes a woman to think woman first.
—Sandra Smoley, County Supervisor,
Sacramento, California

In the larger electoral context outside feminist political organizations, reactions to the women's-rights movement span the poles
from extreme opposition to warmest support. Spillover effects, both
direct and indirect, attest perhaps better than anything else to feminism's powerful influence on various sectors of the society. In both
women's and men's campaigns during the 1970s the women's-
rights movement became a complicated issue—really a tangle of
separate issues lumped together and jeeringly called "women's lib"
by detractors or proudly proclaimed as "feminism" by supporters.
At times these supporters even included opposing female and male
candidates each vying for the title of best local feminist.[1] Most
often, however, women's rights were treated as a set of related
issues covering a wide range of demands, some of which could be
supported safely in some districts, and some of which politicians
could support publicly almost nowhere in the country.

Among the many reactions to the women's-rights movement, two have important consequences for female political candidates. One is generally negative—a backlash response to feminist issues. The other is largely positive—widespread support among individual women everywhere for women in politics.

BACKLASH

The greatest external impact of the contemporary feminist political movement has been to create a climate of acceptance for the idea of women holding office. It is a critical contribution. But while the general public has accepted the belief that wider opportunities should be available to women in politics and other nontraditional activities, society at large has yet to adopt women's-rights issues as top-priority concerns. On the other side, increasingly vocal political forces have focused negatively on some women's-rights issues in order to oppose what they consider to be destructive social change. Insofar as individual political candidates are seen as linked to feminist issues or organizations, their races sometimes have been subject to special scrutiny and challenge. By the mid-seventies, a number of women campaigning, particularly liberals and progressives, were forced to contend with this new by-product of women's struggle for equality—a backlash comprised of people who view the women's-rights movement as part of a threat to valued traditions and social customs.

The challenge for liberal female candidates with feminist inclinations has been to steer clear of appearing suspect in their support of fundamental American values. While liberal male candidates also must handle conservative opposition, some political women believe that it is easier for men to avoid the controversial issues specifically associated with the feminist movement. As one seasoned political woman explains, for example, "Male politicians aren't comfortable with the abortion issue, and it's easier for them to stay away from it." She is convinced that the abortion issue is stronger for women because "we get pregnant—people think of it when they see women, and throughout the country women have been fighting a battle about it."

Indeed, during a time when women's rights have become a visible and often controversial social issue, a female candidate is almost bound to encounter questions related to her sex and to feminist issues even when she considers them irrelevant to her credentials for public office and to her platform on public policy issues. As political realists, women running for office try to avoid being pigeonholed because they know that their success and effectiveness in the public world depend on broad-based support and a grasp of diverse issues. But they also face up to the fact that being female means being seen as a "politician who is a woman," and that during campaign season some feminist issues are apt to come up, as are antifeminist reactions.

Most female candidates stress that they are running as qualified office seekers—not as women. While they are loath to label themselves "feminists," they are concerned about a broad range of issues which usually include some considered as being women's issues. Responses to the inevitable questions often sound like this one from a municipal councilwoman in New Jersey: "I don't think of myself as a real strong feminist, but certainly I am for the ERA, and I believe in a woman's right to choose, and the society does have to face the fact of inequities in salaries, and in appointments to government agencies."[2] Former State Assemblywoman Greta Kiernan of New Jersey, a woman who has been sympathetic to the women's movement but does not consider herself formally identified with it, remarked to a reporter, "I'm not a feminist, I'm a 'personist.'"[3]

Call themselves what they might, on the issue of "women," female candidates walk through a minefield, never knowing when a seemingly mild reference, or a personal decision to retain one's own professional name, or an old speech dredged up by the opposition will set off headline explosions. For example, Arizona's U.S. Senate aspirant Carolyn Warner played down any feminist leanings during her 1976 primary campaign out of fear that feminism would cost her votes. She campaigned as a businesswoman, wife, mother, and administrator who had reduced paperwork and increased efficiency during her first two years as state superintendent of education. She ran as a fiscal conservative and a humanist. She played up her image as a wife and the mother of a large, happy family whose members—dressed in red, white, and blue—were working in her campaign. Warner's support of such issues as the Equal Rights Amendment was so muted that she did not get enthusiastic backing from the state's feminists, who wanted a louder voice speaking for them in an unratified state. They were worried that she would not be a leader on the issue.

Nonetheless, when Warner did make a mild feminist-sounding remark, the reaction was fast and furious. During a campaign speech to a businesswomen's group, Warner noted that all members of the U.S. Senate were male, and suggested, "It's time a qualified woman was elected to the Senate." Her chief opponent, Dennis DeConcini, retaliated by charging that "a political campaign has reached a new low when a candidate finds it necessary to appeal to race, religion or sex." That story made page one of the state's largest newspaper, *The Arizona Republic,* with the headline "DeConcini says Mrs. Warner begs election because of sex."

For those who had watched Warner's careful maneuvering around feminist issues, the headline could not have been more ironic. Warner's husband, a key staff member of her campaign, commented, "She just said it was time we had a qualified woman in the Senate. She didn't even say it should be herself. I don't call that pleading for votes. Carolyn has never, ever pushed the feminine aspect of her role. She has been hard-hitting, and her campaign has dealt with the issues—such as government bureaucracy, Arizona's water shortage, and solar energy." Indeed, Warner had been an issue campaigner. She lost the election to DeConcini by twenty thousand votes.

If one's predominant motive in running is to be elected, rather than to use the campaign to talk about feminist issues, whether one should emphasize such issues depends very much on the nature of the district. In Oregon during 1976 Maxine Hays, a 48-year-old Republican, was unexpectedly defeated in her bid for a nomination to seek a legislative seat. In her role as national president of the 170,000-member Federation of Business and Professional Women's Clubs (BPW), Hays had been active nationally on behalf of women's issues. Despite the fact that BPW placed passage of the Equal Rights Amendment as a top priority, Hays deliberately chose not to campaign on any women's issues in her largely conservative district. She had reason to be cautious. A week before the election she appeared on a radio talk show where she candidly answered a caller's question about the ERA by stating "I wholeheartedly endorse it." The answer brought a raft of angry phone calls. In an upset, she lost the primary to her male opponent, who was a political unknown.

As in Carolyn Warner's defeat in Arizona, there is no hard evidence for determining whether Hays' feminist proclivities—her presidency of BPW and her pro-ERA position—contributed to a significant loss of votes. There are simply shared campaign experiences from women across the country running for all levels of office. In recent years these experiences reveal the ways in which the "woman's issue" has been used, confused, and sometimes made to seem dangerous.

Insofar as feminism is perceived as controversial, candidates are wary about close association with its visible spokespersons, and they ask—sometimes explicitly, often implicitly—that activist feminists understand their motivations and deal sensitively with their precarious situations. Mutual understanding and sensitivity seem likely to benefit everyone in the long run, as was the case in a Nevada campaign. Concerned that antifeminist opposition would attempt to make her look like a "radical woman" because she had led Nevada's delegation to the National Women's Conference in 1977, Jean Ford was careful to keep her 1978 state senate race separate from an ERA referendum campaign. Her support for feminist issues was solid, and she assumed—as did many other political women in the 1970s—that she could make a greater contribution to the community as an elected official than as a defeated candidate. As a result of her successful race, Ford was the one woman serving in Nevada's senate at the end of the decade.

As differentiated from an antiwoman vote to keep female candidates out of public office, the antifeminist vote is tied to specific issues rather than to gender per se. In the 1970s these issues covered a range of subjects. Beginning with the Equal Rights Amendment and abortion rights, controversy also raged about issues of publicly supported child care, divorce laws and alimony rights, military service for women, veterans' preference in civil service employment, and other issues associated with the women's-rights movement. When a candidate was linked to a liberal position on these matters, she or he became vulnerable to special attack from a vocal opposition. Some political women were able to win elections despite these attacks; others were not.

In Minnesota, a candidate defeated for the state senate in 1976 had gone on record supporting the Supreme Court decision on abortion. It was a political judgment she made knowing that there was heated controversy in her district over a family-planning clinic.

Her campaign workers were told by voters that they had received calls in which the caller had said, "Oh, you're in favor of her. She's an abortionist." Her campaigners also said that some volunteers refused to hold coffee parties for her after receiving threats. Some early supporters who had accepted her lawn signs claimed they were being harassed and said, "Please, I'm going to vote for you, but take down the lawn sign."

Two other state legislative candidates in Minnesota's 1976 elections worked hard to keep their support of feminist issues out of public debate—one because she feared that if women's rights became a focal point in the campaign, her race would be hurt by it; the other because she felt that the typical voter in her district would have trouble understanding her feminist perspective. The latter candidate believed that many voters would not know what the Equal Rights Amendment was about, and that the best strategy was for her to get elected and then try to educate the electorate. Both candidates' attitudes and strategies are typical of the ways in which women sympathetic to promoting women's rights and opportunities often choose to handle themselves during campaigns.

Candidates committed to women's issues themselves, who feel it would be political folly to emphasize subjects like the ERA or abortion during election season, tend to express their feminism quietly to safe audiences. For the most part, they keep feminist leanings underground unless someone specifically asks. With reference to what she called her "back-door approach," one candidate remarked, "My election would be much more evidence of what equal rights can mean than ten speeches." In general, effective political women are realists. While many express a genuine, even profound idealism about the principles and functions of a democracy, as politicians they know that idealism must be directed through a filter of pragmatism in order to further instrumental goals.

Organized Right-Wing Opposition

Yet even pragmatic political women cannot always survive heavy, direct attacks when right-wing groups make a special point of targeting candidates for defeat by "exposing" liberal positions on controversial matters. The opposition, which has steadily increased its level of energy since the mid-1970s, is concerned about a variety of domestic- and foreign-policy items. Among those re-

ceiving greatest attention have been some issues initially advanced
by the women's-rights movement. Positions advocated by feminists
are viewed by ultraconservative forces as inimical to social stability.
While not yet top priority for society in general, feminist issues
have served as red flags which right-wing leaders have used to rouse
and organize support. In the minds of some antifeminists, being for
the Equal Rights Amendment means being for abortion, and both
are viewed as related to a spate of ancient shibboleths, including
atheism, homosexuality, familial decay, child neglect, and so on. In
response to a journalist's question about why his antiabortion group
had begun active opposition to the ERA, Paul Brown, director of
the Life Amendment Political Action Committee, was quoted as
saying, " 'If women have equality, what will happen to the unborn
child?' "[4]

The one subject initially raised by the women's-rights movement which excites more reaction than any other is abortion rights,
about which controversy has continued to grow. One of the most
divisive social issues of recent times, it has affected campaign politics from the presidential level down to the smallest local races.
Most political candidates of both sexes try to avoid the topic, but
more and more often it is thrust upon them by organized opponents
of legalized abortion. "I know that's what did it," says Iowa's
Minette Doderer in assessing her primary election defeat in 1978.
Doderer had served in elective office for almost fifteen years, first
as a member of Iowa's lower house in the legislature, and from
1969 to 1978 as a state senator. One of a handful of women to hold
a leadership position as a state legislator, in 1978 she announced
her statewide campaign for lieutenant governor.

Minette Doderer had always been supportive of the women's-
rights movement, joining the Women's Political Caucus, the National Organization for Women, and the Women's Equity Action
League as well as holding membership in more traditional women's
organizations like the League of Women Voters and the Business and
Professional Women's Clubs. But neither feminism per se nor Doderer's specific affiliations were matters of emphasis in her statewide
campaign. In fact, the campaign ran smoothly until the issue of abortion was raised in the last three weeks before election day. In poll
results announced by the *Des Moines Register* the week before the
election, Doderer had a narrow lead over Bill Palmer, her Demo-

cratic primary opponent and a colleague in the state senate who supported the right-to-life position on abortion.

On the last weekend of the campaign, a group called Iowans for Right to Life distributed approximately sixty thousand pamphlets in churches around the state, most of them Catholic churches. In some churches, the pamphlet was inserted in the Sunday program; in others, it was placed behind windshield wipers on cars parked in church lots during services. The pamphlet, illustrated with a picture of a fetus, contained the message: "This little guy wants you to vote on June 6 so he can live. Vote for Bill Palmer." Leaving the impression that Minette Doderer donned surgical gloves and herself performed abortions, the pamphlet referred to her as a "leading abortionist" in the state.

In addition to the church distribution, a massive mailing in the state asked voters how they felt about abortion—whether they thought babies should be killed, and whether citizens should be paying the costs of abortions.

Minette Doderer had not been an outspoken advocate of abortion. She had responded carefully to questions raised about abortion rights by saying that she was not in favor of empowering the government to make those kinds of decisions about citizens' private lives. She believes she did not mince words over the years on the issue, but she says that her reputation was not attached to it and that it hardly arose at meetings she addressed until the "last-minute scare tactic" shot it into the campaign. Voters interviewed at polling places on election day were quoted as saying, "I voted *against* Doderer," more often than "I voted *for* Palmer," according to Doderer. She believes that a negative tactic produced a negative vote. One of Doderer's supporters said that a woman told her, "I didn't vote for her." When the supporter asked why not, the voter replied, "Because I got that pamphlet and I didn't know anything else about her."

In the statewide race, Doderer's $30,000 campaign received $2,000 from the Women's Campaign Fund and $300 from the Iowa Women's Political Caucus. Feminist groups did not work very hard on the campaign "because they all thought I was okay," says Doderer. The last-minute attack took everyone by surprise.

On June 6, Minette Doderer lost her primary race by approximately 3 percent of the vote cast. On the night after the election, she told reporters that the "abortion issue did it to me" because she wanted to warn other candidates about a situation they might well be facing. She says that the right-to-life group did indeed take credit for her defeat.

In many campaigns, opposition or support from a well-organized single-issue constituency can turn out to be a significant factor in the race. This is true even when the issue itself has little or nothing to do with the duties or powers of the office a candidate is seeking, as was the case regarding abortion rights in Doderer's bid for the lieutenant governorship. By 1980 the right-to-life movement had developed considerable clout in single-issue politics across the country. It had even polled the fourth highest number of votes in New York's 1978 gubernatorial election, consequently winning status as a recognized political party within the state. As a result of the 1978 elections, in which New York's Right to Life Party polled almost 131,000 votes, the state's ballot for future elections listed the Right to Life Party above the Liberal Party, which won only 123,457 votes in 1978.

Of course, antiabortion groups often sustain defeats themselves in districts where they are weak or poorly organized or find little incentive to spend resources supporting any of a field of candidates who are all relatively unsympathetic to their position. Such was the case, for example, in a New Jersey legislative district during the 1979 elections, where one-term Democratic incumbent Barbara McConnell won a tough reelection race in a traditionally Republican district despite opposition from those who abhorred her liberalism regarding abortion. Never underestimating the potential damage an organized right-to-life effort could inflict on her candidacy, McConnell conducted an intense, highly effective professional campaign that built in all possible safeguards against surprise attacks. Aware of her vulnerability on the abortion controversy, McConnell took it very seriously throughout the campaign even though her Republican opposition did not offer right-to-life interests a clear ideological alternative on the issue. In addition to reaping the rewards of careful planning and organization, McConnell also benefited from her solid reputation as a knowledgeable and respected politician who had been an outstanding first-term legislator. "If you anticipate the problem, organize, and never take anything for granted," says McConnell, "you can survive these attacks."

It seems to be more and more important for political candidates to be alert and prepared for possible opposition from energetic special-interest groups. Former Congresswoman Martha Keys of Kansas concurs with Minette Doderer in believing that moderate and liberal political candidates are facing increasingly potent challenges from well-financed negative campaigns conducted by coalitions of arch-conservative single-issue groups. After serving in the U.S. House of Representatives for two terms, Keys was defeated in the 1978 general election by a Republican opponent whom she describes as "a candidate marketed by right-wing groups." Noting that his campaign expenditure was $340,000 compared with her $125,000, she says that no one had ever spent that kind of money in her congressional district, and that his resources came from the new right-wing movement across the country which utilizes sophisticated computerized fund-raising techniques operated by direct mail experts like Richard Viguerie.*

The campaign against Keys stressed six or seven negative issues which were called to voters' attention through what Keys describes as a series of "lies and distortions." Among these issues was the question of her district and continued residence in Kansas after she married a congressman from Indiana, the issue of veterans' preference in federal hiring, and the abortion issue. With regard to veterans' preference, Keys was charged with voting to eliminate veterans' preference in federal hiring, which she describes as a "lie" since the issue never arose that way in the Congress. Even after one of the state's leaders of a veterans organization came to her defense, the opposition continued to distort her position on this. Keys says that the issue of abortion was used as a "subterranean issue underneath the surface of the campaign." Right-to-life leaflets were distributed in the parking lots of Catholic churches during the last two weekends before election day despite the protests of a church leader who repudiated any connection between the church and a group called Catholics for a Pro-Family Congress. According to Keys, in addition to doing extensive leafleting in the district, the group conducted a direct mail campaign targeted at two heavily Catholic rural counties away from media centers. "While it was not the only factor, it was one of the negative issues that took a toll," says Keys of a race which she lost with about 49 percent of the vote.

Keys is concerned about the "marketing approach" to elec-

---

*The Viguerie Company of Falls Church, Virginia, specializes in mailing lists for conservative causes and candidates.

tions and about the right wing's ability to raise substantial funds through massive direct mail techniques. Funds are raised nationwide and then channeled into districts where liberal and moderate candidates can be opposed with extraordinarily expensive and aggressive media campaigns. In that type of politics, women have little chance of increasing their numbers in public office. While Martha Keys believes that the 1978 campaign to unseat her was not motivated by a plan necessarily to oppose women and that male politicians are equally subject to serious opposition from organized reactionary groups, she does stress that women particularly are unable to compete with the kind of money that was used to defeat her. Concluding that public financing of campaigns is the key to increasing the numbers of women in electoral politics, the former congresswoman states that "public financing is the most important step we can take to bring wild spending and the marketing approach under control."

The women's-rights movement and the organized antifeminist backlash have been confronting each other on a range of issues and in a variety of political arenas. In 1977 a great deal of energy from both sides went into influencing the outcome of the National Women's Conference in Houston. The national plan of action ultimately adopted in Houston reflected the feminist perspective on issues related to women's lives. In 1979 and 1980 both sides were involved in the White House Conference on Families, with antifeminist groups (identifying themselves as "pro-family") representing positions "against ratification of the proposed equal rights amendment, legalized abortions, feminism in all forms and access for teenagers to contraception and sex education in the schools" and describing themselves "as 'grass roots,' and as religious."[5]

The women's-rights movement has developed ties with some liberal and progressive political groups; the antifeminists are linked to groups at the opposite end of the political spectrum. Nadine Brozan's *New York Times* January 1980 report about a schism between factions preparing for the White House Conference on Families notes that "apart from ideological disagreement, the moderates are also critical of the ties between the 'pro-family' movement and what is often referred to as the political 'new right,' an ultraconservative movement favoring drastic reduction in the role of government." She quotes an active member of several antifeminist organizations on the issue of the federal government: " 'It interferes by increasing inflation. That makes it necessary for women to leave their homes to go to work and makes them abrogate the roles they really want as wives and mothers. Then the government uses the fact that they are in the work force to create day care. Day care is powerful. A program that ministers to a child from six months to six years has over eight thousand hours to teach beliefs and behavior. The family should be teaching values, not the government or anyone in day care.' "[6]

Whereas political feminists favor increasing the numbers of female candidates as a matter of principle, right-wing groups appear largely unconcerned about recruiting women to seek office. For both sides, however, support or opposition in campaigns depends on the candidates' positions on issues. The twist in the knot for female candidates is this: among the increasing numbers of women who now see themselves as political candidates, many are liberals encouraged to seek office in a climate of opportunity created by contemporary feminism. When confronted by an opposition aiming to punish liberal candidates, these women probably are more vulnerable than men. As a new group of political contenders, women in politics generally have less protected, rooted strength in the established system to hold them in place during heavy attack from an active opposition.

WOMEN SUPPORTING WOMEN

On the positive side, as a result of the feminist movement, individual women of all types are supporting other women in an arena which a short decade earlier had been accepted by nearly everyone as the exclusive territory of men. From the woman on the street to women in the political parties who support female candidates to the women elected to public office who pull others along into politics, a woman's consciousness is finding a variety of ways to express itself in campaign politics.

Before she was sworn into office in 1979, Congresswoman-elect Geraldine Ferraro said, "When I win again, I'd like to bring some more women with me." And New York's Carol Bellamy explains, "I like to support and endorse competent candidates, but at this point a woman is going to have a better chance. I'm willing to make many more accommodations for a female candidate than a man at this point."

On election night 1978 in Iowa, when it was clear that Minette Doderer had lost her statewide primary race, some of the young, college-aged women who had worked hard and enthusiastically on her campaign broke down and cried. "They went to pieces," Doderer recalls. They told her they had lost faith in politics. They were going to give it up. The candidate's own feelings were also raw, but she held herself in check and told them, "I didn't run so you could quit!"

Quite the opposite. Doderer, Bellamy, Ferraro, and many other political women are teaching by message and example important lessons about participation. Whether they encounter opposition to their liberalism, to their advocacy of specific women's-rights issues, or simply to their presence as candidates; whether they have more or less campaign support from established political interests, or even from the organized women's political movement; whether they win or lose—everywhere they run for office, they bring some new women into politics with them, and they inspire other women to discover a new identification with the political process because of them. Women supporting women—a theme which has found strong expression because of the women's-rights movement—is important to the story of women's life in electoral politics.

In addition to the publicized activity of women's organizations and feminist leaders willing to endorse female candidates, there are individual gestures which indicate a consciousness among political women of each other's needs, and there is evidence of keen interest and support among female citizens everywhere. Individual gestures such as that made by Sandra Richards, who received a $700 contribution from the House Democratic Caucus in Oregon during her successful legislative race in 1976—she returned $200 of it earmarked for the campaign of Joyce Cohen, another legislative candidate. Keen interest and support such as that cited by Madelene Van Arsdell's campaign manager in describing the candidate's 1976 reelection campaign for the Arizona state senate—"Organized women are a minor factor in her race," said Van Arsdell's manager, "but women *are* her campaign." A one-term incumbent and a Democrat in a targeted Republican district, Van Arsdell was defeated by a Republican businessman despite an intensive door-to-door campaign on her part. "Of the hours spent in this campaign," reported her manager, "95 percent are woman-hours." She explained, "That's not because we only do things during the daytime when some women might be free. Men will come to the campaign meetings, tell us the way to the beach, and disappear. Mostly we need volunteers for canvassing, and we've had about fifty. Almost all of them are women."

In Clemson, South Carolina, a small town of seven thousand, Catherine Smith had been a member of the city council for eight years and had decided not to run again in 1974. Five days before the municipal elections, a group of young women in their thirties approached her and convinced her to consider the mayoralty. Since it was too late to file for the race, they asked if she would accept the position if she won on a write-in vote. She agreed and overnight they organized enough support to give her a two-to-one margin of victory on the write-in. A woman in her sixties, Smith was serving in her third term as mayor of Clemson at the end of the decade.

Scratch a woman and you find a woman who knows she is a woman. That is what has been most significant about the various kinds of support women have been giving each other recently in campaign politics. Because the amount of women's direct financial contributions has not been overwhelming and because women collectively have not surged forward to achieve revolutionary transformations in the political system or in women's levels of representation, it is easy to miss a common theme arising from incidents and anecdotes told by women campaigning in all types of election districts. They describe instances of moral support and enthusiasm, active involvement in campaigns as workers, volunteer efforts to organize voters, ballot support on election day, and a new interest in politics and political issues related to a sense that perhaps women can bring something special to government.

After her successful statewide race in 1978, Vermont's Madeleine Kunin said, "I got more positive than negative feeling on the street because I was a woman." Kunin recalls that during one of her campaign visits to the northern part of Vermont, the boss at a lumber company stated that he believed more women should be in politics because they would make the system better. Demurring, Kunin remarked, "We can't blame it all on men." "Yes we can.

They'd blame it on us!'' exclaimed an elderly woman standing nearby.

During Kunin's campaign for lieutenant governor, many women—especially middle-aged and older women—went "through a kind of ritual with me, saying 'I'm not a women's libber, or one of those.' Then they'd come through very strongly in support of me *as* a woman, and often they'd be anti-male." In Kunin's estimation, women running for office have acquired "symbolic importance" for female voters. She does not have a breakdown by sex of people who voted for her in 1978, but she says that her victory as a Democrat had to be supported by many Republicans and Independents who crossed over to elect her to office with a Republican governor. While she received over 50 percent of the vote on general election day, the Democratic candidate for governor received only about 30 percent.

Kunin's observations are echoed by other candidates. Commonly they express the view that women are interested in supporting other women—particularly with their votes. According to a *New York Times* poll, for example, four out of every ten women voted for Bella Abzug in New York's 1976 Senate primary, while only three men did. For Daniel Patrick Moynihan, her major opponent in the primary, the ratio was reversed. Attempts to collect evidence documenting signs of gender-based voting have been meager to date, but many women running for office believe that there are indications of a women's vote for women. Some of it has begun to be realized in recent elections; much more of it may be waiting to be tapped. "It was said that women wouldn't vote for a woman, but as women felt better about themselves, they could vote for women," says Los Angeles City Councilwoman Pat Russell.

Support for women by women has even outweighed party loyalties—a difficult potential conflict. In the voting booth, one's decision can remain a private matter, but it has to be handled with the utmost care in the glare of public spotlights by political practitioners, whose partisan credentials are subject to scrutiny. In Oregon, many people believe that Republican Norma Paulus could not have been elected secretary of state in 1976 without the ballot-box support of Democratic women. As a state legislator, Paulus was known as having played a significant role in Oregon's passage of the Equal Rights Amendment, in reform of the state's divorce laws and passage of legislation banning sex discrimination in credit. Her actions earned her the backing of Democratic female colleagues in the legislature. Although none was willing to endorse her campaign publicly, some did support it privately.

The extent to which Democratic women crossed party lines to vote for Paulus in the general election is unknown, as no polling data were taken. But in a state where Democrats have a 281,000 voter registration edge, and in a race where Republican Paulus won 60 percent of the general election vote, it is assumed that women were crossing over to pull the lever for her. Norma Paulus herself is convinced that crossover voting by women was "very significant" in her victory.

Active support from veteran partisan women within a candidate's party has also been an important sign of the times, signaling an interest among women in women's leadership and the development of political women's networks. In 1976 when Bella Abzug, who was holding a relatively secure seat in the lower house of the Congress, decided to give it up and enter the New York Democratic primary race for a U.S. Senate nomination, she took a big risk and sustained an agonizingly close defeat. Her decision to seek what would have been an important victory for women was reinforced by her conviction that women ought to be represented in the nation's highest lawmaking body, and by her knowledge that many women would be on her side. Perhaps the single largest campaign contribution made by women came from those who were old hands in local partisan politics, who took pride and satisfaction in being able to organize substantial support for a woman they admired.

From the very beginning, the Abzug campaign had called upon the Women's Division of the Democratic Party in New York to provide county contacts and county coordinators. The Women's Division Steering Committee, which endorsed Abzug, also supplied the campaign with the list of fifteen hundred women who attended their most recent state conference. Letters were sent by the campaign to these women asking them to contribute money and to participate in a variety of ways.

In general it "was very easy to get upstate supporters among women, but not among men," said one of Abzug's organizers. The campaign made it a policy to have a male and female co-chairperson in every county. Nonetheless, three-quarters of the counties were in fact organized by women. The women were Democratic Party women, some of whom had run for local offices. Since many of the upstate New York counties are controlled by the Republican Party, and because the Democratic Party was receptive to women running in losing races, an impressive number of upstate Democratic women had experience as candidates. It was experience they brought to organizing for Bella Abzug.

In one county, women's political experience and support won a major victory for Abzug. Erie County in upstate New York is the home of the city of Buffalo. It is also the home of Joseph Crangle, a Democratic Party leader and chief supporter of Daniel Moynihan, Abzug's main rival in the primary campaign. In Erie County there is also a "female boss" in the Democratic Party. The "boss," Irene Drajem, founded the Greater Democratic Women's Club in the 1950s and has been its only president ever since. She claims the club has a membership of 750 women, who "usually go along with me. They know I would only support good candidates. I didn't have any opposition."

Drajem had worked cooperatively with Joe Crangle within the party and was state committeewoman from her assembly district. But she had a falling out with Crangle when he neglected to give her "girls" some jobs, in particular when he reneged on an offer he had made to her. "He couldn't push me around," she said.

Two years before, Drajem had helped to elect Mary Anne Krupsak as lieutenant governor of New York. Considering Krupsak a friend, she was receptive when the lieutenant governor asked her to assist Abzug's race. She had already heard Abzug speak and had been impressed with her.

To help Abzug's campaign, Drajem recruited the women in her Democratic Women's Club to look up phone numbers of registered party members and call them. She claims 475 women made forty thousand phone calls in the three weeks preceding the election. Bella Abzug won Erie County by several hundred votes. It was claimed as a major victory.

Seasoned political practitioners like Irene Drajem are potentially formidable allies. Their presence can serve as a source of encouragement for women seeking office. As political realists, they know the rules of the game and are willing to play accordingly. They pay their debts, remember broken promises, trust their lead-

ers, value loyalties, and work in a highly coordinated, tightly organized manner. Women with Drajem's stature and strength are still
few and far between in party politics. But those few who are scattered across the country in counties with strong party organizations
can be helpful partners for female candidates without a long history
of relationship to local parties.

It makes a big difference to have team support at the very
earliest stages of a candidacy. Men often have been invited to run
for office by those in positions to influence the selection of nominees. Political women are beginning to seek out their own potential nominees, thus supporting each other at a critical and sensitive
point in women's development as candidates—the moment of decision to compete in the electoral process.

Ruth Shack, a member of Florida's Dade County commission,
recalls the circumstances which launched her successful candidacy.
An incumbent on the commission was indicted, and Shack received
several phone calls from women legislators whom she had supported and for whom she had worked. They asked if she wanted
her name submitted for appointment to the unexpired term. Saying
"Yes," Shack also decided she would run for the seat in the next
election. While Shack did not get the appointment because local
political leaders did not want to give any candidate the advantage
of incumbency, she began campaigning from that day forward. She
stresses that the women officials who sought her out for office
played an important part in influencing her candidacy.

Often the inspiration comes simply because women with the
potential for political participation can now find someone like themselves to imitate. "You made me believe that it was possible to do
it," said a woman who ran successfully for the New York legislature
in 1978 after watching Karen Burstein serve in the state senate.
Similar statements have been made to pioneering political women
everywhere. Speaking from personal experience as a visible candidate and seasoned officeholder who has come into contact with
many women seeking office for the first time in recent years, Maryland's state legislator Pauline Menes says that more and more
women are "willing to take a gamble because they see other women
being elected and know that they have a chance." Indirect but
effective, just *being there* is itself an act supportive of other women.

It has been common, perhaps convenient, in the past to think of women as not particularly interested in each other's advancement. No one has proved that case or the opposite for then or now. But the impressionistic evidence from a decade popularly called narcissistic is that, to the contrary, women's developing self-confidence and consciousness of themselves as women is resulting in a new freedom to turn to each other for giving and receiving support. Women on the street collar candidates to say, "I'm so proud you're running." They are encouraging their daughters to set new goals. A candidate vividly recalls the voter who approached her with this announcement: "I'm a pots-and-pans wrestler. But I want my daughter to have a chance!" In politics now women can find other women to admire and support. They have begun to take chances for themselves and to grant chances to one another.

Conclusion
The Beginning of
a Difference

If liberty and equality, as is thought by some, are chiefly to be found in democracy, they will be best attained when all persons alike share in the government to the utmost.

—Aristotle
Politics, Bk. IV, ch. 4

In political life women's status is in transition. Change has begun. Yet women are well aware that no welcome mat awaits them at the entranceway to electoral power, and that the forces of history and custom will influence the ratio of women to men among political candidates in the years to come. They know that ingrained images of women still function to restrict their behavior in competitive activities, and that the typical patterns of women's private lives are difficult to mesh with political candidacies. Having learned that coveted nominations are apt to be reserved for political insiders, women are challenged to build credibility as candidates from the outside. They see the route to victory carpeted with political dollars and other resources controlled by established sources of influence and power, and they are learning that resources available from the organized women's political movement for support of female candidates are very helpful but likely to remain in small supply and difficult to obtain. Because of these and other conditions of campaigning experienced by today's female candidates, it will take time as well as positive effort and steady encouragement before enough

250

women are running at all levels of the political system to create a balance of sexes in public life.

If the inroads for women in politics made during the seventies are to continue, a great many more women must seek and win election in the years ahead. Young women these days do admit to political ambitions more often and more comfortably than a decade ago. Cautiously optimistic, New York's Carol Bellamy awaits the next generation of women in politics, but she and her peers are concerned that "politics is so low on everyone's list of what to do" even with so many more choices for women today. "I hate government and love it all at once," states Bellamy. "It's the broadest and most exciting and complex place to be." She is looking down the road to find the young women taking advantage of new opportunities to reach for candidacies and to take an active part in shaping the world they inhabit. "Today's political environment is dreadful," she admits, then adds: "In my most optimistic moments, I hope that the incredible vacuum in leadership can be filled by women."

"Each of us has a responsibility in the events that occur," reflects her friend Karen Burstein. In 1978 after Burstein moved over from elective office in the New York state senate to take an appointive position on the state's Public Service Commission, she continued to visit schools, address women's meetings, and speak out on the importance of women's participation in public affairs wherever she found an appropriate forum. She and Bellamy even co-teach evening courses on such subjects as "Political Power for Women." Says Burstein, "I still do it all the time because the struggle isn't over." Burstein and Bellamy are two of the corps of ambitious and socially responsible women emerging in the public limelight who care about bringing other women forward with them.

The fate of women's collective aspirations in public life is tied to individual women taking the responsibility for helping to change their political status. Real progress depends on more women everywhere being willing to take risks—with themselves, and for each other. Experienced women must continue to extend a hand to political novices. They must find, motivate, and educate many other women to enter politics. Women must promote each other's ambitions and provide direct, hard support for each other's candidacies.

To ignore this set of interrelated responsibilities for advancement as a group is to risk sacrificing a steady expansion of new opportunities and political power for a few scattered, limited, anomalous, and temporary successes.

What has begun during the decade of the seventies can stagnate at the level of recent gains or it can be nurtured and advanced further. While the latter course will not be an easy one, women's increased participation in politics will have a significant impact on many other women and on the democratic process. For the foreseeable future, women in leadership positions carry special responsibilities in the public arena and can make special contributions in shaping and implementing policy. Furthermore, women's sheer presence in political life gives evidence that basic principles of equality and participatory democracy are still healthy and still functioning for the well-being of the entire society.

"I want to stress the importance of having more women in elective office at all levels of government if we are to have a true democracy," says Harriet Keyserling. After serving for two years in South Carolina's house of representatives, she came to believe that it is "tragic to have male representatives making decisions about women's minds, women's bodies, women's work, and women's status as citizens with little or no input from female colleagues." Stressing that the majority of the population "is hardly represented in the decision-making process of our country," Keyserling hits a familiar theme which implies that one important reason more women are needed in political life is that they will contribute a female perspective to matters of public interest. Because she knows what it feels like to be a woman, the female officeholder is more likely than her male counterpart to notice how public issues, policies, and institutions affect the quality of life for the female population.

Indeed, women are making a difference. Early indications from the recent increases in women's political participation do suggest that a change in the sexual composition of the public world will bring with it changes in the public agenda. "Why does anyone think that certain matters such as day-care facilities, nursing-home care, battered wives, the problems of divorced women and displaced homemakers—just to mention a few—are surging forward into the consciousness of the nation as issues that need to be addressed?" inquires Pat Bailey, the sole woman serving on the Federal Trade Commission in 1980. "Certainly, I don't think it is some new-found altruism among male policymakers, although many of them are sensitive and supportive." Bailey believes that women "are more sensitive to issues and decisions that are made as they will affect women."[1]

Her view finds support in evidence from councils, legislatures, and other governing bodies or executive and administrative offices where women have begun to gain a voice. In Connecticut, Maryland, Missouri, Oregon, and other states, for example, elected women in the state capitals have established caucuses or informal groups to consider and promote legislative issues affecting women. Connecticut's female legislators organized formally in 1979, calling themselves a Group of Women Legislators. In regularly scheduled meetings they agreed to support a number of bills of special concern to them. Issues identified by the group include: increasing funding to assist battered women; developing objective job evaluations based on the principle of equal pay for work of equal worth; finding methods to credit volunteer work experience as a credential for employment; providing counseling services for displaced homemakers; requesting annual reports on upward mobility for women in state service; printing a summary of laws affecting women. The Women's Caucus of the Maryland Legislature takes positions on bills that fall into its established legislative priority areas—among them, property rights of married women, pension and insurance equity for widows and divorced women, strengthening the state's human-relations commission, and reform of statutes dealing with rape and related sexual offenses. At the federal level, in 1977 the Congresswomen's Caucus was founded to deal with the "rights, representation and status of women." In 1979 all women serving in the Congress were members of the caucus—evidence that its concern with women's issues appealed to Representatives from diverse geographic constituencies, across party lines, and notwithstanding differences in political ideology.[2]

Interest in issues considered especially important to women places an additional burden of responsibility on the shoulders of female politicians. Sought out by a women's constituency, female candidates are expected to be particularly sensitive and responsive to its concerns. Once in office, a woman discovers that she is viewed as representing a constituency well beyond her district. "Because she's a woman and because there are so few elected women, Elizabeth Holtzman has an additional constituency," said Rod Smith, Holtzman's administrative assistant. He noted that while in the House of Representatives, Holtzman had "an interest and a sensitivity men may lack—she's concerned with issues of profound importance to women in areas which interest her because she's a woman herself." Smith pointed out that about one-third of the time of Holtzman's congressional office was taken up with women's issues. Ohio's Congresswoman Mary Rose Oakar devotes about the same percentage of time to women's issues, as do others among the small number of women holding highly visible elective positions.

The concern with legislation, executive orders, and governmental regulations responsive to a female perspective is not limited just to issues of women's rights, but also includes less obvious policy matters, both large and small. In one state legislature's heated discussion of Sunday closing laws, for example, the women legislators found themselves unanimously opposed and on the other side of the issue from many of their male colleagues. Without prior discussion, each woman had understood that working women needed stores open on weekends when they could shop.

On the campaign trail and in elective office, political women do have special responsibilities. Taking on these responsibilities can be viewed as an opportunity to make a truly valuable new contribution in public life. Or they can be shouldered or shirked as unfortunate burdens added to the already heavy pressures of candidacy and officeholding. Indeed, they are additions to the typical demands of daily political life encountered by any ambitious woman. In order to be accepted as an able public leader by the voters and her peers, she must satisfy the usual great expectations for knowledge and performance. She must function as a full-fledged public leader, fulfilling the duties and establishing the presence which that position requires. On top of all that, at this moment in history, she cannot forget her special responsibility for being woman qua woman. It is a debt she owes to her own heritage and must pay in order to build a different future for herself and new generations. It is one major reason why her continued and growing presence among public leaders is so important.

Women are still so small a factor in the equation of political power that no one can describe in detail or with confidence how a large, continuous increase in women's public presence might reshape governmental institutions or affect societal priorities in the long run. It will take ever larger numbers of female candidates and public officials even to continue changing the world for women. It will take massive increases in numbers before anyone can judge whether the future will look different from the past which was molded by men. Some observers do believe that women are likely to create new patterns of behavior and performance for the larger society. Idealistic partisans of women's advancement envision women refusing to participate in cutthroat career patterns; redefining standards for success; advocating flexible work schedules which leave room for private and family life; creating space to acknowledge emotions and express feelings; promoting the concept of service and concern for people's welfare above the demands of the profit motive; using political power to advance issues rather than to further private business interests or personal status—in general, adhering to values and supporting programs which lay stress on humanizing the society.

If such contributions to the quality of life are possible, they cannot come from a few isolated, overburdened, exceptional women who break into political life by defying the odds against them and then devote great energy to proving their competence, often in the face of doubts and disparagement. Only when so many women occupy public leadership positions that the burdens and also the benefits of being special fade will the right conditions exist in which to assess women's general contribution to governing society.

At present, the most one can speculate is that it seems probable that a large influx of women into the places of public power would have a noticeable impact on the entire society. Gender is hardly an insignificant component of anyone's personal identity and individual experiences. Recognizing the richness of a mixture of women *and* men debating public issues and guiding public policies, we would do well to favor recruiting more women into the ranks of political candidates. Concerned about the caliber of current public leaders, the nation might also welcome potential sources of new leadership from hitherto underrepresented groups of citizens.

There will never be enormous proportions of citizens who are very active politically for more than short periods at a time. But there should be room for all who wish to participate. If a democracy has one overwhelming mandate it is to cultivate people who care about participation and responsible leadership—people like the political women described in this book.

The experiences of these women and others like them are lessons which can benefit many other women in the years ahead. This legacy may be a greater contribution to society than any individual among them can make in her own public career. Even now their example has taught that while women face formidable obstacles in entering the public world, those obstacles can be confronted and overcome. Multiple and various in their talents and interests, today's political women stand as convincing evidence that women represent no less diversity than men. And while the effect of a great influx of women into public life cannot be foreseen, there is no sign that increased political activity by women like those who have placed themselves in the running thus far will do anything but benefit the democracy.

It has already been benefited. Because women are making themselves a visible part of the political process, their races have called attention to some strengths and weaknesses of our electoral system as a vehicle for choosing leaders. They have attracted other newcomers to political participation. And they have won de facto acceptance of a principle of equality. That principle has been established now regardless of the outcome of specific controversies about particular issues. These accomplishments to their credit, political women have gone on to contribute new perspectives to the development of public policy. All of that adds up to a significant beginning, no less and no more. With much begun and nothing finished, there is all the more reason for many others to join these women in the running.

Reference Notes

Chapter 1
THE ADVANCE GUARD

1. Martin Gruberg's *Women in American Politics: An Assessment and Sourcebook* (Wisconsin: Academia Press, 1968) is a reference book which identifies the female officials elected and appointed to fairly high-level public offices during most of this period.

2. In a paper entitled "Women Candidates and Support for Women's Issues: Closet Feminists," delivered in April 1979 at the Annual Meeting of the Midwest Political Science Association, Susan Carroll concludes from her study of female candidates in 1976: ". . . many women might most appropriately be characterized as 'closet feminists.' They are intensely committed to women's issues and to the goals of the feminist movement, but, in large part, their feminism remains hidden from public view—at least during the campaign stage of their public careers." The substance of this paper and the data on which its findings are based are incorporated in Carroll's doctoral dissertation, cited below in note 18.

3. Quoted in an interview with Ellen Malcolm in *Women's Political Times* (Washington, D.C.: National Women's Political Caucus), Vol. IV, No. 1, February 1979.

4. Figures are from surveys conducted by Louis Harris and Associates. They are reviewed in a roundup of national public opinion data on women in American society in "The Modern Woman: How Far Has She Come?" *Public Opinion* (January/February 1979) 35–39.

5. These figures, from surveys conducted by the American Institute

of Public Opinion (Gallup), are reviewed in "The Modern Woman: How Far Has She Come?" (note 4 above).

6. Jeane J. Kirkpatrick's *The New Presidential Elite: Men and Women in National Politics* (New York: Russell Sage Foundation and The Twentieth Century Fund, 1976) analyzes the results of a survey of delegates to the 1972 presidential nominating conventions. In *Clout: Womanpower and Politics* (New York: Coward, McCann & Geoghegan, 1974), Susan and Martin Tolchin report on the confrontations between feminists and the McGovern campaign in Miami (see pages 31–59).

7. At the time that the National Women's Political Caucus and other women and men who supported improvements in women's political status began to exert pressure for change, both the Democratic and Republican parties were involved in reform efforts aimed at opening the parties to increased participation by various underrepresented groups. The McGovern-Fraser Commission in the Democratic Party and the Republican Party's committee on delegates and organization, chaired by Rosemary Ginn of Missouri, played important roles in promoting reform within the parties.

8. *The Macon Telegraph* (Georgia), May 2, 1979.

9. Unless otherwise cited, figures about female elected officials here and elsewhere in the book are from the National Information Bank on Women in Public Office, a project of the Center for the American Woman and Politics of the Eagleton Institute of Politics at Rutgers— The State University of New Jersey.

10. The only woman ever to have been elected lieutenant governor before the mid-seventies was Consuelo N. Bailey; lieutenant governor of Vermont in 1955–56. See Martin Gruberg (note 1 above), p. 190.

11. In 1979 the following women were holding office as lieutenant governors: Nancy Dick (Colorado), Evelyn Gandy (Mississippi), Jean S. King (Hawaii), Madeleine Kunin (Vermont), Nancy Stevenson (South Carolina), Thelma Stovall (Kentucky). Since only forty-two states have lieutenant governors, women in 1979 were holding 14 percent of the positions at a level of elective office where no woman served at the beginning of the decade.

12. The cities are: Phoenix, Arizona; San Jose, California; San Francisco, California; San Antonio, Texas; Chicago, Illinois.

13. Throughout this book, figures about female candidates in the 1970s are based largely on information collected and supplied by Women's Election Central, a project of the National Women's Education Fund, 1410 Q Street, NW, Washington, DC 20009. The project has been conducted in cooperation with the National Women's Political Caucus and the Women's Campaign Fund. The figures about congres-

sional candidates are also drawn from a systematic listing of female candidates to the U.S. House of Representatives between 1916 and 1976 prepared by Professor G. Lane Van Tassell of the Department of Political Science at Georgia Southern College, Statesboro, Georgia.

14. David S. Broder, "Women in Congress: Still Scarce," *The Washington Post,* October 18, 1978.

15. In 1980 women fared somewhat better, receiving 14 percent of nominations for open U.S. House seats—six out of forty-three. However, with one exception, these nominations were for seats long held by the political party opposite to that of the women candidates in 1980.

16. Quoted in *Time,* May 21, 1979.

17. The sketch of female officeholders is based on a national survey of women holding office at federal, state, county, and local levels of government, conducted by the Center for the American Woman and Politics. Findings are reported and analyzed by Marilyn Johnson and Susan Carroll, "Statistical Report: Profile of Women Holding Office, 1977," in *Women in Public Office: A Biographical Directory and Statistical Analysis, Second Edition,* compiled by the Center for the American Woman and Politics (Metuchen, New Jersey: The Scarecrow Press, 1978).

Their analysis is based on responses to mailed questionnaires received from over 3,200 women serving in elective offices in 1977. Their comparative analyses of women and men holding office in 1977 are based on data from a subsample of female officeholders constructed from this main sample and matched with a sample of male officeholders serving as state legislators and county commissioners in sixteen states and mayors and local councilmen in eight of the sixteen states, representing a diversity of region. The findings about male officeholders referred to later in this profile are based on responses to a mailed questionnaire from 366 men holding elective office in 1977.

18. Figures about federal- and state-level female candidates in the 1976 elections come from a national survey of women running in primary and general election races conducted by Susan Carroll for *Women as Candidates: Campaigns and Elections in American Politics,* a Ph.D. dissertation in the Department of Political Science, Indiana University, Bloomington, Indiana, 1980.

19. Organizational affiliations and political party activity of women in office are reported in Parts II and III of Johnson and Carroll (see note 17). An earlier report from the first national survey of women holding federal, state, county, and local offices, conducted in 1975 by the Center for the American Woman and Politics, describes women's organiza-

tional affiliations in Marilyn Johnson and Kathy Stanwick, "Profile of Women Holding Office," *Women in Public Office: A Biographical Directory and Statistical Analysis* (New York: R. R. Bowker, 1976). In addition, political woman as a joiner is discussed in a book about women state legislators in the early 1970s: Jeane J. Kirkpatrick, *Political Woman* (New York: Basic Books, 1974).

20. The description of similarities and differences between women and men in elective office is based on data reported from the 1977 survey of officeholders cited in note 17 above. As described there, for purposes of comparison a matched sample of female and male elected officials, constructed from respondents to mailed questionnaires, consisted of women and men holding similar offices in the same states: state legislators and county commissioners in sixteen states and mayors and local councilpersons in eight of the sixteen states. My discussion of comparisons between political women and men generalizes from this study, using its figures based on a sample of officials in several elective offices to describe the general population of officeholders in the United States.

Chapter 2
THE RIGHT IMAGE

1. Joyce Purnick, "Senate 1980: See How They Run," *New York* (March 19, 1979), 42.

2. The observations about the double standard appeared in Leslie Bennetts, "On Aggression in Politics: Are Women Judged by a Double Standard?" *The New York Times,* February 12, 1979.

3. Eric Fettmann, "The City Politic: Why Getting Elected Is a Primary Concern," *New York* (September 4, 1978), 12.

4. Tom Buckley, "Woman Odds-On Favorite as Connecticut Governor," *The New York Times,* April 24, 1974.

5. Ann R. Willner, "Nancy," *The New York Times,* November 13, 1978.

Chapter 3
PRIVATE LIFE/PUBLIC WORLD

1. National survey data from over 3,200 women serving in municipal, county, and state legislative offices in 1977 indicate that a large majority of women in office are married:

	State Senate %	State House %	County Commission %	Mayoralty %	Local Council %
Married	72	80	81	76	78
Divorced/ Separated	11	8	5	7	5
Widowed	8	6	10	11	12
Single	9	6	4	6	5
Total number respondents	(64)	(278)	(282)	(290)	(2,173)

Figures are from Johnson's and Carroll's "Profile of Women Holding Office" (see citation in Chapter 1, note 17), Table 13, p. 13A.

2. In Part II of their "Profile of Women Holding Office," Johnson and Carroll (see citation in Chapter 1, note 17) report that women holding municipal, county, and state offices in 1977 indicated strong support from their husbands, with 60 percent of local council members, 62 percent of mayors, and between 75 and 77 percent of county and state officials saying that their husbands "actively encourage" their officeholding. After comparing survey data from both women and men holding office in 1977, Johnson and Carroll comment that their analysis "suggests the hypothesis that family approval is a far more important selective criterion for the political participation of women than of men. It is likely that women whose families disapprove of their political activity fail to seek office in the first place, resulting in a high degree of family support among those who enter office." Findings from their research on this issue lead to the conclusion: "Finally, and perhaps most critical in understanding the process of political recruitment of women, relatively few married women enter politics without the support and encouragement of their husbands but a relatively large group of men in politics lack the support of their wives."

3. The comment by Jasper Dorsey appeared in the *Atlanta Journal and Constitution* in a column entitled "Charm Is More Important than Talent In Personality Contest of Politics."

4. Among women responding to Susan Carroll's national survey of female candidates in primary and general election races for congressional, statewide, and state legislative offices in 1976 (see citation in Chapter 1, note 18), only 19 percent of congressional candidates, 30 percent of statewide candidates, 20 percent of state senate candidates, and 21 percent of state house candidates were mothers of children under age 12.

In Part II of their "Profile of Women Holding Office" in 1977,

Johnson and Carroll (see citation in Chapter 1, note 17) find that while most elected women are mothers, the majority in almost every office have no children under 18 years of age. In comparing the parental status of a matched sample of female and male officeholders, the researchers report: "Female and male officeholders are equally likely to be parents, and they have approximately the same numbers of children. However, a higher percentage of men are parents of young children, under 12 years of age. The differences are not large: in the total sample, 34% of the men and 24% of the women have children under 12 years. Differences widen at the state legislative level, however, where 35% of men but only 16% of women have young children, even though legislators do not differ in marital status."

Chapter 4
OUTSIDERS

1. Harold J. Wiegand, "Women are not invited," *The Philadelphia Inquirer,* March 21, 1979.

2. Michael Daly and Henry O'Hagan, "Runnin' Scared," *The Village Voice,* May 16, 1977.

3. As recounted by Martindell, the incident occurred at a dinner at the New Zealand Embassy in Washington, D.C. Martindell said afterward that "the remark had 'astounded' her and that, as a result, her efforts at conversation with the New Zealand leader 'ended for a while.' " Reported by Edward C. Burks, "The Prime Minister Vs. 'Lady Politician,' " *The New York Times,* New Jersey Weekly Section, July 1, 1979.

4. *Time* (November 6, 1978), 35.

5. The breakdown was as follows:

Very Important	Fairly Important	Slightly Important	Not Important	Don't Know
28%	24%	16%	30%	2%

Chapter 5
LAYING THE GROUNDWORK

1. This route to office was noted in an Associated Press release printed in *The New York Times* on November 19, 1978. Entitled "Many New Congress Members Had Capitol Hill Staff Positions," the article noted that "at least eight of the 97 congressional candidates elected for

the first time Nov. 7 had worked on the Capitol Hill staffs of senators or representatives."

2. Quoted by John Feinstein in "Women Seize Solid Hold on Md. Politics," *The Washington Post,* November 9, 1978.

3. Quoted by Tom Price in "Treasurer Donahey may shoot for higher office," the Dayton *Journal Herald,* May 5, 1977.

4. In Feinstein (see note 2 above).

5. Quoted by Debra Leff in "Survey Shows Women 'Political Novices,'" *Women's Political Times* (Washington, D.C.: National Women's Political Caucus), Vol. III, No. 2 (Summer 1978), 7.

Chapter 6
GETTING AND SPENDING RESOURCES

1. Time, people, and money as critical campaign resources are identified and examined for practical use in women's campaigns by Betsey Wright in *Campaign Workbook* (Washington, D.C.: National Women's Education Fund, 1978).

2. Ward's campaign and the candidate's quotes were reported by Mary Thornton in "Holt, Ward Both Woo Democratic Voters," *The Washington Star,* October 16, 1978. Congresswoman Holt shared her views in a separate interview with the author of this book in March 1979.

3. Reported by Tom Griffin in "Schulenburg quips through school race," *Press Connection* (Madison, Wisconsin), March 22, 1979.

4. For an excellent step-by-step review of how to plan and organize a campaign efficiently as well as establish a headquarters operation, assess staff needs, and recruit and utilize volunteers, see Chapters 1 and 4 of *Campaign Workbook* (note 1 above).

5. Campaign experts differ in their opinions about the advantages and disadvantages of staffing campaign organizations with large numbers of volunteers. Paid professional consultants often feel negative toward relying heavily on volunteers, especially for key positions. For example, David Garth views "volunteers in general" as a "big problem in terms of costing lots of campaign money" (in David Novis, "An Interview with David Garth," *Princeton Spectrum,* February 15, 1978). Of course, the issue relates to that of a campaign's financial resources as well as to how well volunteers are managed and utilized during campaigns. It is an important issue for women's campaigns, especially since female candidates may be particularly successful in attracting volunteer workers.

6. An excellent, detailed guide to fund raising appears in Chapter 8 of *Campaign Workbook* (see note 1 above).

7. To date no substantial, hard evidence has been gathered for a comprehensive study of differences in fund-raising experiences and amounts raised by comparable female and male political candidates. It is an area of research which requires attention.

8. Reported by Warren Weaver, Jr., "Spending on Senate Campaigns Averaged $900,000," *The New York Times,* January 9, 1979.

9. Figures for amounts of money raised and spent by House leaders in 1978 campaigns are cited by Warren Weaver, Jr., in "Special-Interest Units Contributed $927,000 to 8 Leaders in Congress," *The New York Times,* January 4, 1979.

10. Campaign costs for mayoralty races in New York City in 1977 were discussed by Ken Lerer in "The Race for Mayor: A $1-Million Tab," *New York,* May 2, 1977.

11. Reported by Warren Weaver, Jr. (see note 9).

12. "Statement of the Women's Campaign Fund and the National Women's Political Caucus Regarding Campaign Finance Laws," delivered to the Rules Committee of the United States Senate, May 5, 1977.

13. Quoted by Dale Koch in "Learning the Political Ropes," *Feminist Bulletin* (Scarborough, New York), October 1977.

14. The Sharp incident and Eskind's remark were reported in "Is a Woman's Place in the House?" *Time,* November 6, 1978.

15. B. Drummond Ayres, Jr., "Five New Senators are Millionaires," *The New York Times,* December 27, 1978.

16. Joyce Purnick, "Senate 1980: See How They Run," *New York,* March 19, 1979.

Chapter 7
ORGANIZED SUPPORT

1. National organizations sponsoring special workshops, distributing position papers, or developing other educational materials and services include: National Women's Education Fund; National Women's Political Caucus; National Federation of Business and Professional Women's Clubs; League of Women Voters; National Organization for Women; special-issue groups concerned with such issues as the Equal Rights Amendment and abortion. Women's clubs and divisions in the Democratic and Republican parties at national and state levels have also sponsored workshops and conferences with special sessions devoted to teaching campaign skills, as have university- and college-based pro-

grams such as the Center for the American Woman and Politics at Rutgers University and the Public Leadership Education Network (a group of small women's colleges which develop educational programs to introduce their students to opportunities in public leadership).

2. In 1978 a *New York Times* political analysis of declining political party power and rising special-interest-group power lists, without ado, the women's movement among other organized special interests as having an impact on the composition of the U.S. Congress by affecting the tenure of individual members. (John Herbers, "Interest Groups Gaining Influence at the Expense of National Parties," *The New York Times,* March 26, 1978.)

3. The Women's Campaign Fund gives money and technical assistance exclusively to female candidates. In 1978 its Board of Directors adopted a candidate-assistance policy as follows: "The WCF will continue to focus on national races, and priority will be given in the allocation of resources to campaigns for the U.S. Senate and House of Representatives.

"The WCF will establish a fund for nonfederal races which have special significance to the advancement of women in politics. Special consideration will be given to: 1) Pro-ERA women running against anti-ERA opponents for state legislative seats in unratified states where ratification is possible; 2) Candidates for statewide office; 3) Candidates whose successful races for nonfederal offices could position them as strong congressional aspirants; 4) Minority women candidates."

By 1980, the Women's Campaign Fund made a strong commitment to support women running for state and local offices. The fund had come to recognize that at local levels women could gain credibility, expertise, and experience which would be critical to their political mobility. In May 1980, the fund's newsletter to contributors stated the new policy: "WCF has made a new and important commitment to developing that pool of talented women officeholders at the nonfederal level, by seeking out and supporting effective candidates for any significant office. We are determined to help women gain the campaign and government experience they need at whatever level they choose. We want to put competent women in decision making bodies at every level and we want to help them 'pay their dues' at the lower levels of office before seeking a congressional or U.S. Senate seat."

4. As reported in the October 1979 issue of the National Women's Political Caucus' *Women's Political Times,* the Democratic Women's Task Force launched its 1980 national election strategy with a platform entitled "Fair Share for American Women." The platform calls for "candidates and elected officials to commit themselves to active work for

ratification of the Equal Rights Amendment, to fight inflation, to increase employment, to assure civil rights of all citizens, to appoint larger numbers of women to policymaking positions in government and to put a woman on the United States Supreme Court." The platform also calls for the Democratic National Committee "to pledge itself to the short-term goal of electing at least 50 women to Congress and to substantially increase the number of elected and appointed women at all levels of government. The party should continue to pledge itself to the long-term goal of equal representation by men and women in all elective and appointive offices, to actively recruit women to seek elective office, and support them with financial and technical assistance at all levels."

5. It has been possible for the organized women's political movement to endorse both Democratic and Republican candidates for public office based on feminist criteria. In general, Democrats have been more likely to support key women's issues, but active political women in both major parties have been more positive on feminist issues than the men in their parties. Among a national sample of women and men holding public office in 1977, 76 percent of Democratic women and 63 percent of Democratic men favored passage of the federal Equal Rights Amendment compared with 59 percent of Republican women and 33 percent of Republican men. On the issue of abortion, 70 percent of Democratic women and 75 percent of Republican women compared with 62 percent male Democrats and 55 percent male Republicans did not favor a constitutional ban on abortion. Concerning social security coverage for homemakers, 69 percent female Democrats and 52 percent female Republicans compared with 49 percent Democratic men and 34 percent Republican men approved. Women in office from both major parties also agreed more closely with one another than with the men in their parties that government and private industry should be doing more to advance women's rights—84 percent Democratic women and 72 percent Republican women compared with 63 percent Democratic men and 55 percent Republican men approved of greater support for women's rights from private industry.

The national survey of women and men holding public office in 1977 was conducted by the Center for the American Woman and Politics. For a description of the study, with full citation, see Chapter 1, notes 17 and 20. Figures describing partisan response to women's-rights issues appear on p. 36A of the study.

6. In October 1979, an editorial in the *National NOW Times* (the organization's official monthly publication) explained the organization's policy regarding its Political Action Committee (PAC): "In establishing the NOW Political Action Committee in 1977, the National Organiza-

tion for Women entered a new arena of feminist politics. In two years, the PAC has played an increasingly important role in the fight for ratification of the Equal Rights Amendment and election of public officials who will continue to battle for achievement of feminist goals. . . . The philosophy of NOW/PAC states guiding principles to be used to establish support for candidates or campaigns:

- independence of any political parties;
- support of incumbent friends;
- support of female and male candidates according to their ability to achieve NOW goals;
- development of NOW strategy on a statewide, areawide, or nationwide basis for the achievement of NOW's political purposes.

"Overall analysis of the political structure to be affected is imperative if wise choices are to be made for the use of limited resources. . . . We will not endorse the lesser of two evils, nor will we always endorse the woman candidate. NOW must determine if the particular race will work to further or achieve our goals, and only then will NOW decide whether to support a candidate in a given race. Frequently, the NOW unit may choose to support no one because it is not in accordance with NOW plans and priorities.

"National NOW/PAC currently has prioritized funding in accordance with NOW's established first priority, ratification of the Equal Rights Amendment. All PAC funding and the manner of funding is in keeping with ERA Strike Force policies and plans. . . .

"In 1978, in addition to ERA state ratification electoral effort, because of the ERA extension drive, federal Congressional campaigns were given limited support, where needed. In federal races, 'right to life' targets and incumbent Congressional feminists have been supported, especially if leadership in key committees was involved."

Chapter 8
THE LARGER CONTEXT

1. Where they were contending for votes from people sympathetic with women's efforts to obtain equal rights, both male and female candidates presented themselves as feminists, with liberal male candidates frequently arguing that they had done more for women's rights than their female opponents. This type of situation arose, for example, in two of Maryland's 1976 congressional races, as well as in this race in southern California: A local television station assigned a reporter to

do a brief report for the evening news on some female legislative candidates. The reporter decided that under the fairness rule, she should offer a chance for the men running against the women candidates to be on the show also. One man declined. But Charles (Chip) Post, a Democrat running against moderate Republican Marilyn Ryan, accepted the invitation.

Post's statement on television attracted quite a bit of attention. In effect, he said that he—not Ms. Ryan—was the stronger feminist. "Occasionally I run into someone who says it's stupid for a woman to vote for a man," he said, and he strongly challenged that kind of thinking. "That's sexist," he said. "I support more women in the work force, humane treatment in rape areas—that is a crime of violence rather than sex—more day care, expanding roles for women, ERA, that sort of thing. The message that is important is if [voters] . . . are interested in women's issues . . . [they should] find out who's a feminist and vote for that candidate—whether he's a man or a woman."

There were some chuckles at the awkward word choice, but many people could sympathize with Post's position. While Ryan did win the election, there was no evidence of a big crossover of women voters from the Democratic side. Yet at that point in the campaign it seemed a distinct possibility. "I'd bet there are a lot of Democratic women who would vote for a moderate Republican woman [such as Ryan]," agreed the television reporter. "I can understand his frustration."

2. The statement, made by Councilwoman Patricia Lagay of Metuchen, New Jersey, was quoted by Patricia Mack in *The News Tribune* (Woodbridge, New Jersey), December 5, 1978.

3. Quoted by James F. Lynch in "A 'Practical Pragmatic' Assemblywoman," *The New York Times*, New Jersey Weekly Section, January 14, 1979.

4. The quote appeared in Lisa Cronin Wohl's August 1979 *Ms.* magazine article entitled "Decoding the Election Game Plan of the New Right." Wohl describes the "new right" as a coalition of special-interest groups united around a program of opposition: "Opposition to gun control, the Equal Rights Amendment, organized labor, affirmative action, the Panama Canal treaty, the SALT talks, environmental protection, gay rights, and, perhaps the most lucrative of all in terms of dollars and votes, opposition to abortion rights."

5. Reported by Nadine Brozan in "White House Conference on the Family: A Schism Develops," *The New York Times*, January 7, 1980. Brozan describes the "pro-family" interests as "working through so-called right-to-life and other groups that oppose the rights amendment [ERA]. One key group seems to be the National Pro-Family Coalition

on the White House Conference on the Family. It has brought together more than 150 organizations including Moral Majority, the National Christian Action Coalition, Family America, FLAG, for Family, Life, America, God; and the Eagle Forum, Phyllis Schlafly's powerful national organization."

6. Brozan (see note 5).

Conclusion
THE BEGINNING OF A DIFFERENCE

1. These remarks are from a speech delivered on June 14, 1980, in Washington, D.C., at a Conference for Leaders of Organizations of Women Public Officials sponsored by the Office of Policy Development and Research of the U.S. Department of Housing and Urban Development, and conducted by the Center for the American Woman and Politics of the Eagleton Institute of Politics, Rutgers University.

2. The Congresswomen's Caucus issued a statement eighteen months after its inception describing its interest in mounting a "sustained effort on Capitol Hill and within the federal bureaucracy to improve the rights, representation and status of women": "Using a broad range of techniques, from joint meetings with key Cabinet members to the promotion of specific legislation, the Caucus has attempted to inject consideration of women's rights into the major issues before the Congress and the Executive Branch. It not only supports legislation affecting women but also monitors federal government programs that deeply influence the opportunities available to women." Issues which have absorbed the Congresswomen's Caucus include extending the time period for ratification of the Equal Rights Amendment, employment opportunities for women, reform of the Social Security system to eliminate inequities affecting women, health issues of special concern to women, counseling and training for displaced homemakers, assistance for women business owners, and protection and counseling for battered wives and abused children.

Index

271